os cherries CILANTRO fava beans FIDDLEHEAD FERNS

DISHES rhubarb SALAD GREENS scallions SORREL

oranges

GRAPEFRUIT

GREENS kale

RUTABAGAS

celery root

COLLARD

quince

LUEBERRIES boysenberries BLACKBERRIES currants

s eggplants FIGS garlic BASIL dill PARSLEY mint

es OKRA peaches SWEET PEPPERS plums

VERBENA

CARROTS

LIMES cranberries

POTATOES

parsnips

cabbage winter

BLOOD ORANGES lemons

BEET GREENS chard LEEKS

fresh

FROM THE FARMERS MARKET TO YOUR KITCHEN

FROM THE EDITORS OF GOURMET

Food Photographs by Romulo A. Yanes

Condé Nast Books   Random House

New York

Copyright © 1999
The Condé Nast Publications Inc. All rights
reserved under International and Pan-
American Copyright Conventions.
Published in the United States by Random
House, Inc., New York, and simultaneously
in Canada by Random House of Canada
Limited, Toronto.

LIBRARY OF CONGRESS
CATALOGING-IN-PUBLICATION DATA

Main entry under title:
GOURMET'S FRESH/ the editors of *Gourmet*.
Gourmet's Fresh/ from the editors of
Gourmet; food photographs by
Romulo A. Yanes.
       p. cm.
   Includes index.
   ISBN 0-375-50341-2 (alk. paper)
   1. Cookery, American. 2. Farm produce.
I. Gourmet.
TX715.G7147
641.5973—dc 21   99-21109

Random House website address:
www.atrandom.com

Some of the recipes in this work were
published previously in *Gourmet* Magazine.

Printed in the United States of America
on acid-free paper.

98765432
First Edition

Box information was written by Jane Daniels
Lear. All other informative text was written
by Diane Keitt and Caroline A. Schleifer.

Front Jacket: Watermelon Pimm's Cup
(page 87); Zucchini and Yellow Squash
with Pesto (page 63); Fig and Arugula
Salad (page 64).
Back Jacket: Herbed Tomato Tarts (page 72)
and Roasted Poussins with Lemon Thyme
(page 63).

FOR CONDÉ NAST BOOKS
Lisa Faith Phillips, *Vice President/General Manager*
Tom Downing, *Associate Direct Marketing Director*
Mark Lutz, *Operations Manager*
Colleen P. Shire, *Direct Marketing Manager*
Angela Lee, *Assistant Direct Marketing Manager*
Meredith Peters, *Direct Marketing Assistant*
Margaret McCreary, *Direct Marketing Assistant*
Serafino J. Cambareri, *Quality Control Manager*
Richard B. Elman, *Production Supervisor*

FOR GOURMET BOOKS
Diane Keitt, *Director*
Caroline A. Schleifer, *Editor*

FOR GOURMET MAGAZINE
Ruth Reichl, *Editor-in-Chief*

Zanne Early Stewart, *Executive Food Editor*
Kemp Miles Minifie, *Senior Food Editor*
Alexis M. Touchet, *Associate Food Editor*
Lori Walther Powell, *Food Editor*
Elizabeth Vought, *Food Editor*
Katy Massam, *Food Editor*
Shelton Wiseman, *Food Editor*
Alix Palley, *Food Editor*

Romulo A. Yanes, *Photographer*
Marjorie H. Webb, *Style Director*
Nancy Purdum, *Senior Style Editor*

Produced in association with
MEDIA PROJECTS INCORPORATED
Carter Smith, *Executive Editor*
Anne B. Wright, *Project Editor*
John W. Kern, *Production Editor*
Marilyn Flaig, *Indexer*

Salsgiver Coveney Associates Inc.
Jacket and Book Design

The text of this book was set in MrsEaves
by Media Projects Incorporated. The four-
color separations were done by American
Color and Applied Graphic Technologies.
The book was printed and bound at R. R.
Donnelley and Sons. Stock is Somerset
Gloss, S.D. Warren.

acknowledgments

The idea of creating a farmers market cookbook excited everyone in *Gourmet*'s kitchen. New recipes were developed by: Shelley Wiseman and Alix Palley (spring chapter); Katy Massam (summer menus); Liz Vought (additional summer recipes); Alexis Touchet (fall chapter); Lori Walther Powell (winter menus); Liz and Shelley (additional winter recipes). Zanne Stewart, Executive Food Editor, and Kemp Minifie, Senior Food Editor, acted as tasters and consultants, while Gerald Asher, *Gourmet*'s Wine Editor, chose regional American wines to accompany the menus.

Gourmet photographer, Romulo Yanes; prop-stylist, Susan Victoria; and food stylists, Liz Vought and Alix Palley, created a jacket that captures the flavors of summer. Throughout the book, more than 60 other images, photographed by Romulo and prop-styled by Marjorie Webb and Nancy Purdum, present seasonal dishes. Additional photographs were contributed by Cotten Alston, Richard Bowditch, Mark Ferri, Elisabeth Hughes, Marry Kim, Geoff Lung, Minh + Wass, Steven Mark Needham, Julian Nieman, Mathias Oppersdorff, and Riley + Riley.

For years we've admired Jane Daniels Lear's clever informational "boxes" in *Gourmet*, and luckily she agreed to adapt many here. More insight about produce and farmers markets came from Joel Patraker of New York City's Union Square Greenmarket. Hobby McKenney Coudert and Kathleen Duffy Freud offered editorial assistance, while Anne Wright and John Kern professionally handled all production matters. Finally, we'd like to thank Karen Salsgiver for her artful "fresh" design.

recipe key

tips for success with *Gourmet's Fresh*

Read each recipe through before beginning to cook.

All produce should be washed and dried before proceeding with a recipe.

Measure liquids in glass or clear plastic liquid-measuring cups.

Measure dry ingredients in nesting dry-measuring cups (usually made of metal or plastic) that can be leveled off with a straightedge such as a knife.

Measure flour by spooning (not scooping) it into a dry-measuring cup and leveling off with a straightedge without tapping or shaking cup.

Do not sift flour unless specified in recipe. When sifted flour is called for, sift the flour before measuring it.

Measure skillets and baking pans across the top, not across the bottom.

"Large" eggs are labeled as such. Do not substitute extra-large or jumbo.

contents

The scent of ripe strawberries filled the air. Bees hummed. Off in the distance we could see the corn, blowing gently in the wind. Alice Waters stood with her feet in the dirt and her face in the sun. Taking a deep breath she said, "All I really want is a restaurant where you give people good bread and good wine and good olive oil and then you lead them to a wonderful garden and say, 'There it is—help yourselves.'"

That was more than 20 years ago, and it seemed like a ridiculous dream. In those days most salads were made of iceberg lettuce, tomatoes had no taste, and if you wanted a decent strawberry you had to grow your own.

These days it seems a lot less absurd: Gardens are sprouting all over America. Great tomatoes and good strawberries have never been so easy to find. Who do we have to thank for this?

A number of people. The first great American food revolution began with the teachers. The most important was certainly Julia Child who taught us the technical skills required to create a great cuisine while urging us to have the courage to cook. But an even more important lesson was yet to come. For once we had mastered the techniques of soufflés and sautés, we uncovered the most important secret of cooking: Every great meal begins with great products.

Once they realized this, young chefs like Alice Waters set out to do something about it. No longer satisfied with old fish that had not seen the water for weeks and hard peaches bred for their ability to travel without bruising, they took the obvious next step. They created networks of producers, who would plant gardens, raise animals, and go foraging and fishing just for them. It wasn't easy; I know because when I wrote an article about the incipient farm movement in 1980 one of Alice's suppliers told me he thought she was nuts. "I'm growing baby vegetables for her," he said, "but I don't understand why she wants those little ones when she could have big ones for less money."

Crazy or not, the movement grew. And its impact was profound. Because once we had those wonderful ingredients, we realized that they wanted nothing more than to be left alone. Chefs who had worshipped at the altar of haute cuisine began learning the lessons of the Mediterranean. They began to simplify, to let the great ingredients speak for themselves. Our tastes changed. And then the movement came home.

It started very slowly, but farmers soon found that cooks in cities all over America were eager to buy the wonderful fruits and vegetables they were tasting in restaurants. The farmers planted more and brought the surplus to farmers markets. Little by little the movement grew. The result? Today there are few large American cities that do not have a farmers market.

This is a book for people who love those markets. For people who are happy to wander through the streets of their cities and come upon places where the air smells of peaches and corn and farmers sell fruits and vegetables they pulled from the dirt only hours earlier. It is, above all, a book for people who understand that good products demand only one thing of a cook: Respect.

Because great produce makes so few demands, many of our recipes are fast and easy. Lori's Heirloom Tomato Salad (opposite) is simply dressed with garlic-oil, which allows the sweet taste of the tomatoes to come shining through.

Some recipes, such as Parsley Spätzle, suggest new uses for familiar foods. Others feature some of the out of the ordinary fruits and vegetables, like tatsoi, purslane, and persimmons, that are starting to turn up in the markets. And because fruits and vegetables that were bred for flavor instead of longevity are a new experience for many of us, we have sprinkled information on buying, storing, and preparing produce throughout the book.

We also offer a collection of seasonal menus. After all, cooking from the farmers market means following the seasons and it may change the way you eat. It may also change the way you shop, because dropping in at the farmers market is a very different experience than a trip to the supermarket. It is always unpredictable.

Flip through *Gourmet's Fresh* to find ideas before you set off for the market. Think of it as a beginning, a blueprint for your meals. Should you arrive to discover better or more interesting fruits and vegetables than you had anticipated, buy them; *Gourmet's Fresh* will help you revise the recipe when you get home.

Because in the end, one of the nicest things about shopping at the farmers market is that you never know what you will find. A market is a lot like a garden: There is always a surprise.

Ruth Reichl
Editor-in-Chief

apricots ARTICHOKES asparagus AVOCADOS cherries CILANTRO fava beans FIDDLEHEAD FERNS garlic chives MINT peas PEA SHOOTS purslane RADISHES rhubarb SALAD GREENS sorrel SCALLIONS spinach SPROUTS strawberries TARRAGON tatsoi

spring

Spring Lunch for Two

- ✻ Chilled Sorrel, Pea, and Leek Soup
- ✻ Asparagus, Ham, and Cheese Melts
- ✻ Brandied Cherries with Vanilla Ice Cream
- ✻ *McRostie Carneros Chardonnay 1997*

CHILLED SORREL, PEA, AND LEEK SOUP ☺+

Sorrel, sometimes called sour dock or sour grass, resembles spinach but adds a suprising jolt of tart, lemony flavor to soups, salads, and sauces.

      3   leeks (about ¾ pound total; white and
           pale green parts only)
   1½   tablespoons olive oil
      1   small boiling potato (about ¼ pound)
   1½   cups chicken broth
   1½   cups water plus additional to thin soup
      ½   cup shelled fresh peas (about ½ pound
           in pods) or thawed frozen peas
      ¼   pound sorrel
      ⅓   cup sour cream
      1   teaspoon fresh lemon juice, or to taste

GARNISH
chopped hard-boiled egg and
thin strips of sorrel

Chop leeks and in a bowl of cold water wash leeks well. Lift leeks from water into a colander to drain. In a large saucepan cook leeks in oil with salt and pepper to taste over moderately low heat, stirring, until softened. Peel potato and cut into 1-inch cubes. Add potato, broth, and 1 cup water to leeks and simmer, covered, about 10 minutes, or until potato is tender. Stir in peas and simmer, uncovered, about 5 minutes, or until peas are tender.

While potato mixture is simmering, discard sorrel stems. Cut leaves crosswise into thin strips (about 3 cups loosely packed). In a blender purée potato mixture with sorrel in 2 batches until very smooth, transferring to a bowl. Whisk in sour cream and ½ cup water, adding enough water to thin soup to desired consistency. *Chill soup, covered, until cold, at least 2 hours, and up to 1 day.*

Just before serving, stir in lemon juice and salt and pepper to taste. Garnish soup with egg and sorrel. Makes about 4½ cups, serving 2 generously.

ASPARAGUS, HAM, AND CHEESE MELTS ☺

      ½   cup freshly grated Parmesan
      ¼   cup mayonnaise
      1   pound thin asparagus
      4   slices Italian or other white bread
      2   teaspoons unsalted butter, softened
      ¼   pound sliced cooked ham

Preheat broiler.

In a small bowl stir together Parmesan and mayonnaise. Trim asparagus to fit bread and arrange asparagus in a skillet large enough to hold it in one layer. Add ½ inch salted cold water and cook asparagus, covered, over moderately high heat 5 minutes, or until just tender. In a colander drain asparagus well.

Arrange bread on a baking sheet and butter top of each slice. Broil bread about 6 inches from heat until golden, about 2 minutes. Turn bread over and arrange ham on it, folding or trimming to fit if necessary. Arrange asparagus on ham and spread with Parmesan mixture. Broil open-faced sandwiches about 3 inches from heat until golden, 1 to 2 minutes. Serves 2.

Photo opposite

BRANDIED CHERRIES WITH VANILLA ICE CREAM ☺

      ⅓   pound sweet cherries
      ¼   cup plus 1 tablespoon brandy
      ¼   cup sugar
   1½   cups vanilla ice cream

Halve and pit cherries, transferring to a bowl. In a small heavy saucepan bring ¼ cup brandy and sugar to a boil, stirring until sugar is dissolved, and boil, without stirring, until reduced to about ¼ cup, about 2 minutes. Stir in cherries with their juices and cook over moderately low heat 1 minute, or until cherries are just heated through. Stir in remaining tablespoon brandy.

Scoop ice cream into 2 small bowls and top with brandied cherries. Serves 2.

SPRING DINNER for Four

* Pea Shoot Salad with Avocados and Bacon
* Seared Rosemary Scallops
* Mango Cucumber Salsa
* Purple Potato, Sugar Snap Pea, and Mint Salad
* Strawberry Crème Caramel Tart
* *Chalk Hill Sauvignon Blanc 1997*

Pea Shoot Salad with Avocados and Bacon

Once found only in Asian markets (and sometimes only if asked for by their Cantonese name, dau miu), pea shoots are increasingly available at farmers markets. Pea shoots are the tips of green-pea vines, consisting of a few inches of delicate tendril and tender top leaves. They have a subtle flavor that is similar to watercress or spinach with a hint of peas.

FOR DRESSING

- ⅓ cup sour cream
- ¼ cup fresh orange juice
- 1½ tablespoons fresh lime juice
- 1 garlic clove
- 2 teaspoons Dijon mustard
- ½ teaspoon brown sugar

- 3 bacon slices
- 2 small heads Boston lettuce (about ⅓ pound total)
- ½ pound pea shoots
- 2 ripe California avocados

Make dressing:
In a blender blend together dressing ingredients and salt and pepper to taste.

Cook bacon until crisp and transfer to paper towels to drain. Tear lettuce and pea shoots into bite-size pieces and in a large bowl toss together. Peel and pit avocados and cut into ½-inch pieces. Toss greens and avocados with dressing until combined well.

Serve salad with bacon crumbled on top. Serves 4.

Seared Rosemary Scallops

- 8 rosemary branches (12 inches long) or bamboo skewers (10 inches long)
- 2 teaspoons chopped fresh rosemary leaves
- ½ teaspoon paprika
- ¼ teaspoon cayenne
- 32 medium sea scallops (about 1½ pounds)
- about 4 tablespoons olive oil

If using rosemary branches, remove leaves from all but top 3 inches of each branch. In a small bowl stir together chopped rosemary, paprika, and cayenne. Remove tough muscle from side of each scallop if necessary and pat scallops dry. Season scallops with salt and sprinkle with rosemary mixture. Thread 4 scallops onto each rosemary branch or bamboo skewer.

In a large nonstick skillet heat 2 tablespoons oil over moderately high heat until hot but not smoking and sauté half of scallops until golden and just cooked through, 1 to 2 minutes on each side. Transfer scallops to a heated plate and sauté remaining scallops, adding more oil if necessary. Serves 4.

Photo opposite

Mango Cucumber Salsa

- 1 firm-ripe large mango
- ⅔ English cucumber
- ¼ cup finely chopped scallion
- ¼ cup fresh orange juice
- 2 teaspoons fresh lime juice
- 1 teaspoon extra-virgin olive oil

Peel mango and cut flesh from pit. Cut mango into ¼-inch dice and transfer to a bowl. Halve cucumber lengthwise and seed. Cut cucumber into ¼-inch dice and add to mango. Stir in remaining ingredients until combined well and season with salt and pepper. Serves 4.

Photo opposite

PURPLE POTATO, SUGAR SNAP PEA, AND MINT SALAD

 1 pound small purple or other boiling
    potatoes (about 10)
 ½ pound sugar snap peas
20 fresh mint leaves
 1 tablespoon plus 1 teaspoon balsamic vinegar
 1 tablespoon plus 1 teaspoon extra-virgin
    olive oil

In a small heavy saucepan cover potatoes with salted cold water by 1 inch and simmer until tender, 15 to 20 minutes.

While potatoes are simmering, trim snap peas. With a slotted spoon transfer potatoes to a colander to drain and cool 10 minutes. Return water in pan to a boil and blanch snap peas until crisp-tender, about 1 minute. In a colander drain snap peas and refresh under cold water. Drain snap peas and pat dry with paper towels.

Cut potatoes lengthwise into quarters and thinly slice mint leaves. In a bowl toss together potatoes, snap peas, mint, vinegar, oil, and salt and pepper to taste. Serves 4.

Photo on page 14

STRAWBERRY CRÈME CARAMEL TART

We slightly dried the small strawberries in this recipe so that their excess juice would not affect the crème caramel. If using wild strawberries, they do not need to be dried before using here. Both the crème caramel and the crust may be made ahead, but, to ensure a crisp crust and shiny caramel, do not assemble the tart until shortly before serving.

FOR CRÈME CARAMEL

1¼ cups whole small strawberries (about 30)
1¼ cups granulated sugar
1½ cups heavy cream
1 whole large egg
3 large egg yolks
1 teaspoon vanilla

FOR PASTRY CRUST

5 tablespoons unsalted butter
1 cup all-purpose flour
2½ tablespoons packed brown sugar
¼ teaspoon salt
2 tablespoons ice water

GARNISH
small strawberries

Make crème caramel:
Preheat oven to 225° F.

Trim strawberries and spread on a baking sheet. Bake strawberries in middle of oven 30 minutes to dry slightly and cool strawberries on baking sheet on a rack.

Increase temperature to 350° F.

In a dry heavy saucepan cook 1 cup sugar over moderately low heat, stirring slowly with a fork (to help sugar melt evenly), until melted and pale golden. Cook caramel, without stirring, swirling pan, until deep golden. Immediately pour caramel into a 9-inch glass pie plate, tilting plate to coat bottom and sides evenly. Put pie plate in a baking pan.

In a saucepan heat cream just to a boil and remove pan from heat. In a bowl whisk together whole egg, yolks, remaining ¼ cup sugar, vanilla, and a pinch salt until combined well and add warm cream in a stream, whisking. Skim off any froth and carefully pour custard into pie plate. Arrange dried strawberries decoratively on their sides in custard (custard should completely cover strawberries) and add enough hot water to baking pan to reach halfway up side of pie plate. Bake *crème caramel* in middle of oven about 40 minutes, or until custard is just set but still trembles slightly (custard will continue to set as it cools). Remove plate from pan and cool custard completely on a rack. *Chill crème caramel, loosely covered with plastic wrap, at least 4 hours and up to 1 day.*

Make crust:
Cut butter into pieces and soften slightly. In a large bowl with your fingertips or a pastry blender blend together flour, brown sugar, salt, and butter until mixture resembles coarse meal. Add 1 tablespoon ice water and toss mixture with a fork until incorporated. Add enough remaining ice water, ½ tablespoon at a time, tossing with fork, until mixture just begins to form a dough. On a work surface with heel of your hand smear dough in 3 or 4 forward motions to help distribute butter. Form dough into a ball and flatten to form a disk. *Chill dough, wrapped in plastic wrap, 1 hour.*

Preheat oven to 350° F.

On a lightly floured surface roll out dough into a 10-inch round (about ⅛ inch thick) and transfer to a baking sheet. Using a 9-inch plate as a guide, trim dough to a 9-inch round. Prick round all over with a fork. *Chill round 30 minutes.* Bake round in middle of oven until golden, about 30 minutes, and cool completely on baking sheet on a rack. *Crust may be made 1 day ahead and kept, loosely covered with foil, at room temperature.*

Assemble tart just before serving:
Have ready a flat serving plate at least 10 inches in diameter with a slight lip. Run a thin knife around edge of *crème caramel* and rotate pie plate back and forth to make sure *crème caramel* is loosened. Slide crust on top of *crème caramel* and invert serving plate on top of crust. Invert tart onto serving plate (caramel will run to edges of plate) and garnish with strawberries.

Photo opposite

SPRING DINNER FOR SIX

* Asparagus Soup with Saffron
* Herbed Roast Leg of Lamb
* Mixed Baby Vegetables
* White Bean Gratin with Garlic
* Strawberry and Lemon Curd Tarts
* *Pellegrini North Fork of Long Island Cabernet Sauvignon 1995*

ASPARAGUS SOUP WITH SAFFRON

 5 cups vegetable or chicken broth
¼ teaspoon crumbled saffron threads
⅓ cup shelled natural pistachios or
   pine nuts
3½ pounds asparagus (about 3 large bunches)
 1 large russet (baking) potato
½ stick (¼ cup) butter
½ cup packed fresh flat-leafed parsley leaves

In a small saucepan bring ½ cup broth
to a boil and remove pan from heat. Stir
saffron into hot broth and steep, stirring
occasionally, 15 minutes.

In a dry heavy skillet toast nuts over moderate heat, stirring, until fragrant. Chop nuts.

Have ready a large bowl of ice and cold
water. Trim asparagus and cut into 2-inch
pieces, reserving tips separately. In a large
saucepan of boiling salted water blanch
tips 2 minutes, or until crisp-tender, and
transfer with a slotted spoon to ice water to
stop cooking. Drain tips well and pat dry.

Peel potato and cut enough into ½-inch
cubes to measure 1½ cups. In a 4-quart
kettle cook asparagus stalks in butter over
moderate heat, stirring, 3 minutes. Stir in
potato, saffron infusion, and 4 cups broth
and simmer, covered, until vegetables are
very tender but not falling apart, about
20 minutes.

In a blender or food processor purée mixture in batches until smooth (use caution
when blending hot liquids), transferring
to a bowl. In kettle stir together purée and
enough of remaining ½ cup broth to reach
desired consistency. Add half of asparagus
tips and bring soup to a simmer. While
soup is heating, chop parsley. Season soup
with salt and pepper.

Serve soup topped with nuts, parsley,
and remaining asparagus tips. Serves 6.

Photo opposite

HERBED ROAST LEG OF LAMB

¼ pound pearl onions (preferably red;
   optional)
2½ pounds plum tomatoes (about 15)
 1 yellow onion
 2 shallots
 1 head garlic
 2 fresh rosemary sprigs
 2 fresh oregano sprigs
 2 fresh thyme sprigs
 6 tablespoons olive oil
 a 6-pound leg of lamb, trimmed by butcher

GARNISH
fresh mint sprigs

Preheat oven to 450° F.

In a saucepan of boiling water blanch pearl
onions 3 minutes. Drain pearl onions in
a colander and peel. Cut tomatoes into
thick slices. Peel and halve yellow onion.
Peel shallots and garlic cloves. In a large
roasting pan stir together pearl onions,
tomatoes, yellow onion, shallots, garlic,
rosemary, oregano, and thyme sprigs,
¼ cup oil, and salt and pepper to taste.

Trim any remaining fat from lamb and
pat dry. Arrange lamb on top of vegetable
mixture. Drizzle lamb with remaining
2 tablespoons oil and season with salt and
pepper. Roast lamb and vegetables in
middle of oven 15 minutes. Reduce
temperature to 350° F. and roast lamb
and vegetables, basting lamb and stirring
vegetables every 20 minutes, 1 hour and
20 minutes more, or until lamb registers
145° F. on an instant-read thermometer
for medium-rare meat.

Transfer lamb to a cutting board and let
stand, loosely covered with foil, 15 minutes.
Reserve pearl onions for mixed baby vegetables (recipe on page 20) or to serve on the
side. In a blender purée remaining vegetables
with pan juices in batches and pour through
a fine sieve into a bowl, pressing on solids.

Garnish lamb with mint and serve with sauce
and, if desired, pearl onions. Serves 6.

Photo on page 20

MIXED BABY VEGETABLES

¾ pound baby carrots
½ pound *haricots verts* (thin French green beans) or regular green beans
½ pound baby zucchini and/or baby yellow squash
½ pound yellow and/or green baby pattypan squash
1 large boiling potato (about ½ pound)
2 tablespoons olive oil
¼ pound cooked pearl onions (preferably reserved from herbed roast leg of lamb, recipe on page 19)
2 tablespoons minced fresh dill and/or mint leaves, or to taste

Have ready a large bowl of ice and cold water. Peel and trim carrots. Trim beans. In a kettle of boiling salted water cook separately carrots, beans, zucchini and/or yellow squash, and pattypan squash until crisp-tender, transferring vegetables as cooked with a slotted spoon to ice water to stop cooking. Drain vegetables and pat dry. Peel potato and cut into ½-inch cubes. Cook potato in boiling water until just tender and drain well. *Vegetables may be prepared up to this point 1 day ahead and chilled in sealable plastic bags.*

In a large skillet heat 1 tablespoon oil over moderately high heat until hot but not smoking and sauté half of vegetable mixture and half of pearl onions 3 minutes, or until heated through. Stir in half of herbs and salt and pepper to taste and sauté mixture, stirring, 1 minute. Transfer sautéed vegetables to a bowl and sauté remaining vegetable mixture, onions, and herbs in remaining tablespoon oil in same manner. Return sautéed vegetables in bowl to skillet and sauté, stirring, until heated through. Serves 6.

Photo left

White Bean Gratin with Garlic

2   heads garlic
1½ cups dried white beans such as
    Great Northern or navy
¾   cup chicken broth
½   cup fine dry bread crumbs
3   tablespoons unsalted butter, softened

Separate garlic heads into cloves (do not peel). Pick over beans and in a 4-quart kettle combine with garlic and enough cold water to cover beans by 2 inches. Gently simmer bean mixture, adding more water as necessary to keep beans covered, until beans are tender, about 1½ hours. Drain bean mixture in a colander. Remove garlic and peel. In a small bowl mash garlic with a fork and gently stir into beans. *Bean mixture may be made 1 day ahead and chilled, covered. Bring mixture to room temperature before proceeding.*

Preheat oven to 400° F.

In a 2-quart nonreactive baking dish gently stir together bean mixture, broth, and salt and pepper to taste. In a bowl with your fingertips blend together bread crumbs and butter. Sprinkle crumb mixture evenly over bean mixture and bake in middle of oven until golden and bubbly, about 20 minutes. Serves 6.

Strawberry and Lemon Curd Tarts

FOR SHORTBREAD CRUSTS
2   tablespoons sugar
½   cup all-purpose flour
½   stick (¼ cup) cold unsalted butter

FOR LEMON CURD
4   large egg yolks
⅓   cup sugar
⅓   cup fresh lemon juice
3   tablespoons unsalted butter

2   cups strawberries

Preheat oven to 375° F.

Make crusts:
In a food processor pulse together sugar and flour. Cut butter into small pieces and add to flour mixture, pulsing until mixture forms a crumbly dough, about 15 seconds. Roll out dough between 2 sheets of wax paper to form a 12-inch circle (about ¼ inch thick). Remove top sheet of wax paper and using a 4-inch round cutter cut out 6 rounds. Invert rounds onto an ungreased baking sheet and carefully remove wax paper. Remove excess dough and trim rounds to make neat circles. Bake rounds in middle of oven until pale golden, about 8 minutes. Cool shortbread crusts on sheet on a rack 5 minutes and transfer crusts to rack to cool completely. *Shortbread crusts keep in an airtight container at cool room temperature 2 days.*

Make lemon curd:
In a 2-quart heavy saucepan whisk together curd ingredients until combined well. Cook mixture over moderately low heat, whisking constantly, until it reaches a boil, about 10 minutes (do not let boil), and immediately remove pan from heat. Pour curd through a fine sieve into a bowl and cool, its surface covered with a buttered round of wax paper. *Chill curd, covered, at least 2 hours and up to 2 days.*

Trim strawberries and cut into ⅛-inch-thick slices. Spread curd evenly onto crusts and decoratively top with strawberry slices. Serves 6.

ELEGANT SPRING DINNER FOR SIX

* Mushroom Consommé with Morels and Pastry "Hats"
* Herb-Roasted Veal Chops
* Polenta with Sage and Parmesan
* Minted Spring Vegetables
* Mango Fool
* *Buttonwood Santa Ynez Valley Cabernet Sauvignon 1995*

MUSHROOM CONSOMMÉ WITH MORELS AND PASTRY "HATS"

Although morels add a woody flavor to the consommé, they are not essential. You can substitute other dried mushrooms such as porcini or shiitake. Also, while the pastry "hats" are festive, the consommé is delicious on its own.

FOR CONSOMMÉ
2 pounds fresh white mushrooms
2 onions
2 quarts cold water
1 teaspoon salt
¾ ounce dried morel mushrooms*
   (about 1 cup)
1½ cups boiling-hot water
¾ cup Sercial Madeira

2 tablespoons 1-inch pieces fresh chives

FOR PASTRY "HATS" (OPTIONAL)
2 puff pastry sheets (from one 17¼-ounce package frozen puff pastry sheets), thawed
1 large egg
1 teaspoon water

SPECIAL EQUIPMENT
six 12-ounce "truffle soup bowls" or 9- to 10-ounce ovenproof ramekins, each measuring 3½ to 4 inches across top

*available by mail order from Marché aux Delices, tel. (888) 547-5471

Make consommé:
In a food processor finely chop white mushrooms. Chop onions. In a 6 quart stockpot or kettle simmer white mushrooms, onions, cold water, and salt, uncovered, 2 hours. Pour consommé through a large fine sieve lined with a dampened paper towel into a large saucepan, pressing gently on solids, to yield about 5 cups consommé (if there is not enough, add water to make 5 cups; if too much, boil consommé until reduced to 5 cups). Season consommé with salt and pepper.

While consommé is simmering, in a small bowl soak morels in boiling-hot water 20 minutes, or until soft. Remove morels with a slotted spoon, reserving soaking liquid, and in a small saucepan simmer morels and Madeira, covered, 5 minutes.

Add morel mixture to consommé. When solids in soaking liquid have settled, slowly pour liquid into consommé, being careful to leave last tablespoon (containing sediment) in bowl. Simmer consommé, covered, 3 minutes. *Consommé may be made 2 days ahead and chilled, covered.* Bring consommé to room temperature.

Preheat oven to 400° F.

Divide consommé, including morels, and chives among bowls or ramekins.

Prepare pastry "hats":
On a lightly floured surface roll out 1 pastry sheet into a 12-inch square and with a round cutter at least ¾ inch larger than diameter of bowls cut out 4 rounds. Roll out second pastry sheet and cut out 2 more rounds in same manner. Brush any excess flour from both sides of rounds.

In a small bowl lightly beat egg with water. Working with 1 pastry round at a time, brush a ½-inch border of egg wash around edges of rounds and invert rounds over bowls or ramekins, carefully stretching ½ inch down side and pressing to seal.

When all bowls or ramekins are covered with pastry, brush tops with remaining egg wash. *Pastry-covered consommé may be prepared up to this point 4 hours ahead and chilled. (Pastry will not rise quite as high when going straight from refrigerator to oven.)* Arrange bowls or ramekins on a large baking sheet and bake consommé in middle of oven until pastry "hats" are puffed and golden, 12 to 18 minutes. Serves 6.

Photo opposite

HERB-ROASTED VEAL CHOPS

Veal chops from a butcher shop are usually about 1 1/4 inches thick and weigh 12 to 14 ounces each. Those available at the supermarket are often thinner and smaller, ranging from 8 to 10 ounces each, and would only need to be roasted 12 to 15 minutes in this recipe.

4   large garlic cloves
2   tablespoons chopped fresh sage leaves
2   tablespoons chopped fresh rosemary leaves
2   teaspoons kosher salt
1   teaspoon freshly ground black pepper
5   tablespoons olive oil
6   veal rib chops (each 1 1/4 inches thick and 12 to 14 ounces)
1   cup dry white wine
1   cup chicken broth
2   tablespoons cold unsalted butter

Finely chop garlic and in a small bowl stir together with herbs, salt, pepper, and 2 tablespoons oil. Pat chops dry and rub with all but 1 teaspoon herb mixture, reserving remainder for sauce. *Chill chops, covered, at least 1 hour and up to 1 day.*

Preheat oven to 375° F.

Pat chops dry if necessary. In a 12-inch nonstick skillet heat 1 1/2 tablespoons oil over moderately high heat until hot but not smoking and brown 3 chops, about 3 minutes on each side and a few seconds on edges. Transfer browned chops to a shallow baking pan and brown remaining chops in same manner, adding remaining 1 1/2 tablespoons oil as needed. Roast chops in middle of oven until an instant-read thermometer inserted horizontally into a chop registers 160° F., 15 to 20 minutes.

While chops are roasting, pour off any fat from skillet (do not wipe clean). Add wine and reserved herb mixture and deglaze skillet over high heat, scraping up brown bits, 1 minute. Boil wine mixture until reduced to about 1/4 cup, about 4 minutes. Add broth and boil until liquid is reduced by half, about 5 minutes.

Transfer chops to a heated platter. Pour any juices from baking pan into sauce and bring to a boil. Cut butter into pieces and add to sauce, swirling skillet until sauce is slightly thickened and butter is incorporated.

Serve chops with sauce. Serves 6.

POLENTA WITH SAGE AND PARMESAN

This recipe is based on Marcella Hazan's "no-stirring" method from her book Essentials of Classic Italian Cooking.

8   fresh sage leaves
6   cups water
1 1/2   teaspoons salt
1 1/2   cups cornmeal
1/3   cup freshly grated Parmesan (about 1 ounce)

Chop sage leaves. In a 3- to 4-quart heavy saucepan bring water with sage and salt to a boil and gradually add cornmeal in a thin stream, whisking. Cook polenta over moderate heat, whisking, 2 minutes. Gently simmer polenta, covered, stirring for 1 minute after every 10 minutes of cooking, 45 minutes total. Stir in Parmesan. Remove pan from heat and cover to keep warm. *Polenta will keep warm, covered, about 20 minutes.* Stir polenta before serving. Makes about 5 cups, serving 6.

MINTED SPRING VEGETABLES ◔

*Asian eggplants (long, thin, and pale purple) or
Italian eggplants (deep purple) may be used here.
If using the more common Italian variety, choose
the smallest ones available.*

3   small thin eggplants (about ¾ pound total)
¾   pound yellow squash (about 2 medium)
2   bunches radishes (about 20)
1   large garlic clove
6   tablespoons extra-virgin olive oil
2   tablespoons chopped fresh flat-leafed
    parsley leaves
1½ tablespoons chopped fresh mint leaves
1   teaspoon fresh lemon juice
½   teaspoon kosher salt

Cut eggplants diagonally into ⅓-inch-
thick slices. Cut squash diagonally into
¼-inch-thick slices. Trim radish tops to
¼ inch and halve large radishes lengthwise.
Mince garlic.

In a 12-inch nonstick skillet heat 3 tablespoons oil over moderate heat until hot but
not smoking and cook half of eggplant until
golden on each side. Transfer cooked eggplant to a bowl and cover with foil to keep
warm. Cook remaining eggplant in remaining 3 tablespoons oil in same manner and
transfer to bowl. In oil remaining in skillet
cook garlic, stirring, 30 seconds, and add
to eggplant.

In a steamer set over boiling water steam
squash, covered, until crisp-tender, about
2 to 3 minutes. Add squash to eggplant
and cover to keep warm. In steamer
steam radishes, covered, until crisp-tender
but still pink, about 1 to 2 minutes. Add
radishes to squash mixture with parsley,
mint, and juice. Season vegetables with
kosher salt and pepper and toss to combine.
Serves 6.

Photo below

MANGO FOOL ◔

*This creamy dessert can be served immediately or
chilled for a firmer texture.*

2   ripe mangoes (about 1½ pounds total)
2   tablespoons fresh lime juice, or to taste
¼   cup plus 1 tablespoon sugar, or to taste
1   cup well-chilled heavy cream

Peel mangoes and cut flesh from pits. In
a food processor purée mangoes with lime
juice and ¼ cup sugar, or to taste. In a
large bowl beat cream with remaining
tablespoon sugar until it just forms stiff
peaks. Fold in mango purée gently but
thoroughly. *Fool keeps, covered and chilled,
2 days.*

Serve fool in goblets. Serves 6.

spring recipes

FRESH PEA SOUP WITH TARRAGON ◔

An aromatic herb with strong licorice flavor, tarragon has long, narrow, green leaves. Tarragon is distinctive and assertive, but it mixes perfectly with the likes of parsley, chives, and chervil. Pull the tender leaves from the coarse central stalk before chopping them.

1 large onion
2 teaspoons unsalted butter
3 cups shelled fresh peas
  (about 3 pounds in pods)
2½ cups low-salt chicken broth
2 teaspoons chopped fresh tarragon leaves
  freshly ground white pepper
⅓ cup well-shaken buttermilk

ACCOMPANIMENT
toasted crusty bread

Chop enough onion to measure ¾ cup and in a saucepan cook in butter, covered, over moderate heat, stirring occasionally, 5 minutes, or until tender. Add peas and broth and simmer, uncovered, 5 minutes, or until peas are tender. Stir in tarragon.

In a blender purée soup until smooth (use caution when blending hot liquids). Pour soup through a coarse sieve back into pan and heat over moderate heat until hot. Remove pan from heat. Add white pepper and salt to taste and stir in all but 2 teaspoons buttermilk.

Divide soup between 2 bowls and gently spoon half of remaining buttermilk decoratively onto each serving. Serve soup with crusty bread. Makes about 3 cups, serving 2.

Photo opposite

STUFFED RADISHES

1 pound radishes (about eighteen 1¼ inch)
½ cup Kalamata or other brine-cured
  black olives
1 tablespoon drained bottled capers
4 ounces cream cheese, softened
2 tablespoons minced fresh parsley leaves

GARNISH
small fresh parsley sprigs

Have ready a bowl of ice and cold water. Halve radishes crosswise and trim rounded end of each half to enable it to stand upright. With a small melon-ball cutter hollow out a ¾-inch cavity in each half, dropping halves as hollowed into ice water. Pit olives and mince. Finely chop capers. In a bowl beat cream cheese until creamy and stir in olives, capers, parsley, and salt and pepper to taste. Transfer mixture to a pastry bag fitted with a ½-inch plain tip. Transfer radishes, hollowed sides down, to paper towels and drain 5 minutes.

Pipe cream cheese mixture into radish cavities and garnish each stuffed radish with a parsley sprig. *Radishes may be stuffed 1½ hours ahead and chilled, covered.* Makes about 36 hors d'oeuvres.

Photo below

salad greens

 When you get home from the farmers market, examine the greens carefully and discard any wilted, bruised, or broken leaves—they're a breeding ground for decay. If a head of lettuce is held together by a wire or rubber band, this should also be discarded. Make sure the greens are dry before storing them in bags in the refrigerator. Some people swear by muslin bags for storage, but perforated plastic bags work well, too—the key is to retain the greens' moisture and allow air to circulate. (Wrap delicate greens such as *mesclun*, *tatsoi*, and sorrel loosely in paper towels first.) Always wash and dry greens carefully before using—even those labeled "prewashed."

Bear in mind that salad dressing will wilt greens in no time flat, so dress salads just before serving. This is especially important for tender, young spring lettuces—all you really need is some good olive oil and a little *fleur de sel* and freshly ground black pepper.

—Jane Daniels Lear

TATSOI AND CRUNCHY SPROUT SALAD

A thick spoon-shaped Asian green, tatsoi lends a sturdy bite to salads and is often included in mesclun mixes. Tatsoi is usually sold loose, like baby spinach, which can be substituted.

- ¼ cup seasoned rice vinegar
- 2 tablespoons soy sauce such as Kikkoman
- 2 tablespoons vegetable oil
- 1 tablespoon sugar
- 2 teaspoons grated peeled fresh gingerroot
- 2 cups crunchy sprouts such as pea and lentil (about ½ pound)
- ⅓ pound *tatsoi* (about 6 cups) or baby spinach leaves

In a large bowl whisk together vinegar, soy sauce, oil, sugar, and gingerroot until combined well. Add sprouts and toss until coated. *Marinate sprouts 30 minutes.* Add *tatsoi* and toss until combined well. Serves 4.

STUFFED EGGS WITH CAVIAR ⊙+

This recipe can be made with either quail eggs or chicken eggs. The alternative amounts provided in the ingredient list correspond to the type of egg used.

12	quail eggs or 6 large eggs
1½	teaspoons or 5 tablespoons mayonnaise
1	teaspoon or 1 tablespoon minced shallot
¾	teaspoon or 2 teaspoons minced fresh tarragon leaves
1¾	ounces caviar

In a saucepan cover eggs with cold water by 1 inch and bring water just to a boil. Remove pan from heat and let eggs stand, covered, 7 minutes if using quail eggs or 17 minutes if using large eggs. Drain hot water from pan and run cold water over eggs, cracking shells against side of pan. Peel eggs.

Cut a paper-thin slice off both ends of each egg to enable it to stand upright. If using quail eggs, cut one third off narrow end of each, discarding tops; if using large eggs, halve crosswise. Carefully remove yolks from whites and in a bowl mash yolks with a fork. If using quail eggs, stir in smaller measures of mayonnaise, shallot, and tarragon. If using large eggs, stir in larger measures of same ingredients. Season yolk mixture with salt and pepper. Spoon yolk mixture into whites and smooth tops. *Chill stuffed eggs, covered with plastic wrap, at least 30 minutes and up to 4 hours.*

Just before serving, top eggs with caviar. Makes 12 stuffed eggs.

Photo below

WARM ARTICHOKES WITH GOAT CHEESE DIPPING SAUCE

4	medium artichokes
2	lemons
6	ounces soft mild goat cheese
2	tablespoons extra-virgin olive oil
⅓	cup heavy cream

With a sharp knife cut off top 2 inches of artichoke leaves and discard. Cut stems flush with bottoms and discard stems. With scissors trim tips of remaining leaves. Cut 1 lemon in half and rub cut surfaces of artichokes with lemon halves. Discard lemon halves.

In a 5-quart kettle bring 1 inch salted water to a boil and steam artichokes, covered, over moderate heat until tender, 20 to 25 minutes.

While artichokes are steaming, grate zest from remaining lemon and squeeze 2 tablespoons juice. In a small heavy saucepan heat zest and juice with remaining ingredients over moderately low heat, stirring to break up cheese, until sauce is smooth and heated through. Season sauce with salt and pepper. Invert artichokes onto a plate to drain. When artichokes are just cool enough to handle, remove inner purple leaves and choke with a teaspoon and discard. Spoon sauce into centers of artichokes. Serves 4.

RISOTTO WITH FRESH HERBS ◔

1½ cups mixed fresh herbs such as parsley,
    basil, oregano, and chives
1   medium onion
1   large celery rib
6   cups chicken broth
3   tablespoons unsalted butter
1½ cups Arborio rice
½   cup dry white wine
⅓   cup freshly grated Parmigiano-Reggiano
    (about 1 ounce)

Coarsely chop herbs. Finely chop onion and celery. In a saucepan bring broth to a simmer and keep at a bare simmer.

In a 4-quart heavy saucepan or kettle cook onion and celery in butter over moderately low heat, stirring, until softened. Add rice and cook, stirring, 2 minutes. Add wine and cook, stirring, 1 minute. Stir in ½ cup simmering broth and cook over moderate heat, stirring constantly and keeping at a strong simmer throughout, until absorbed. Continue cooking at a strong simmer and adding broth, about ½ cup at a time, stirring constantly and letting each addition be absorbed before adding next, until rice is tender and creamy-looking but still *al dente*, 18 to 20 minutes total. (There may be some broth left over.) Stir in herbs, cheese, and salt and pepper to taste and serve risotto immediately. Serves 6 as a first course.

SHRIMP AND ARTICHOKES IN PEPPERY BUTTER SAUCE

2   large artichokes (each about ¾ pound)
1   stick (½ cup) cold unsalted butter
1   large garlic clove
1   tablespoon fresh lemon juice, or to taste
1   tablespoon freshly ground black pepper
2   teaspoons Worcestershire sauce
½   teaspoon Tabasco
½   teaspoon dried basil, crumbled
½   teaspoon salt, or to taste
¼   teaspoon dried oregano, crumbled
¼   teaspoon cayenne
½   pound small shrimp in their shells
    (preferably with heads; about 24)
3   scallions

ACCOMPANIMENTS
crusty bread
lemon wedges

With a sharp knife cut off artichoke stems and discard. With scissors trim tips of leaves. In a large saucepan of boiling salted water cook artichokes 30 to 45 minutes, or until bottoms are tender when pierced with a knife.

While artichokes are cooking, preheat oven to 500° F.

Cut butter into bits. Drop garlic into a food processor with motor running and mince. Turn motor off. Add lemon juice, black pepper, Worcestershire sauce, Tabasco, basil, salt, oregano, and cayenne and pulse to combine. Add butter and blend until combined well.

Spread shrimp in 3-cup shallow baking dish large enough to hold them in one layer. Mince scallions and sprinkle over shrimp. Drop spoonfuls of butter mixture evenly over top and bake, stirring once or twice, until shrimp are cooked through, about 5 minutes.

Invert artichokes onto paper towels to drain. Divide artichokes and shrimp with butter sauce between 2 soup plates and serve with bread and lemon. Serves 2.

Photo opposite, top

FARFALLE WITH ROASTED GARLIC AND PEA PURÉE

Tender young green peas have a brief season before the summer heat sets in and makes them large and tough. Since peas, like corn, begin to convert their sugars to starch as soon as they're picked, they're best cooked on the day of purchase. If substituting frozen peas, be sure to use the ones marked "baby" peas since many of the regular-sized ones can be mealy and bland.

1 head garlic
4 cups shelled fresh peas
  (about 4 pounds in pods)
2 cups water
1 tablespoon unsalted butter
3 tablespoons fresh lemon juice
1 tablespoon chopped fresh tarragon leaves
¾ pound *farfalle* (bow-tie pasta)
½ cup fresh snow-pea or pea shoots

Preheat oven to 425° F.

Cut ½ inch off top of garlic head, exposing cloves, and wrap garlic tightly in foil. Roast garlic in middle of oven 30 minutes, or until very soft, and cool. Squeeze roasted garlic from head into a blender.

In a saucepan boil peas in 2 cups salted water until just tender, about 5 minutes. In blender purée garlic, peas with cooking liquid, butter, lemon juice, tarragon, and salt and pepper to taste. Transfer purée to a saucepan and keep warm, covered.

In a 6-quart kettle bring 5 quarts salted water to a boil and cook pasta, stirring occasionally, until *al dente*. Drain pasta in a colander and in a bowl toss with sauce, snow-pea or pea shoots, and salt and pepper to taste. Serves 4 as a main course.

Photo left, bottom

cutting hard vegetables

First things first: Use a freshly sharpened knife! To cut a long vegetable such as a carrot into julienne strips: Cut it crosswise into pieces of desired length, then make a flat surface on a long side by cutting a thin strip from one side of each piece. With the flat side down, cut each piece lengthwise into ⅛-inch-thick slices. Stack two or three slices and cut them lengthwise into ⅛-inch-thick strips. (Alternatively, cut the carrot diagonally into ⅛-inch-thick slices. Stack two or three slices and cut lengthwise into ⅛-inch strips.)

To cut a round or oval vegetable such as a turnip or potato into julienne strips: Cut it in half to create a flat surface (so that it won't roll). With the flat side down, cut the halves into slices and, working with a stack of several slices, cut them into strips. (If you need to slice large quantities, a *mandoline* or other manual slicer would be useful.)

To make cubes (½ inch or larger) or dice (smaller than ½ inch): Cut vegetables into slices and then strips of desired width. Cut stacks of strips crosswise into even pieces.

It's easy to dismiss the precision involved in this kind of task as merely cosmetic; in fact, it's an excellent way to ensure that all your vegetables will cook at the same rate.

—Jane Daniels Lear

STIR-FRIED BEEF WITH BABY BOK CHOY ◒

a   1-pound piece flank steak
1   tablespoon dry Sherry
2   tablespoons soy sauce
    such as Kikkoman
2½ teaspoons cornstarch
5   tablespoons vegetable oil
1⅓ pounds baby bok choy
    (8 to 12 heads)
3   large garlic cloves
1   bunch scallions
½   cup chicken broth
2   teaspoons sugar
1   teaspoon salt
2   tablespoons finely chopped peeled
    fresh gingerroot

ACCOMPANIMENT
cooked white rice

Cut flank steak in half lengthwise along grain and cut crosswise into ⅛-inch-thick strips. In a bowl stir together Sherry, 1 tablespoon soy sauce, 2 teaspoons cornstarch, and ½ tablespoon oil until cornstarch is dissolved. Add beef and toss to combine well.

Quarter bok choy lengthwise. Thinly slice garlic. Diagonally cut scallions into 1-inch pieces. In a small bowl stir together chicken broth, sugar, and salt.

Heat a wok or deep 12-inch heavy skillet (preferably cast iron) over high heat until a bead of water dropped on cooking surface evaporates immediately. Add 1½ tablespoons oil, swirling wok or skillet to coat evenly, and stir-fry beef mixture until beef is no longer pink, 1 to 2 minutes. Transfer beef to a plate and clean wok or skillet.

Heat wok or skillet over moderately high heat until a bead of water dropped on cooking surface evaporates immediately. Add remaining 3 tablespoons oil and stir-fry garlic, scallions, and gingerroot 10 seconds. Add bok choy and stir-fry until coated with oil, about 1 minute. Add broth mixture and cook, covered, until bok choy is crisp-tender, 4 to 5 minutes. Add beef, tossing to combine, and stir-fry until heated through, about 30 seconds.

With a slotted spoon transfer beef and bok choy to a platter and bring liquid remaining in wok or skillet to a boil. In a cup stir together remaining ½ teaspoon cornstarch and remaining tablespoon soy sauce until cornstarch is dissolved and stir into boiling liquid. Boil sauce, stirring, until slightly thickened and pour sauce over beef and bok choy.

Serve stir-fry with rice. Serves 4.

Glazed Salmon
with Sautéed Chanterelles,
Fava Beans, and Frisée

1   pound fresh fava beans in pods
½   pound fresh chanterelle mushrooms*
1   head *frisée* (French curly endive; about 5 ounces)
½   pound shallots
3   large garlic cloves

FOR SALMON GLAZE
1   tablespoon soy sauce such as Kikkoman
1   tablespoon Sherry vinegar
1   tablespoon packed light brown sugar
¼   teaspoon salt

¼   pound thick bacon slices
4   pieces skinless salmon fillet (6 ounces each)
1   tablespoon olive oil
3   tablespoons chicken broth
3   tablespoons Sherry vinegar
½   teaspoon granulated sugar

available seasonally at some farmers markets and specialty produce markets and by mail order from Marché aux Delices, tel. (888) 547-5471

Shell fava beans and have ready a bowl of ice and cold water. In a kettle of boiling salted water cook favas 2 minutes and drain in a colander. Transfer favas to ice water to stop cooking. Drain favas and gently peel away outer skins. With a pastry brush gently

brush chanterelles to remove any grit and trim any tough stems. Halve chanterelles lengthwise if large. *Favas and chanterelles may be prepared up to this point 1 day ahead and chilled, separately, in sealable bags.*

Preheat oven to 400° F.

Separate *frisée* leaves, discarding any dark green or discolored leaves. Leaving some of root end of shallots intact, quarter lengthwise. Mince garlic.

Make glaze:
In a very small saucepan bring glaze ingredients to a boil, stirring, and remove pan from heat.

Lightly oil a shallow baking pan.

Cut bacon crosswise into ¼-inch-wide strips and in a 12-inch nonstick skillet cook over moderate heat until browned. Remove skillet from heat and transfer bacon with a slotted spoon to paper towels to drain, reserving fat in skillet. Season salmon with salt and pepper and arrange, skinned side down, in baking pan. Brush salmon with 1 tablespoon reserved bacon fat and bake in upper third of oven until just cooked through, about 10 minutes.

Sauté vegetables while salmon is baking: Discard all but 1 tablespoon fat from skillet. Heat fat and oil over moderate heat until hot but not smoking and cook chanterelles, shallots, and garlic with salt and pepper to taste, stirring, 5 minutes. Add chicken broth and cook, covered, until shallots are softened and chanterelles are tender, about 3 minutes. Stir in bacon, favas, vinegar, granulated sugar, and salt and pepper to taste and sauté, uncovered, over moderately high heat, 1 minute. Remove skillet from heat and stir in *frisée* (it will wilt slightly).

Brush baked salmon with glaze. Divide vegetables among 4 plates and top with salmon. Serves 4.

SCRAMBLED EGGS WITH FRESH MORELS ◎

A simple preparation is the best way to enjoy the earthy flavor of morels. Always rinse morels first by swishing them around in a bowl of water to remove sand and grit, then gently pat them dry with paper towels.

1   small onion
¼   pound fresh morel mushrooms*
5   large eggs
1   tablespoon unsalted butter

GARNISH
chopped fresh chives

ACCOMPANIMENT
buttered toast

available seasonally at some farmers markets and specialty produce markets and by mail order from Marché aux Delices, tel. (888) 547-5471

Finely chop onion. Wash mushrooms and pat dry. Quarter mushrooms lengthwise. In a bowl whisk together eggs and season with salt and pepper. In a nonstick skillet heat butter over moderately high heat until foam subsides and sauté onion, stirring, until softened. Add mushrooms and sauté, stirring, until tender. Add eggs and cook, stirring constantly, until eggs are just set, about 1 minute.

Garnish eggs with chives and serve with toast. Serves 2.

GRILLED CHICKEN WITH MUSTARD SORREL SAUCE ◎

a   3-pound chicken, quartered
¼   cup extra-virgin olive oil plus additional for brushing chicken
2   cups sorrel leaves (about ⅓ pound)
1   tablespoon Dijon mustard
1   tablespoon water

Prepare grill.

Brush chicken with oil and season with salt and pepper. Grill chicken, skin sides down, on an oiled rack set 5 to 6 inches over glowing coals 10 to 15 minutes on each side, or until cooked through. (Alternatively, grill chicken in a hot oiled well-seasoned ridged grill pan over moderately high heat.)

In a blender purée sorrel with remaining ¼ cup oil, mustard, water, and salt and pepper to taste until smooth.

Serve chicken with sorrel sauce. Serves 4.

LINGUINE AND CLAMS WITH GARLIC CHIVE SAUCE ◎

Also known as Chinese chives, garlic chives are wider and flatter than regular chives and have a pungent, garlicky scent. They are available at Asian markets and some farmers markets.

24   small hard-shelled clams such as littlenecks (less than 1½ inches in diameter)
½   pound dried linguine
2   tablespoons unsalted butter
⅓   cup dry white wine
1   small bunch garlic chives

Scrub clams well. In a 4-quart kettle bring 3 quarts salted water to a boil for linguine. Cook pasta in boiling water until *al dente*. Reserve ½ cup cooking water and drain pasta in a colander.

While pasta is cooking, in a large skillet heat butter over moderately high heat until foam subsides and add clams and wine. Steam clams, covered, over moderately high heat 5 to 8 minutes, checking them every minute after 5 minutes and transferring with tongs as they open to a serving bowl. (Discard any clams that are unopened after 8 minutes.) Pour liquid in skillet through a fine sieve into bowl.

Cut enough garlic chives (including bulbs) into 2-inch pieces to measure about ½ cup. In a blender purée garlic chive pieces with reserved cooking water. Toss clams with pasta, chive sauce, and salt and pepper to taste. Serves 2 as a main course.

CRUNCHY CUCUMBER AND RADISH SALAD ○

Piles of small new onions (sometimes called spring, green, or bunching onions), with their greens still attached, are readily available at the farmers market. Their bright, fresh flavor is a nice addition to this salad.

½ pound Kirby cucumbers (about 2)
½ pound radishes (about 8)
 2 new onions (about 2 inches in diameter)
¼ cup fresh lime juice
 1 teaspoon salt
 1 bunch fresh chives
¼ cup packed fresh cilantro leaves

With a manual slicer or sharp knife cut cucumbers and radishes crosswise into ⅛-inch-thick slices. Stack slices and cut into ⅛-inch-thick julienne strips. Trim green shoots from onions and halve onions lengthwise. Cut halves lengthwise into ⅛-inch-thick slices and separate onion layers.

In a bowl toss together cucumbers, radishes, onions, lime juice, and salt. Cut chives crosswise into 1½-inch pieces and chop cilantro. Add herbs to vegetables and toss to combine well. Serves 4.

coriander or cilantro?

Coriandrum sativum—coriander—is commonly called by its Spanish name, cilantro; it also is referred to as Chinese or Mexican parsley. This herb owes its popularity in the U.S. to the ever-broadening array of foods from many cultures cropping up in American homes, from Thai or Chinese takeout to guacamole and chips. With a bold, grassy aroma and taste, cilantro is integral to cuisines around the world—including those of Southeast Asia, China, India, Spain, Portugal, Central Africa, Mexico, Central America, and South America.

Fresh cilantro may be rolled in a dampened paper towel and stored in the fridge for a few days. Wash it carefully just before using as sometimes the leaves can be very sandy. When added at the very end of cooking, cilantro (leaves and thin stems) imparts a clean tang to a dish. It's also wonderful in a crisp salad. The seeds are a standard ingredient in pickling spices and marinades, and in Southeast Asian curry pastes even the roots are used.

—Jane Daniels Lear

ASPARAGUS WITH BROWN BUTTER SAUCE AND HAZELNUTS

Trim thin asparagus by gently bending the lower stalk until it snaps—it will automatically break where the tough and tender parts meet. Cut thick asparagus with a knife just above the point where there's a change of color on the stalk. Discard the tough white end and peel a few inches of the stalk with a vegetable peeler if it seems tough or stringy.

½ cup hazelnuts (about 4 ounces)
2 pounds asparagus
1½ tablespoons unsalted butter
1½ tablespoons Sherry vinegar

Preheat oven to 350° F.

In a shallow baking pan toast hazelnuts in middle of oven until pale golden, 7 to 10 minutes. Wrap nuts in a kitchen towel and rub to remove any loose skins (do not worry about skins that do not come off). Chop nuts.

Trim asparagus. Bring a kettle of salted water to a boil and cook asparagus until crisp-tender, about 2 minutes. Drain asparagus in a colander and pat dry. In a large nonstick skillet cook butter over moderately high heat until it just turns golden brown. Add vinegar, asparagus, and salt and pepper to taste and sauté asparagus, stirring gently, until just tender. Add nuts and toss to combine. Serves 4.

SPRING VEGETABLE RAGOUT

Spiral-shaped fiddleheads, the curled fronds of ostrich ferns, make a very brief appearance in spring farmers markets. Their flavor is often compared to asparagus or green beans.

½ pound fiddleheads*
½ pound baby pattypan squash
½ pound baby carrots
½ pound pearl onions, unpeeled
¾ cup shelled fresh peas (about
    ¾ pound in pods)
½ stick (¼ cup) unsalted butter
2 fresh thyme sprigs
1 bay leaf
1 cup chicken broth
¼ pound fresh morel mushrooms*
1 large garlic clove
3 tablespoons minced fresh parsley leaves
1½ tablespoons minced fresh mint leaves

available seasonally at some farmers markets and specialty produce markets and by mail order from Marché aux Delices, tel. (888) 547-5471

Bring a kettle of salted water to a boil and have ready a large bowl of ice and cold water. With your fingers rub off any dry brown casings on fiddleheads. Soak fiddleheads in cold water, changing water several times to remove any grit, and drain. Trim squash. Peel and trim carrots.

Cook fiddleheads in boiling water 4 minutes, or until crisp-tender, and transfer with a slotted spoon to ice water to stop cooking. Transfer fiddleheads to paper towels to drain. Cook squash and carrots in boiling water 3 minutes, or until crisp-tender, and transfer with slotted spoon to ice water. Transfer squash and carrots to paper towels to drain. Cook pearl onions in boiling water 1 minute and transfer with slotted spoon to a bowl. Cook peas in boiling water 2 to 3 minutes, or until just tender, and drain.

Peel and trim pearl onions. In a large heavy skillet simmer onions, 2 tablespoons butter, thyme, bay leaf, ¼ cup broth, and salt and pepper to taste, covered, 5 minutes.

While onion mixture is simmering, wash morels and pat dry. Trim morels and halve lengthwise or slice crosswise. Add morels and ½ cup remaining broth to onion mixture and simmer, covered, 10 minutes, or until morels are tender. Add fiddleheads, squash, carrots, and remaining ¼ cup broth and simmer, covered, 1 minute. Mince garlic and add to mixture with peas, parsley, and mint. Simmer ragout, covered, 1 minute. Cut remaining 2 tablespoons butter into bits and add to ragout, stirring until butter is just melted. Discard bay leaf and thyme sprigs and season ragout with salt and pepper. Serves 6 as a side dish.

Photo opposite

SAUTÉED PURSLANE WITH GARLIC AND BALSAMIC VINEGAR ◌

Though often considered a garden weed, purslane is a highly nutritious green that grows easily in moist areas. It has small, thick, succulent leaves, and its edible green stems are tinged with ruby. Purslane is mild-tasting and can be cooked briefly as it is here, or enjoyed raw in salads.

1 pound purslane
2 garlic cloves
2 tablespoons extra-virgin olive oil
1 tablespoon balsamic vinegar

Discard coarse stems from purslane. Mince garlic and in a large nonstick skillet cook in oil over moderate heat, stirring, until fragrant. Add purslane and cook, tossing with tongs, until just wilted, 2 to 3 minutes. Stir in vinegar and season purslane with salt and pepper. Serves 4.

SUGAR SNAP PEAS AND SPINACH WITH GINGER ◯

½ pound sugar snap peas
¾ pound spinach
1½ teaspoons vegetable oil
1 tablespoon grated peeled fresh gingerroot
1 teaspoon soy sauce such as Kikkoman
½ teaspoon Asian sesame oil

Trim peas and cut diagonally into ½-inch-thick pieces. Discard coarse stems from spinach and in a colander rinse leaves.

In a large nonstick skillet heat vegetable oil over moderately high heat until hot but not smoking and sauté gingerroot, stirring, 30 seconds. Add peas and sauté, stirring, 2 minutes. Add spinach and soy sauce and sauté, stirring, until spinach is wilted and peas are crisp-tender, about 1 minute.

Serve peas and spinach drizzled with sesame oil. Serves 4.

SESAME PEA-SHOOT SALAD ◯

Sugar snap peas (sometimes called sugar peas) have such tender pods that there is no need to shell them. In fact, their appeal is the contrast of crisp sweet pod and tender pea. Thin snow peas, with barely developed peas in a supple pod, have more crunch and are less sweet. (See headnote on page 15 for pea shoot information.)

1 cup sugar snap peas
½ cup snow peas
½ cup shelled fresh green peas (about ½ pound in pods)
2 teaspoons sesame seeds
1 tablespoon rice vinegar
1 tablespoon Asian sesame oil
½ to 1 tablespoon packed light brown sugar
2 teaspoons soy sauce such as Kikkoman
6 cups pea shoots

In a kettle of boiling salted water cook sugar snap peas 2 minutes. Add snow peas and green peas and cook 1 minute. Drain peas in a colander and rinse under cold water. Pat peas dry between paper towels.

In a dry small skillet toast sesame seeds over moderate heat, stirring, until golden. In a small bowl whisk together sesame seeds, vinegar, oil, brown sugar, and soy sauce until sugar is dissolved.

In a bowl toss pea shoots and peas with dressing. Serves 4.

Photo opposite

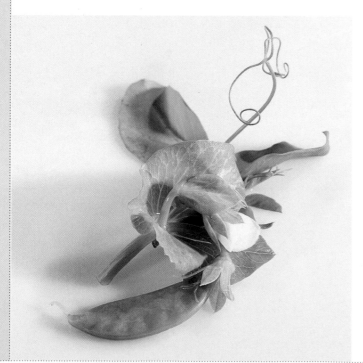

SNOW PEA SHOOT WITH POD

STRAWBERRY SHORTCAKE

Depending on the ingredients you have at hand, you can make either cream or buttermilk biscuits. White Lily flour produces a very light biscuit, but no one will be disappointed by the results of using regular all-purpose flour.

    3   pints strawberries
   1/3   cup granulated sugar, or to taste
    1   cup well-chilled heavy cream
   1/3   cup sour cream
  1 1/2 tablespoons confectioners' sugar,
         or to taste
    1   teaspoon vanilla
    8   cream or buttermilk biscuits
         (recipes follow)

Hull strawberries and quarter lengthwise. In a large bowl combine strawberries and granulated sugar and with a potato masher mash berries gently until they release their juices, being careful not to crush them to a pulp. *Let mixture stand at room temperature, stirring occasionally, 1 hour.*

In a bowl with an electric mixer beat heavy cream with sour cream and confectioners' sugar until it holds a soft shape and beat in vanilla. Split biscuits horizontally with a fork. Arrange bottom halves on 8 plates and spoon strawberry mixture over them. Top strawberry mixture with some whipped cream and arrange biscuit tops on cream. Serve remaining cream on the side. Serves 8.

Photo right

CREAM BISCUITS ◷

    2   cups White Lily* or other all-purpose flour
    1   tablespoon baking powder
   1/2   teaspoon salt
  1 1/4 cups heavy cream plus additional for
         brushing biscuits

*available by mail order from The White Lily Foods Company, tel. (423) 546-5511

Preheat oven to 425° F. and lightly grease a baking sheet.

Into a bowl sift together flour, baking powder, and salt and add 1 1/4 cups cream. Stir mixture until it just forms a dough and gather into a ball. On a lightly floured surface knead dough gently 6 times and pat out 1/2 inch thick. Cut out as many rounds as possible with a 3-inch round cutter dipped in flour and invert rounds onto baking sheet. Gather scraps and pat out dough. Cut out more rounds to make 8 rounds total and invert onto sheet.

Brush tops of rounds with additional cream and bake biscuits in middle of oven 12 to 15 minutes, or until pale golden. Transfer biscuits to a rack and cool to room temperature. Makes 8 biscuits.

BUTTERMILK BISCUITS

2 cups White Lily* or other all-purpose flour
2 teaspoons baking powder
½ teaspoon baking soda
½ teaspoon salt
½ cup vegetable shortening
¾ cup buttermilk
   milk for brushing biscuits

Preheat oven to 425° F. and lightly grease a baking sheet.

Into a bowl sift together flour, baking powder, baking soda, and salt and with your fingertips or a pastry blender blend in shortening until mixture resembles meal. Add buttermilk and stir mixture until it just forms a dough. Gather dough into a ball. On a lightly floured surface knead dough gently 6 times and pat out ½ inch thick. Cut out as many rounds as possible with a 3-inch round cutter dipped in flour and invert rounds onto baking sheet. Gather scraps and pat out dough. Cut out more rounds to make 8 rounds total and invert onto sheet.

Brush tops of rounds with milk and bake biscuits in middle of oven 12 to 15 minutes, or until pale golden. Transfer biscuits to a rack and cool to room temperature. Makes 8 biscuits.

MAPLE ICE CREAM

"Grade B" (dark amber) pure maple syrup is preferred in this recipe for its robust maple flavor. Throughout the spring in the Northeast, farmers markets offer new maple syrup soon after the trees have been tapped.

2½ cups heavy cream
1 cup pure maple syrup
   (preferably Grade B, dark amber)
¼ teaspoon salt

In a large bowl stir together all ingredients until combined well. Freeze mixture in an ice-cream maker. Transfer ice cream to an airtight container and put in freezer to harden. *Ice cream keeps 1 week. Makes about 1 quart.*

APRICOT ALMOND CAKE

½ stick (¼ cup) unsalted butter
1 teaspoon vanilla
¼ teaspoon almond extract
¾ cup sliced blanched almonds
⅔ cup plus 1 tablespoon superfine granulated sugar
½ cup all-purpose flour
3 fresh apricots
4 large egg whites
¼ teaspoon salt

ACCOMPANIMENT
lightly sweetened whipped cream or vanilla ice cream

Preheat oven to 400° F. and butter an 8-inch round cake pan.

In a small saucepan melt butter over moderate heat and let cool. Stir in vanilla and almond extract. In a food processor finely grind almonds with ⅔ cup sugar and flour. Halve and pit apricots. Cut halves into thin slices and in a small bowl toss with remaining tablespoon sugar. In a bowl with an electric mixer beat whites with salt until they just hold stiff peaks. Fold in almond mixture gently but thoroughly and fold in butter mixture (batter will deflate slightly). Spread batter in cake pan and arrange apricot slices evenly on top.

Bake cake in middle of oven 20 to 25 minutes, or until golden and a tester comes out clean. Invert cake onto a plate and cool, fruit side up, on a rack 5 minutes.

Serve cake warm with whipped cream or ice cream. Serves 6.

cherries

In very late spring cherries take pride of place at many farmers markets. It's almost impossible to leave without a sackful! When buying cherries, look for firm, shiny ones. Green stems signify that they are freshly picked.

Fresh sweet cherries are usually eaten out of hand, but if you use them in a recipe you can remove the stones with a small sharp knife or a hand-held cherry pitter—a kitchen tool that resembles a hole-puncher. A cherry pitter works on the fleshier tart, or sour, cherries as well, but because these cherries are so soft you can also pit them by hand: Working over a bowl to catch the juices, simply squeeze the stones out through the stem ends.

Pitted cherries freeze well and keep up to 6 months. Simply freeze them on paper towel-lined baking sheets and, when they are hard, double-bag them in heavy-duty sealable plastic bags and tuck them into the coldest part of your freezer.

—Jane Daniels Lear

RICE PUDDING WITH POACHED APRICOTS

Scented geranium (pelargonium; not common geranium) comes in many scents—apple, lime, rose, and straw-berry among others. We chose lemon-scented leaves, which imbue our poached apricots with a hint of gentle citrus flavor. Some farmers markets may carry the plants, but it's unlikely that you will find them as cut herbs. Lemon verbena or lemon zest can be substituted.

FOR RICE PUDDING
- 1 orange
- 3 cups whole milk
- 1 cup long-grain white rice
- ½ cup sugar
- 1½ cups well-chilled heavy cream
- ½ teaspoon vanilla

FOR POACHED APRICOTS
- 1 pound fresh apricots
- ⅓ cup sugar
- ¼ cup water
- 5 scented geranium leaves (nontoxic and pesticide-free), optional

Make rice pudding:
With a vegetable peeler remove zest from orange in long strips. In a 3-quart heavy saucepan simmer milk, zest, rice, and ¼ cup sugar, covered, stirring occasionally, until rice is tender and most of milk is absorbed, about 30 minutes. Discard zest and cool rice mixture to room temperature. In a large bowl with an electric mixer beat cream with vanilla and remaining ¼ cup sugar until it holds soft peaks and fold into cooled rice mixture. *Chill pudding, covered, until cold, at least 2 hours, and up to 2 days.*

Make poached apricots:
Halve and pit apricots and quarter them. In a 2-quart heavy kettle simmer sugar, water, and geranium leaves 2 minutes. Add apricots and simmer, covered, 5 minutes. Cool poached apricots to room temperature and discard geranium leaves. *Poached apricots may be made 2 days ahead and chilled in an airtight container.* Serve rice pudding topped with poached apricots. Serves 4 to 6.

RHUBARB APPLE PIE

*Although rhubarb is a vegetable, it's usually treated like
a fruit and sweetened with lots of sugar to tame its
extreme acidity. Look for crisp ruby-red stalks and discard any leaves that are attached as they can be toxic.*

2 recipes pastry dough (recipe on page 128)
1¾ pounds Granny Smith apples
1¼ pounds rhubarb
1 cup plus 1 tablespoon sugar
3 tablespoons all-purpose flour
¾ teaspoon cinnamon
½ teaspoon freshly grated nutmeg

On a lightly floured surface with a lightly
floured rolling pin roll out 1 disk of dough
into a 14-inch round (about ⅛-inch thick)
and fit into a 9-inch (1-quart) glass pie
plate. Trim edge, leaving a ½-inch overhang. Roll out remaining disk of dough
in same manner and transfer to a baking
sheet. *Chill shell and pastry round 30 minutes.*

Preheat oven to 350° F.

Peel and core apples. Trim rhubarb,
discarding any leaves. Cut apples and
rhubarb into ½-inch pieces and in a large
bowl toss with 1 cup sugar, flour, cinnamon, and nutmeg to coat. Pour rhubarb
mixture into shell and cover with pastry
round. Trim dough, leaving a ¾-inch
overhang, and fold overhang under edge
of bottom shell, pressing to seal. Crimp
edge decoratively. Sprinkle pie with
remaining tablespoon sugar and with a
sharp knife cut three ¾-inch-long slits
on top of pie to form steam vents.

Bake pie in middle of oven until crust
is golden, about 1½ hours. Transfer pie
to a rack to cool. Serve pie warm or at
room temperature. Serves 6 to 8.

RHUBARB STRAWBERRY COMPOTE WITH CARDAMOM CREAM

FOR CARDAMOM CREAM
1 cup well-chilled heavy cream
2 tablespoons sugar
¼ teaspoon ground cardamom

1 pound rhubarb
1 pint strawberries
1 cup water
1 cup sugar
8 shortbread rounds such as
Walkers Shortbread Highlanders,
or other shortbread

Make cardamom cream:
In a bowl with an electric mixer beat cream
with sugar and cardamom until it just holds
stiff peaks. *Cardamom cream may be made 3 hours
ahead and chilled, covered.*

Trim rhubarb, discarding any leaves, and
cut crosswise into 1-inch pieces. Hull
strawberries and quarter lengthwise, transferring to a large bowl. In a 12-inch heavy
skillet bring water and sugar to a boil,
stirring until sugar is dissolved, and boil
1 minute. Add rhubarb in 1 layer and cook
at a bare simmer, gently stirring once or
twice, until rhubarb is tender but not
falling apart, about 10 minutes. With a
slotted spoon transfer rhubarb to bowl
with strawberries and gently stir to combine. Boil syrup until reduced to about
¾ cup, about 3 minutes.

Divide shortbread rounds among 4 plates
and top with compote and cardamom
cream. Drizzle plates with syrup. Serves 4.

avocados FAVA BEANS green beans BLUEBERRIES blackberries BOYSENBERRIES raspberries CURRANTS celery SOUR CHERRIES corn CUCUMBERS eggplants FIGS garlic BASIL dill PARSLEY mint CANTALOUPE honeydew melons WATERMELON nectarines

summer

GRILLED SHRIMP WITH SALSA VERDE ☙

FOR SALSA VERDE
½ cup packed fresh basil leaves
½ cup loosely packed fresh flat-leafed
    parsley leaves
1 small garlic clove
¼ cup extra-virgin olive oil
2 teaspoons red-wine vinegar
¾ teaspoon anchovy paste

12 large shrimp (about 6 ounces)
1 tablespoon extra-virgin olive oil

Make salsa verde:
In a blender purée *salsa verde* ingredients
until smooth and season with salt and pepper. *Salsa verde may be made 1 day ahead and chilled,
covered. Bring salsa to room temperature before serving.*

Prepare grill.

Shell and devein shrimp. Pat shrimp dry.
In a bowl toss shrimp with oil and season
with salt and pepper. Grill shrimp on a
lightly oiled rack set 5 to 6 inches over
glowing coals until just cooked through,
about 2 minutes on each side. (Alternatively, broil shrimp under a preheated
broiler 2 to 3 inches from heat.)

Serve shrimp with *salsa verde.* Serves 2.

SPAGHETTI AND TOMATO SALAD WITH DILL YOGURT DRESSING ☙

*English cucumbers, grown in hothouses, are longer than
American varieties and contain fewer seeds and less
water. These qualities make them ideal for our yogurt
sauce, however, any cukes at the farmers market can be
used provided they're salted and drained for 30 minutes
and then rinsed thoroughly and squeezed dry.*

¼ pound spaghetti
¾ English cucumber
1 garlic clove
⅛ teaspoon salt
2 tablespoons fresh dill sprigs
¼ cup plain low-fat yogurt
¼ cup well-shaken buttermilk
6 ounces vine-ripened cherry tomatoes
¼ cup Kalamata or other brine-cured
    black olives

In a 5-quart kettle bring 3 quarts salted
water to a boil for spaghetti.

Peel and seed ½ cucumber and shred on
large holes of a 4-sided grater. Squeeze
shredded cucumber in a kitchen towel
to remove excess liquid. Seed and dice
remaining ¼ cucumber. Mince garlic
and mash to a paste with salt. Chop dill.
Reserve ½ tablespoon dill and in a large
bowl stir together remaining dill, shredded
and diced cucumber, garlic paste, yogurt,
buttermilk, and salt and pepper to taste.

Halve or quarter tomatoes. Pit olives and
cut into thin slices. In a bowl stir together
tomatoes, olives, reserved dill, and salt
and pepper to taste.

Cook spaghetti in boiling water until *al dente*
and drain in a colander. Rinse spaghetti
under cold water to stop cooking and drain
well. Add spaghetti to yogurt mixture and
toss to coat.

Serve spaghetti topped with tomato mixture.
Serves 2.

Photo opposite

tomatoes

Although tomatoes are available in supermarkets year-round, nothing beats the succulence of one fresh from the garden. These days there are literally hundreds of kinds to choose from, in a wide range of colors, shapes, and sizes. Ask your local growers about any heirlooms they might be cultivating—wonderful old varieties such as Old Brooks, Burbank, Cherokee Purple, and Oxheart won't keep quite as long as hybrids, but they more than make up for the fact in flavor, texture, and nutrition.

Regardless of type, nothing ruins a tomato faster than putting it in the refrigerator: The flesh will lose its firmness, becoming mealy, and much of the flavor will be lost. A sunny windowsill isn't the best place for tomatoes, either—they do best kept stem side up (to prevent bruised shoulders) at normal room temperature and in indirect light. Under these conditions gloriously ripe tomatoes will keep a day or so and underripe ones will take up to a week to reach their peak. If you find yourself with too many ripe tomatoes on hand make a quick marinara sauce for the freezer— you'll congratulate yourself come winter!

—Jane Daniels Lear

CHEDDAR PITA TOASTS

1 pita pocket (a 6-inch round)
2 teaspoons extra-virgin olive oil
⅓ cup freshly grated Cheddar

Preheat oven to 375° F.

Halve pita horizontally to form 2 rounds and brush rough sides with oil. Sprinkle rounds with Cheddar and season with salt and pepper. On a baking sheet bake rounds in middle of oven until cheese is melted and bubbling, about 6 minutes.

Transfer rounds to a cutting board and cut each into 6 wedges. Serve toasts warm. Serves 2.

PEACH PAVLOVAS ⊙+

*This no-cook peach topping is quick and delicious.
Although peaches are highly perishable, it is important to
purchase only ripe ones for the best flavor. The fruit
should be fragrant, not too hard, and have creamy or
golden skin free of any greenish tint. Some varieties have
a crimson hue, but this doesn't indicate ripeness.*

FOR PAVLOVAS
2 large egg whites
½ cup sugar
¾ teaspoon cornstarch
¼ teaspoon vanilla
¼ teaspoon vinegar

FOR TOPPING
2 firm-ripe peaches
2 tablespoons water
1 teaspoon sugar
1 teaspoon fresh lemon juice
⅓ cup well-chilled heavy cream

Make pavlovas:
Preheat oven to 225° F. and line a baking
sheet with parchment paper.

In a large bowl with an electric mixer beat
whites with a pinch salt until they just hold
soft peaks. Gradually add sugar, cornstarch,
vanilla, and vinegar and beat until meringue
holds stiff, glossy peaks. Spoon meringue
into 2 mounds on baking sheet and spread
each into a 3½-inch round, smoothing tops.

Bake pavlovas in middle of oven 45 minutes.
Turn off oven. *Let pavlovas stand in oven 2 hours.*
Transfer pavlovas to a rack to cool completely (pavlovas will be hard outside and
soft inside). *Pavlovas keep in an airtight container
at cool room temperature 1 day.*

Make topping:
Pit peaches and cut into ½-inch-thick
wedges. In a blender purée half of peaches
with water, sugar, and juice until very
smooth. In a bowl with cleaned beaters
beat cream until it just holds soft peaks.

Top pavlovas with whipped cream and peach
wedges and serve with purée. Serves 2.

NECTARINE BASIL LEMONADE ⊙

*The nectarine, originally from China, is related to
the peach and has smooth orange-red skin. Choose
nectarines that yield slightly to gentle pressure.*

2 firm-ripe nectarines
3½ cups water
1 cup loosely packed fresh basil leaves
¾ cup sugar, or to taste
1 cup fresh lemon juice

GARNISH
small fresh basil leaves

Coarsely chop 1 nectarine and in a small
saucepan stir together with 2 cups water,
basil, and sugar. Bring mixture to a boil,
stirring until sugar is dissolved, and simmer
5 minutes. Cool mixture and pour through
a fine sieve into a pitcher, pressing hard on
solids. Thinly slice remaining nectarine and
stir into pitcher with remaining 1½ cups
water and lemon juice.

Serve lemonade in ice-filled tall glasses
and garnish with basil leaves. Makes about
6 cups.

Photo above

Summer Dinner for Four

* Miniature Crab Cakes with Avocado Cilantro Dip
* Grilled Country Ribs with Summer Savory Mustard Marinade
* Green Bean and Red Onion Salad
* Couscous and Cherry Tomato Salad with Basil
* Gingerbread with Nectarines and Cream
* *Cosentino Napa Valley Merlot Reserve 1996*

MINIATURE CRAB CAKES WITH AVOCADO CILANTRO DIP ⊙

California avocados are preferred for their buttery taste. Unlike most other fruits, avocados may be purchased underripe; allow them to soften at room temperature for 2 or 3 days. Ripe avocados will yield when pressed firmly, but shouldn't feel soft.

FOR AVOCADO DIP
1   ripe California avocado
¼   cup packed fresh cilantro leaves
2   tablespoons plain yogurt
½   teaspoon minced garlic
1   teaspoon fresh lemon juice

FOR CRAB CAKES
1   large egg
¾   pound jumbo lump crab meat
½   cup fine fresh bread crumbs
2   teaspoons Dijon mustard
1   teaspoon finely grated fresh lime zest
¼   teaspoon salt
1   tablespoon vegetable oil

Make dip:
Halve and pit avocado. Scoop flesh into a food processor and purée with remaining dip ingredients until smooth. Season dip with salt and pepper and transfer to a bowl. *Dip may be made 2 hours ahead and chilled, covered.*

Make crab cakes:
In a large bowl lightly beat egg. Pick over crab meat to remove any bits of shell and cartilage (being careful not to break up lumps) and add to egg with all remaining crab cake ingredients except oil. Stir mixture until just combined and season with salt and pepper. In a 12-inch nonstick skillet heat oil over moderate heat until hot but not smoking and, working in batches, drop crab mixture by tablespoons into skillet without crowding. Cook crab cakes until golden, about 1 minute on each side, transferring to a plate.

Serve crab cakes with dip. Serves 4.

GRILLED COUNTRY RIBS WITH SUMMER SAVORY MUSTARD MARINADE ⊙

Soft, smooth, inch-long summer savory leaves offer peppery thyme flavor. If you're unable to find fresh leaves, substitute 2 tablespoons crumbled dried leaves.

¼   cup Dijon mustard
2   tablespoons red-wine vinegar
½   cup olive oil
6   tablespoons finely chopped fresh summer savory leaves
2   tablespoons water
4   pounds country-style pork ribs (about 12)

Prepare grill.

In a bowl whisk together all ingredients except ribs and season marinade with salt and pepper. In a baking dish large enough to hold ribs in one layer coat ribs with marinade. Let ribs stand, covered, at room temperature 15 minutes.

Grill ribs on an oiled rack set 5 to 6 inches over hot glowing coals until just cooked through, about 10 minutes on each side. Serves 4.

Photo opposite

GREEN BEAN AND RED ONION SALAD ⊙

1   pound green beans
1   red onion
1   tablespoon plus 1 teaspoon balsamic vinegar
¼   cup extra-virgin olive oil

Trim beans and cut into 1½-inch pieces. On a steamer rack set over boiling water steam beans, covered, until crisp-tender, about 4 minutes. Halve onion lengthwise and slice thin crosswise.

In a bowl whisk together vinegar, oil, and salt and pepper to taste until emulsified and add onion, tossing to combine. Add warm beans and toss to combine well. Serves 4.

Photo opposite

Couscous and Cherry Tomato Salad with Basil ◖

When ripe cherry tomatoes start to appear in the market in abundance, they're at their best. Look for Sweet 100, a very juicy, sweet, low-acid red variety, as well as Yellow Pear, a small yellow or red heirloom pear-shaped variety, known for its sweetness.

1½ cups water
1 teaspoon salt
1 cup couscous
1 medium vine-ripened tomato
1 teaspoon Dijon mustard
2 teaspoons balsamic vinegar
2 tablespoons extra-virgin olive oil
1½ pints vine-ripened red and yellow
cherry tomatoes (about ⅔ pound)
¼ cup packed fresh basil leaves

In a 3-quart saucepan bring water and salt to a boil and stir in couscous. Immediately remove pan from heat and let couscous stand, covered, 5 minutes.

Cut medium tomato into quarters and in a blender purée with mustard and vinegar until smooth. With motor running add oil in a slow stream. Season dressing with salt and pepper. Halve cherry tomatoes and tear basil leaves into bite-size pieces. In a large bowl toss together couscous, dressing, cherry tomatoes, and basil and season with salt and pepper. Serves 4.

Gingerbread with Nectarines and Cream ◖

1 cup all-purpose flour
½ teaspoon baking soda
¾ teaspoon ground ginger
¾ teaspoon cinnamon
½ teaspoon salt
1 large egg
½ cup sugar
½ cup unsulfured molasses
½ cup vegetable oil
½ cup boiling water

FOR TOPPING
4 ripe nectarines
3 tablespoons sugar
1 cup well-chilled heavy cream
½ teaspoon vanilla

Preheat oven to 400° F. Grease and flour an 8-inch square baking pan, knocking out excess flour.

Into a bowl sift together flour, baking soda, ginger, cinnamon, and salt. In a cup lightly beat egg and stir into flour mixture with sugar, molasses, and oil. Add boiling water in a slow stream, whisking until combined well, and pour batter into pan. Bake gingerbread in middle of oven 30 minutes, or until a tester inserted in center comes out clean.

Make topping while gingerbread is baking:
Cut nectarines into ¼-inch-thick wedges and in a bowl toss with 2 tablespoons sugar. In another bowl with an electric mixer beat cream with vanilla and remaining tablespoon sugar until it holds soft peaks.

Cool gingerbread slightly in pan on a rack. Cut gingerbread into quarters and serve topped with whipped cream and nectarines. Serves 4 generously.

Photo opposite

ALFRESCO
SUMMER DINNER
FOR FOUR

* Melon and Prosciutto
* Lobster, Potato, and Corn Salad with Tarragon
* Mesclun and Watercress Salad
* Plum Sorbet
* Almond and Rosemary Biscotti
* *Trefethen Napa Valley Dry Riesling 1997*

MELON AND PROSCIUTTO ☉

*A honeydew and cantaloupe pairing is always delicious,
but any ripe melons—especially the fabulous French
Charentais, the sweet white-meated Persian melon,
or the Israeli hybrids, Galia and Ogen   would work
well here.*

¼ cantaloupe
¼ honeydew melon
1 tablespoon fresh lemon juice
1½ teaspoons extra-virgin olive oil
⅓ pound thinly sliced prosciutto

Discard rind from melons and thinly
slice melon. In a large bowl drizzle melon
with lemon juice and oil and gently toss.
On each of 4 plates decoratively arrange
melon and prosciutto. Serves 4.

LOBSTER, POTATO, AND CORN SALAD WITH TARRAGON

2 tablespoons sea salt
2 large ears corn
2 bay leaves
2 live lobsters (1½ pounds each) or 1 pound
   cooked lobster meat (about 2 cups)
2 pounds boiling potatoes (preferably new)
2 shallots
½ cup extra-virgin olive oil
3½ tablespoons rice vinegar
2 tablespoons heavy cream
⅓ cup loosely packed fresh tarragon leaves,
   or to taste

GARNISH
fresh tarragon sprigs

In a 6-quart kettle bring 4 quarts water
to a boil with sea salt and have ready a bowl
of ice and cold water. Cut enough kernels
from cobs to measure about 1¼ cups. In
boiling water blanch corn 30 seconds and
transfer with a fine sieve to ice water to stop
cooking. Drain corn well. To boiling water
add bay leaves. If using live lobsters, rinse
1 lobster under cold water and plunge head-
first into boiling water. Boil lobster, covered,

2 minutes and transfer with tongs to a bowl.
Return water to a boil and cook remaining
lobster in same manner, leaving it in kettle.
Return first lobster to kettle and remove
kettle from heat. *Let lobsters stand in liquid,
covered, 25 minutes (lobsters will continue to cook).*

While lobsters are standing, in another kettle
cover potatoes with salted water by 2 inches
and simmer until just tender, about 20 minutes. Drain potatoes and cool slightly. When
potatoes are cool enough to handle, peel
and cut into 1-inch pieces. Mince shallots.
In a large bowl whisk together half of shallots,
⅓ cup oil, and 1½ tablespoons vinegar.
Add warm potatoes and salt and pepper
to taste and toss gently but thoroughly.

Transfer lobsters to a cutting board. Break
off claws at body. Crack claws and remove
meat, leaving it intact. Twist off tails and
halve lengthwise. Remove meat from tails
and cut crosswise into ½-inch pieces. Halve
bodies lengthwise along undersides. Break
off legs at body and remove meat from body
cavities near leg joints, discarding bodies
and remaining shells. In a bowl whisk together
remaining oil, remaining 2 tablespoons
vinegar, and cream. Add remaining shallots
and salt and pepper to taste and whisk until
combined well. Add lobster meat and toss
gently to combine well.

Coarsely chop tarragon leaves and add to
potato mixture with corn, lobster mixture,
and salt and pepper to taste, tossing gently.
*Salad may be made 4 hours ahead and chilled, covered.
Bring salad to room temperature before serving.*

Serve salad garnished with tarragon sprigs.
Serves 4.

Photo opposite

corn

Frenzied shoppers stripping husks from ears of corn, then tossing the rejected ears back on the heap for the next person to paw over, are an all-too-common sight. This corn carnage results in ruined ears—the husks preserve the fresh sweetness of the kernels, which begin to dry out as soon as they are exposed to the air. You can tell if plump, even rows of kernels fill out the cob by feeling the top from outside the husk. The occasional worm—a happy sign that the cornfield hasn't been overloaded with pesticides—is easily removed with the silk. Examine the ears carefully for freshness. The stems should look recently cut (not dried out), the husks should be vibrant green and slightly damp, and the medium-brown silk (avoid ears with blackened silk) should feel sticky.

If you can't serve the corn right away, store it, unhusked, in a plastic bag in the coldest part of the fridge—the chill will slow the conversion of sugar to starch that begins the moment the ears are picked. Modern Supersweet varieties, which contain 25 to 30 percent sugar, are bred to slow down the conversion of sugar to starch—they will last up to 2 weeks. If you are among those folks who prefer corn to taste like *corn*, not candy, seek out heirloom varieties such as Golden Bantam, Country Gentleman (also known as Shoepeg), and Black Aztec.

—Jane Daniels Lear

MESCLUN AND WATERCRESS SALAD ☺

Watercress adds peppery taste and crunch to salads. Look for deep green, tender leaves that have no dark or moist spots where the leaves have folded. If wrapped well in a damp kitchen towel, watercress will keep in the refrigerator for 2 days.

- 1¼ cups packed mixed fresh herb leaves such as parsley, thyme, basil, and tarragon
- 1 teaspoon honey
- 1 teaspoon Dijon mustard
- 1½ tablespoons red-wine vinegar
- ½ teaspoon salt
- 3 tablespoons extra-virgin olive oil
- 2 bunches watercress
- 4 cups *mesclun* (mixed baby lettuces; about 4 ounces)

Finely chop ¼ cup mixed herbs and in a small bowl whisk together with honey, mustard, vinegar, and salt until combined. Add oil in a stream, whisking until emulsified.

Discard tough stems from watercress. In a large bowl toss together remaining herbs, watercress, *mesclun*, and dressing and season with salt and pepper. Serves 4.

PLUM SORBET ☺+

By late summer you shouldn't have any trouble finding elongated Italian prune plums (photo opposite). Most of these plums are dried to make prunes, hence their name. Here, the prune plum's sweet yellow flesh and tart dark-blue skin combine to make a delicious sorbet.

- 2 pounds Italian prune plums
- 1 cup packed light brown sugar
- ¼ cup granulated sugar
- 3 tablespoons fresh lemon juice

Halve and pit plums. In a large saucepan cook plums with remaining ingredients over moderate heat, stirring, until plums release their liquid and simmer, stirring, 5 minutes. Cool mixture slightly.

In a blender purée mixture in 2 batches and pour through a fine sieve into a bowl. *Chill mixture, covered, until cold, about 2 hours.*

Freeze mixture in an ice-cream maker. Transfer sorbet to an airtight container and put in freezer to harden. *Sorbet keeps 1 week.* Makes about 5 cups.

Photo right, top

ALMOND AND ROSEMARY BISCOTTI

1½ cups whole almonds (about 7 ounces)
2 cups unbleached all-purpose flour
1 cup sugar
1 teaspoon baking soda
¼ teaspoon salt
4 large eggs
1 tablespoon plus 1 teaspoon chopped fresh rosemary leaves
1 teaspoon vanilla
1 teaspoon water

Preheat oven to 350° F. and butter a large baking sheet.

Coarscly chop almonds and in a shallow baking pan toast in middle of oven until pale golden, about 10 minutes. Reduce temperature to 300° F.

Into a bowl sift together flour, sugar, baking soda, and salt. In another bowl with an electric mixer beat together 3 eggs, rosemary, and vanilla until just combined. Stir in flour mixture and beat until a dough forms. Stir in almonds and halve dough.

Working on baking sheet, with floured hands form each piece of dough into a flattish 12-inch-long log and arrange logs at least 3 inches apart on sheet. In a cup beat together remaining egg and water and brush logs with egg wash. Bake logs in middle of oven until golden, about 50 minutes. Cool logs on baking sheet on a rack, 10 minutes. On a cutting board with a serrated knife diagonally cut logs crosswise into about ⅓-inch-thick slices. Bake *biscotti*, cut sides down, on baking sheet in middle of oven until crisp, about 15 minutes, and cool on rack. *Biscotti keep in an airtight container at cool room temperature 1 week.* Makes about 60 *biscotti*.

MOZZARELLA, GREENS, AND GARLIC BRUSCHETTA ☺

Young arugula leaves have a pleasant nutty flavor; as they mature, they develop a stronger, peppery taste. Here the green is cooked, so the older leaf can be used.

1¼ pounds arugula, spinach, or escarole
6 garlic cloves
½ teaspoon coarse salt
2 tablespoons olive oil
½ cup coarsely grated fresh mozzarella
16 garlic toasts (recipe follows)

Discard coarse stems from greens and coarsely chop enough greens to measure about 6 cups. Mince garlic and mash to a paste with salt. In a large heavy skillet cook garlic paste in oil over moderately low heat, stirring, 1 minute. Add greens and salt and pepper to taste and sauté over moderately high heat, stirring, until wilted and tender, about 3 minutes. Transfer greens mixture to a bowl, discarding any excess liquid, and cool to warm. Stir in mozzarella and mound about 1 tablespoon on oiled side of each toast. Makes 16 *bruschetta*.

Photo on page 69

GARLIC TOASTS ☺

1 loaf crusty Italian bread or *baguette* (12 inches long)
1 garlic clove
about 2 tablespoons extra-virgin olive oil

Prepare grill.

With a serrated knife cut bread crosswise into ½-inch-thick slices. Grill slices on a rack set about 4 inches over glowing coals 1 to 1½ minutes on each side, or until golden brown and crisp outside but still soft inside. (Alternatively, slices may be broiled in batches under a preheated broiler about 4 inches from heat.) Rub 1 side of each toast with garlic and lightly brush same side with oil. *Toasts may be made 1 week ahead and kept in an airtight container at room temperature.* Makes about 22 toasts.

GRILLED PORK TENDERLOINS WITH PEACH CHUTNEY

FOR CHUTNEY
3 firm-ripe peaches
⅓ cup packed light brown sugar
2 tablespoons vegetable oil
1 tablespoon white-wine vinegar
2 teaspoons minced garlic
2 teaspoons mustard seeds
½ teaspoon dried hot red pepper flakes

2 pork tenderloins (¾ pound each)

Make chutney:
Quarter and pit peaches and cut into ½-inch pieces. In a 3-quart heavy saucepan bring peaches and remaining chutney ingredients to a boil over moderate heat, stirring, and simmer, stirring occasionally, 15 minutes. Cool chutney and season with salt and pepper. *Chutney keeps, covered and chilled, 1 week. Bring chutney to room temperature before serving.*

Prepare grill.

Pat pork dry and season with salt and pepper. Grill pork on an oiled rack set 5 to 6 inches over glowing coals, turning every 3 minutes, until an instant-read thermometer diagonally inserted 2 inches into center of a tenderloin registers 155° F., about 15 minutes total. (Alternatively, pork may be grilled in a hot well-seasoned ridged grill pan over moderately high heat.) Transfer pork to a cutting board and let stand 10 minutes.

Slice pork and serve with chutney. Serves 4.

Vegetable Kebabs with Mustard Basting Sauce ◐+

Freshly-picked summer squashes, with tender skins and creamy white flesh, are remarkably delicate and sweet. Feel free to substitute French zucchini, striped Italian cocozelle, or golden zucchini for the green zucchini, and various scallop types—dark green Scallopini, golden yellow Sunburst, or pale green pattypan—for the yellow squash.

16 baby carrots (about 8 ounces)
 2 large red bell peppers (about 9 ounces)
16 yellow baby pattypan squash (about 8 ounces) or ¾ pound regular yellow squash
16 baby zucchini (about 6 ounces) or ¾ pound regular zucchini
16 red or white pearl onions (about 6 ounces)
1½ tablespoons white-wine vinegar
1½ tablespoons Dijon mustard
 2 teaspoons olive oil
 8 bamboo skewers (12 inches long)

Bring a large saucepan of salted water to a boil and have ready a large bowl of ice and cold water. Peel and trim carrots. Cut bell peppers into sixteen 2- by ¾-inch pieces. If using regular yellow squash and zucchini cut into thirty-two ¾-inch pieces total. Cook carrots in boiling water 1 minute. Add yellow squash and zucchini and cook vegetables 5 minutes. With a slotted spoon transfer vegetables to ice water to stop cooking and drain well in a colander. Transfer vegetables to a bowl. Cook pearl onions in boiling water 4 minutes and drain well in colander. When cool enough to handle, peel onions, leaving root ends intact. *Vegetables may be boiled 1 day ahead and chilled in sealable plastic bags.*

In a small bowl whisk together vinegar, mustard, oil, and salt and pepper to taste. *Basting sauce may be made 1 day ahead and chilled, covered.*

Prepare grill. *Soak skewers in warm water 30 minutes.*

Thread vegetables, alternating them, onto skewers. Brush one side of kebabs with about half of sauce and grill, coated side down, on an oiled rack set 5 to 6 inches over glowing coals 5 minutes. Brush kebabs with remaining sauce and turn over. Grill kebabs 5 minutes more, or until squash is tender. (Alternatively, kebabs may be grilled in a hot well-seasoned ridged grill pan over moderately high heat.) Serves 4.

Photo on page 58

Herbed Steamed Rice ◐

¾ cup long-grain rice
 2 garlic cloves
 1 teaspoon salt, or to taste
¼ cup chicken broth
 1 tablespoon minced peeled fresh gingerroot
¼ cup finely chopped scallion
 2 teaspoons fresh lemon juice
 1 teaspoon soy sauce
½ cup packed fresh cilantro sprigs

Bring a kettle of salted water to a boil and add rice. Return water to a boil, stirring, and cook rice 10 minutes. In a large sieve drain rice and rinse. In kettle bring 1 inch water to a boil and set sieve over kettle (rice should not touch water). Steam rice, covered with a kitchen towel and lid, until tender, about 20 minutes (check water level in kettle occasionally, adding water if necessary).

While rice is steaming, mince garlic and mash to a paste with ½ teaspoon salt. In a large bowl stir together garlic paste, remaining salt, broth, gingerroot, scallion, juice, and soy sauce and add rice, tossing until combined well. Cool rice to room temperature. Finely chop cilantro and stir into rice. Serves 4.

Photo on page 58

MIXED BERRY TERRINE ◐+

Any fresh berries found at the farmers market will work here—try yellow raspberries or pink gooseberries for an unusual treat.

4 cups mixed fresh berries such as small strawberries, raspberries, and blueberries (about 1½ pounds total)
2¾ teaspoons unflavored gelatin (less than 2 envelopes)
¾ cup plus 2 tablespoons cold water
1 cup sweet white wine such as Muscat de Beaumes-de-Venise
6 tablespoons superfine granulated sugar
1 tablespoon fresh lime juice

If using strawberries halve them. Decoratively arrange mixed berries in a 1-quart nonreactive terrine or loaf pan.

Have ready a bowl set in a larger bowl of ice and cold water. In a cup sprinkle gelatin over ¼ cup cold water and let stand 1 minute to soften. In a small saucepan simmer wine and sugar, stirring until sugar is dissolved, 2 minutes. Remove pan from heat and stir in gelatin mixture until dissolved. Stir in lime juice and remaining ½ cup plus 2 tablespoons water and transfer mixture to bowl set in ice water. Cool mixture, stirring occasionally, to room temperature. Pour mixture slowly over fruit. *Chill terrine, covered, until firm, at least 6 hours, and up to 2 days.*

Dip a thin knife in hot water and run knife around edge of terrine or loaf pan. Dip terrine or pan into a larger pan of hot water 3 to 5 seconds to loosen. Invert a serving plate over terrine or pan and invert terrine onto plate. Serves 6.

LIME SUGAR COOKIES ◐

1½ cups all-purpose flour
1 teaspoon baking soda
¼ teaspoon salt
1 stick (½ cup) unsalted butter, softened
¾ cup granulated sugar
1½ tablespoons finely grated fresh lime zest (from about 4 limes)
1½ tablespoons fresh lime juice
½ large egg
   confectioners' sugar for dusting cookies

Preheat oven to 350° F. and butter 2 large baking sheets.

Into a bowl sift together flour, baking soda, and salt. In a bowl with an electric mixer beat together butter, granulated sugar, and zest until light and fluffy. Beat in juice and egg until combined well and add flour mixture, beating until just combined.

With lightly floured hands roll tablespoons of dough into balls and arrange about 1½ inches apart on baking sheets. With back of a fork slightly flatten balls.

Bake cookies in upper and lower thirds of oven, switching position of sheets halfway through baking, about 12 minutes total. With a spatula immediately transfer cookies to racks to cool. *Cookies keep in an airtight container at room temperature 4 days.*

Just before serving, dust cookies lightly with confectioners' sugar. Makes about 24 cookies.

ZUCCHINI AND YELLOW SQUASH WITH PESTO ☺

¼ cup packed fresh basil leaves
⅓ cup freshly grated Parmesan (about 1 ounce)
1 tablespoon pine nuts
½ teaspoon salt
1 tablespoon fresh lemon juice
½ cup extra-virgin olive oil
1 pound zucchini (about 2 large)
½ pound yellow squash (about 1 large)

In a food processor purée together basil, Parmesan, nuts, salt, juice, and oil until smooth and season with pepper. *Pesto may be made 1 day ahead and chilled, covered.*

With a *mandoline* or other manual slicer cut zucchini and yellow squash lengthwise into very thin slices. Arrange slices in one layer, overlapping them slightly, on 2 large platters and drizzle pesto over slices. Serves 6 as a first course.

Photo opposite

ROASTED POUSSINS WITH LEMON THYME

Lemon verbena or regular thyme leaves can be substituted for the lemon thyme here with equally delicious results.

1¼ sticks (½ cup plus 2 tablespoons) unsalted butter, softened
2 tablespoons chopped fresh lemon thyme leaves
1 tablespoon finely grated fresh lemon zest
1 teaspoon salt
⅛ teaspoon freshly ground black pepper
6 *poussins* (young chickens; 1 pound each)
½ cup dry white wine

GARNISH
lemon wedges and
lemon thyme sprigs

Preheat oven 475° F.

In a small bowl stir together 1 stick butter, thyme, zest, salt, and pepper until combined. Trim *poussin* necks flush with bodies if necessary. Rinse birds inside and out and pat dry.

Beginning at neck end of each bird, slide your fingers between breast meat and skin to loosen skin (be careful not to tear skin). Divide seasoned butter into 12 portions. Using a teaspoon put 1 portion butter under skin of each breast half and spread butter evenly under skin by pressing outside of skin with your fingers. If desired, tie legs of each bird together with kitchen string and secure wings to sides with wooden picks or bamboo skewers.

Arrange birds in a large flameproof roasting pan (about 18 by 12 by 2 inches). Melt remaining ¼ stick butter and brush onto birds. Season birds with salt and roast in middle of oven until golden brown, about 30 to 40 minutes, or until an instant-read thermometer inserted in fleshy part of a thigh registers 170° F.

Remove string and skewers from birds and pour any juices from inside birds into pan. Transfer birds to a platter and keep warm, loosely covered with foil. To pan add wine and on top of stove deglaze over moderate heat, scraping up brown bits. Skim fat from sauce.

Garnish *poussins* with lemon wedges and thyme sprigs and serve with sauce. Serves 6.

Photo on back of jacket

Fig and Arugula Salad ◑

Most fig varieties are black (sweet and dry); green (thin-skinned and juicy); or purple (juiciest and sweetest of the three). Any ripe figs are appropriate here.

- 1 teaspoon Dijon mustard
- 1 tablespoon honey
- 1 tablespoon fresh lemon juice
- 3 tablespoons vegetable oil
- 10 firm-ripe fresh figs
- 8 cups loosely packed arugula (8 ounces)

In a large bowl whisk together mustard, honey, and juice. Add oil in a slow stream, whisking until dressing is emulsified, and season with salt and pepper.

Halve figs or quarter if large and discard coarse stems from arugula. Toss arugula with dressing until combined and season with salt and pepper. Arrange figs decoratively on salad. Serves 6.

Potato and Roasted Pepper Salad

- 3 red bell peppers
- 3 yellow bell peppers
- 3 pounds small white boiling potatoes (about 2 inches in diameter)
- 1 bunch fresh chives
- 3 tablespoons balsamic vinegar
- 1 teaspoon minced garlic
- ⅛ teaspoon dried hot red pepper flakes
- 3 tablespoons extra-virgin olive oil

Roast and peel bell peppers (procedure follows). Cut peppers into ¾-inch-wide strips. In a kettle cover potatoes with salted cold water by 2 inches and simmer until just tender, about 25 minutes. Drain potatoes in a colander.

Cut chives into ½-inch pieces. In a large bowl whisk together vinegar, garlic, and red pepper flakes. Add oil in a slow stream, whisking until dressing is emulsified, and add salt and pepper to taste. Halve warm potatoes and add to dressing with roasted peppers, chives, and salt and pepper to taste, tossing until combined. Serves 6.

To Quick-Roast and Peel Peppers

Broiler method:
Preheat broiler.
Quarter peppers lengthwise, discarding stems, seeds, and ribs. Put peppers, skin sides up, on rack of a broiler pan and broil about 2 inches from heat until skins are blistered and charred, 8 to 12 minutes.

Gas stove method:
Lay whole peppers on their sides on racks of burners (preferably 1 to a burner) and turn flames on high. Char peppers, turning them with tongs, until skins are blackened, 5 to 8 minutes.

Transfer peppers roasted by either method to a bowl and let stand, covered with plastic wrap, until cool enough to handle. Peel peppers and if necessary cut off tops and discard seeds and ribs. *Peppers may be roasted 2 days ahead and chilled, covered.*

Brown Butter Almond Torte with Sour Cherry Sauce

- 1 stick (½ cup) unsalted butter
- 1 teaspoon vanilla
- 1 cup blanched whole almonds (about 4 ounces)
- ½ cup all-purpose flour
- 1 cup sugar
- ¾ teaspoon salt
- 6 large egg whites
- ⅓ cup sliced almonds

ACCOMPANIMENT
sour cherry sauce

Preheat oven to 375° F. Butter and flour a 9-inch round cake pan, knocking out excess flour.

In a small saucepan melt butter over moderately low heat and continue to heat until golden brown with a nutlike fragrance. (Bottom of pan will be covered with brown specks.) Cool butter to warm and stir in vanilla.

In a food processor finely grind whole almonds with flour, ⅔ cup sugar, and ½ teaspoon salt.

In a large bowl with an electric mixer beat whites with remaining ¼ teaspoon salt until they hold soft peaks. Gradually add remaining ⅓ cup sugar, beating until meringue just holds stiff peaks. Fold in almond mixture gently but thoroughly and fold in butter mixture gently but thoroughly (batter will deflate). Spread batter evenly in cake pan.

Sprinkle top of batter evenly with sliced almonds and bake torte in middle of oven 35 to 40 minutes, or until it begins to pull away from side of pan and a tester comes out clean.

Cool torte in pan on a rack 15 minutes and invert onto rack. Flip torte right side up and cool completely. *Torte may be made 1 day ahead and kept in an airtight container at room temperature.*

Serve torte with sauce. Serves 6 generously.

Photo below

SOUR CHERRY SAUCE

3 cups sour cherries (about 1½ pounds)
½ cup sugar
½ cup plus 1 tablespoon water
1 teaspoon cornstarch

Working over a heavy saucepan, pit cherries. In pan bring cherries, sugar, and ½ cup water to a boil. In a cup stir together cornstarch and remaining tablespoon water until cornstarch is dissolved and stir into cherry mixture. Simmer sauce 2 minutes and cool to room temperature. *Sauce may be made 2 days ahead and chilled, covered. Bring sauce to room temperature before serving.* Makes about 3 cups.

CHILLED TOMATO, ROASTED GARLIC, AND BASIL SOUP ☺+

4 garlic cloves, unpeeled
2¾ pounds vine-ripened tomatoes
1½ teaspoons balsamic vinegar
   Tabasco to taste
⅓ cup fresh basil leaves

In a small heavy skillet dry-roast garlic over moderately low heat, turning occasionally, until skin is browned and garlic is tender, about 20 minutes. Peel garlic and quarter tomatoes. In a blender purée garlic and tomatoes in batches and force through a fine sieve into a bowl. Stir in vinegar, Tabasco, and salt to taste. *Chill soup, covered, until cold, at least 6 hours, and up to 1 day.* Chop basil and stir into soup with salt and pepper to taste. Makes about 4½ cups, serving 4.

Photo opposite, front

CHILLED MINTED ZUCCHINI SOUP ☺+

1½ pounds zucchini (about 5 medium)
1 teaspoon extra-virgin olive oil
3 cups water
¼ cup fresh mint leaves
¾ cup plain low-fat yogurt

Thinly slice zucchini. In a 3½- to 4-quart heavy saucepan heat oil over moderately high heat until hot but not smoking and sauté one third zucchini, stirring occasionally, until golden. Add remaining zucchini and water and simmer until zucchini is very tender, about 15 minutes. Cool mixture slightly and in a blender purée in batches until smooth (use caution when blending hot liquids), transferring to a bowl. Finely chop mint leaves. Stir yogurt until smooth and stir into soup with mint and salt and pepper to taste. *Chill soup, covered, until cold, at least 6 hours, and up to 1 day. If necessary, season soup with salt and pepper.* Makes about 5½ cups, serving 4.

Photo opposite, left

CHILLED CURRIED YELLOW SQUASH SOUP ☺+

1 large leek (white and pale green parts only)
1½ pounds yellow squash (about 3 large)
1 teaspoon extra-virgin olive oil
1 teaspoon curry powder
¼ teaspoon turmeric
4 cups water

ACCOMPANIMENTS
sour cream
Major Grey's chutney

Trim leek and thinly slice enough leek to measure ½ cup. In a bowl of cold water wash sliced leek well and lift leek into a sieve to drain, discarding water. Thinly slice squash. In a 3½- to 4-quart heavy saucepan cook leek in oil over moderately low heat, stirring occasionally, until softened. Add curry powder and turmeric and cook, stirring, until fragrant, about 30 seconds. Add squash and water and simmer, stirring occasionally, until squash is very tender, about 15 minutes. Cool mixture slightly and in a blender purée in batches until smooth (use caution when blending hot liquids), transferring to a bowl. Season soup with salt and pepper. *Chill soup, covered, until cold, at least 6 hours, and up to 1 day. If necessary, season soup with salt and pepper.*

Serve soup with dollops of sour cream and chutney. Makes about 5 cups, serving 4.

Photo opposite, right

CHILLED HONEYDEW AND MINT SOUP IN CANTALOUPE ◔+

When choosing cantaloupes, look for tan or gold (not green) coloring between the raised netting; honeydews should feel velvety smooth, be slightly sticky, and have a creamy pale yellow coloring (without a hint of green). Give the blossom end of each variety a sniff—when ripe they are fragrant.

½ large honeydew melon
1 cup loosely packed fresh mint leaves
3 tablespoons fresh lime juice
1 tablespoon sugar, or to taste
3 cantaloupes

GARNISH
fresh mint sprigs

Cut honeydew into 1-inch pieces, discarding rind. In a blender in batches or in a food processor purée honeydew and mint leaves with lime juice, sugar, and a pinch salt until smooth and transfer to a bowl. *Chill soup, covered, until cold, at least 1 hour, and up to 2 days.*

Halve cantaloupes, discarding seeds, and decoratively trim. Serve soup in cantaloupe halves and garnish with mint sprigs. Makes 6 cups, serving 6.

Photo above

PEPPERED CHICKEN LIVER, SAGE, AND FRIED ONION BRUSCHETTA ◔

1 small onion
2 tablespoons vegetable oil
½ pound chicken livers
2 large garlic cloves
2 large fresh sage leaves
1 teaspoon freshly ground black pepper, or to taste
1 teaspoon coarse salt
a pinch ground allspice, or to taste
16 garlic toasts (page 59)

GARNISH
16 small fresh sage leaves

Halve onion lengthwise and cut into thin slices. In a large skillet heat oil over moderately high heat until hot but not smoking and sauté onion, stirring, until golden. Transfer onion with a slotted spoon to paper towels to drain.

Trim and halve livers. Pat livers dry. Slice garlic and mince sage. Add garlic to skillet and cook over moderate heat, stirring, until pale golden. Add livers and sauté over moderately high heat, stirring, until golden and just springy to the touch, about 1½ to 2 minutes on each side. Stir in sage, pepper, salt, and allspice and in a food processor pulse until coarsely puréed.

Mound about 2 teaspoons liver mixture on oiled side of each toast and top with onions. Garnish *bruschetta* with sage leaves. Makes 16 *bruschetta*.

Photo opposite

TOMATO AND RICOTTA SALATA BRUSCHETTA

Fresh chives add a sweet, mild oniony flavor to these little starters. If the pretty purple flowers are still attached (they blossom in early summer), they can be used in salads and as a garnish.

 2 large shallots
 3 large vine-ripened tomatoes
 2 ounces *ricotta salata* cheese or feta
 1 tablespoon extra-virgin olive oil
 2 tablespoons minced fresh chives, or to taste
 2 teaspoons balsamic vinegar, or to taste
16 garlic toasts (page 59)

Thinly slice shallots. Halve and seed tomatoes. Chop enough tomatoes to measure 2 cups. Cut enough cheese into ¼-inch dice to measure about ⅓ cup. In a small skillet cook shallots in oil over moderate heat, stirring, until softened. Add chopped tomato and salt and pepper to taste and cook, stirring, 30 seconds, or until just heated through.

In a bowl toss tomato mixture with diced cheese, chives, vinegar, and salt and pepper to taste and mound about 1 tablespoon on oiled side of each toast. Makes 16 *bruschetta*.

Photo below

BRUSCHETTA (RECIPES ON PAGES 59, 68, AND ABOVE)

SQUID, POTATO, AND ARUGULA SALAD

   1 pound small boiling potatoes
 1½ pounds cleaned squid
   1 tablespoon olive oil
   2 large celery ribs
   ½ medium red onion
   3 cups packed arugula leaves
   2 small vine-ripened tomatoes
      (about ½ pound total)
   2 garlic cloves
 2½ tablespoons fresh lemon juice
   2 tablespoons extra-virgin olive oil

In a saucepan cover potatoes with water by 1 inch and simmer until tender, about 20 minutes. Drain potatoes and cool to room temperature.

While potatoes are cooking, cut squid bodies into ¼-inch-thick rings and quarter tentacles. In a large nonstick skillet heat olive oil over moderately high heat until hot but not smoking and sauté squid, stirring, just until opaque, about 3 minutes. Transfer squid to a shallow baking pan and chill until cool.

Cut celery into ¼-inch-thick slices. Quarter onion through root end and cut quarters into ¼-inch wedges. In a small bowl cover onion with cold water and let stand 15 minutes. Drain onions in a colander. Remove tough stems from arugula and tear leaves in half. Cut tomatoes and potatoes into ½-inch wedges. Mince garlic.

In a large bowl whisk together garlic, lemon juice, and extra-virgin oil. Add potatoes, squid, celery, onion, arugula, and tomatoes and toss until combined well. Season salad with salt and pepper. Serves 4.

ZUCCHINI, MUSHROOM, AND PASTA PIE

FOR DOUGH

1½ sticks (¾ cup) cold unsalted butter
2½ cups all-purpose flour
1 teaspoon salt
6 to 8 tablespoons ice water

FOR MUSHROOM SAUCE

2 tablespoons unsalted butter
3 tablespoons all-purpose flour
2 cups milk
   freshly grated nutmeg
1 small onion
1 garlic clove
1 pound mushrooms
¾ pound cooked boneless ham steak
3 tablespoons olive oil
2 tablespoons dry white wine
1 cup loosely packed fresh flat-leafed
   parsley leaves
1 teaspoon minced fresh thyme leaves
¼ cup thinly sliced fresh basil leaves
¼ cup thinly sliced fresh mint leaves

2 pounds zucchini
   vegetable oil for deep-frying zucchini
10 ounces dried spinach *tagliatelle* or fettuccine
1¼ cups freshly grated Parmesan
1 large egg yolk
1 tablespoon water

Make dough:
Cut butter into 1-inch pieces. In a food processor pulse together flour and salt. Add butter and pulse until mixture resembles coarse meal. Add 6 tablespoons ice water and pulse just until a dough forms, adding more, 1 tablespoon at a time, if necessary. Turn dough out onto a work surface and divide into 2 pieces, one twice the size of the other. Form each piece into a disk. *Chill disks, wrapped separately in plastic wrap, at least 1 hour and up to 1 day.*

Make mushroom sauce:
In a heavy saucepan melt butter over moderately low heat. Add flour and cook *roux*, whisking, 3 minutes. Add milk and bring mixture to a boil, whisking. Simmer mixture, whisking, 2 minutes. Transfer béchamel sauce to a heatproof bowl and season with salt, pepper, and nutmeg.

Mince enough onion to measure 2 tablespoons and mince garlic. Thinly slice mushrooms. Cut ham into enough ½-inch cubes to measure about 1¾ cups. In a large skillet cook minced onion and garlic in oil over moderately low heat, stirring, until onion is softened. Add mushrooms and salt and pepper to taste and sauté over moderately high heat, stirring, until liquid mushrooms give off is evaporated. Add wine and simmer until evaporated. Mince enough parsley to measure ½ cup. Stir mushroom mixture and ham into béchamel sauce with minced and sliced herbs and salt and pepper to taste. *Mushroom sauce may be made 1 day ahead and chilled, covered.*

Trim zucchini and, using a *mandoline* or other manual slicer, cut zucchini lengthwise into ¼-inch-thick slices. In a large deep skillet heat ¾ inch vegetable oil until it registers 380° F. on a deep-fat thermometer and fry zucchini in small batches, turning it, 2 to 3 minutes, or until golden, transferring with tongs to paper towels to drain. *Zucchini may be fried 1 day ahead and chilled, covered.*

Preheat oven to 425° F. and bring a kettle of salted water to a boil for pasta.

Cook pasta in boiling water until *al dente*. In a colander drain pasta and rinse briefly under cold water. On a lightly floured surface roll out larger piece of dough into an 18-inch round and fit into a 10-inch springform pan, trimming overhang to 1 inch. In shell layer one third pasta, one third zucchini, one third mushroom sauce, and one third Parmesan and repeat layering twice. Roll out remaining piece of dough into an 11-inch round. Drape dough over filling and seal edges, crimping decoratively. In a cup beat together yolk and water and brush dough with egg wash. Prick dough decoratively with a fork to form steam vents.

Bake pie in middle of oven 10 minutes. Reduce temperature to 375° F. and bake pie 40 minutes more, or until top is golden. Cool pie in pan on a rack 10 minutes and remove side of pan. Serve pie warm or at room temperature. Serves 8.

Photo opposite

HERBED TOMATO TARTS ◖

This recipe makes 2 sizable tarts, enough for a light luncheon main course for 4 people. Alternatively, the tarts can be cut into small pieces to serve as an hors d'oeuvre.

1   puff pastry sheet (from a 17¼-ounce package frozen puff pastry sheets, thawed according to package instructions)

1½   pounds small to medium vine-ripened tomatoes (about 8)

1   small red onion

1   tablespoon anchovy paste

1   cup coarsely grated fresh mozzarella (about 4 ounces)

½   cup freshly grated Parmesan (about 1½ ounces)

2   teaspoons chopped fresh rosemary leaves

2   teaspoons chopped fresh thyme leaves

Preheat oven to 425° F.

On a lightly floured surface with a floured rolling pin roll out pastry into a rectangle roughly 17 by 15 inches and trim edges to form a 16- by 14-inch rectangle. Cut pastry in half lengthwise, forming two 16- by 7-inch rectangles. Brush edges with water and fold in edges to form a ½-inch-wide border on each rectangle. With tines of a fork press border to seal. Transfer rectangles to a large baking sheet.

Thinly slice tomatoes. Halve onion length-wise and thinly slice. Divide anchovy paste between rectangles and spread in a very thin, even layer. Sprinkle each tart evenly with ½ cup mozzarella and 2 tablespoons Parmesan. Arrange tomato slices in one layer on cheese. Scatter onion slices and herbs over tomatoes and sprinkle with remaining ¼ cup Parmesan and salt and pepper to taste.

Bake tarts in upper third of oven 12 to 15 minutes, or until crust is golden. *Tarts may be made 2 days ahead and chilled, covered loosely. Crisp tarts in oven before serving.* Serve tarts warm or at room temperature. Makes 2 tarts, serving 4.

Photo left

GRILLED PORK CHOPS WITH GINGERED PLUM BARBECUE SAUCE ◔

This barbecue sauce is also a perfect complement to grilled chicken.

FOR SAUCE
4 black plums (about ¾ pound)
1 garlic clove
1 tablespoon finely grated peeled fresh gingerroot
3 tablespoons hoisin sauce
2 tablespoons packed brown sugar
2 tablespoons water
1 tablespoon soy sauce such as Kikkoman
1 whole star anise or ¼ teaspoon anise seeds
1 tablespoon cider vinegar
2 scallions

4 pork chops (each 1 inch thick)

Prepare grill.

Make sauce:
Halve and pit plums and cut into 1-inch pieces. Chop garlic. In a saucepan simmer all ingredients except vinegar and scallions, covered, stirring occasionally, until plums are falling apart, about 20 minutes. Add vinegar and simmer, uncovered, stirring frequently, until sauce is consistency of ketchup, about 10 minutes. Chop scallions. Discard star anise and stir in scallions. *Sauce keeps, covered and chilled, 2 days.*

Reserve half of sauce for basting. Just before grilling, coat chops with remaining sauce. Grill chops on an oiled rack set 5 to 6 inches over glowing coals, turning every 5 minutes and basting with reserved sauce during last 5 minutes of grilling, about 20 minutes total, or until just cooked through. Serves 4.

Photo right

PENNE WITH EGGPLANT TOMATO SAUCE AND RICOTTA ◔

1 small eggplant (about 1 pound)
2 pounds vine-ripened tomatoes
1 medium onion
2 garlic cloves
½ cup packed fresh basil leaves
1 pound *penne*, rigatoni, or other tubular pasta
2 tablespoons olive oil
1 cup ricotta

Separately cut eggplant and tomatoes into 1-inch cubes. Chop onion and mince garlic. Coarsely chop basil.

In a 6-quart kettle bring 5 quarts salted water to a boil for pasta.

In a 5-quart heavy kettle or deep heavy saucepan heat oil over moderately high heat until hot but not smoking and sauté eggplant and onion, stirring occasionally, until onion is softened and eggplant begins to brown. Add tomatoes and simmer mixture, stirring occasionally, until tomatoes have a saucelike consistency and eggplant is tender, about 15 minutes. Stir in garlic and basil and season sauce with salt and pepper.

While mixture is simmering, cook pasta in boiling water until *al dente*, about 10 minutes. Drain pasta in a colander and add to sauce, tossing to coat.

Serve pasta topped with dollops of ricotta. Serves 4.

SHRIMP AND AVOCADO CAESAR SALAD

1½ pounds large shrimp (about 25)
¼ cup olive oil
2 cups ½-inch bread cubes
¼ cup freshly grated Parmesan

FOR DRESSING
½ cup mayonnaise
4 anchovy fillets
2 tablespoons red-wine vinegar
1 teaspoon Worcestershire sauce
1 tablespoon fresh flat-leafed parsley leaves

1½ heads romaine
2 firm-ripe California avocados

Shell and devein shrimp. In a large saucepan three fourths filled with generously salted boiling water simmer shrimp until just cooked through, about 2 minutes. Drain shrimp in a colander and arrange in one layer on a baking sheet. *Chill shrimp until cold, about 30 minutes.*

In a heavy skillet heat oil over moderate heat until hot but not smoking and cook bread cubes, stirring frequently, until they begin to turn golden. Remove skillet from heat and sprinkle Parmesan over hot croutons. Season croutons with salt and pepper and transfer to paper towels to drain.

Make dressing:
In a blender blend all dressing ingredients until smooth and season with salt and pepper.

Halve shrimp lengthwise. Tear enough romaine into bite-size pieces to measure 2 quarts. Pit and peel avocados and cut into ½-inch cubes.

In a large bowl toss together romaine, avocados, shrimp, croutons, and dressing. Serves 4 as a main course.

STRIPED BASS WITH RATATOUILLE

FOR RATATOUILLE
4 plum tomatoes (about ¾ pound)
1 large onion (about ¾ pound)
1 medium eggplant (about 1 pound)
1 red bell pepper
1 yellow bell pepper
1 medium zucchini (about ½ pound)
½ cup olive oil
¼ cup packed fresh basil leaves

4 striped bass fillets with skin (about 1½ pounds total)
1 tablespoon olive oil
2 tablespoons dry white wine
2 tablespoons water
1 tablespoon fresh lemon juice

GARNISH
basil sprigs

Make ratatouille:
Halve tomatoes lengthwise and seed. Separately cut onion, eggplant, peppers, and zucchini into ¼-inch dice. In a 12-inch heavy skillet heat 2 tablespoons oil over moderately high heat until hot but not smoking and sauté onion, stirring occasionally, until golden. Transfer onion to a large saucepan. In skillet heat 2 tablespoons oil over moderate heat until hot but not smoking and cook eggplant with salt to taste, stirring occasionally, until lightly browned and just tender. Add eggplant to onion. In skillet heat 2 tablespoons oil over moderate heat until hot but not smoking and cook peppers with salt to taste, stirring occasionally, until just tender. Add peppers to vegetable mixture. In skillet heat 1 tablespoon oil over moderately high heat until hot but not smoking and sauté zucchini, stirring occasionally, until golden. Add zucchini to vegetable mixture. In skillet heat remaining tablespoon oil over moderately high heat until hot but not smoking and sauté tomatoes, stirring, 1 minute. Add tomatoes to vegetable mixture. Chop basil and add to vegetables with salt and pepper to taste. Cook *ratatouille* over moderate heat, stirring occasionally, 5 minutes.

Season bass fillets with salt and pepper. In a large nonstick skillet heat oil over moderately high heat until hot but not smoking and sauté fillets, skin sides down, until skin is golden, about 1½ minutes. Turn fillets over and sauté until undersides are golden, about 1 minute more. Add wine, water, and lemon juice and simmer, covered, until fish is just cooked through, about 2 minutes. With a slotted spatula transfer fillets to a plate and keep warm. Boil liquid in skillet until reduced to about 3 tablespoons.

Arrange some of *ratatouille* (warm or room temperature) on 4 plates and top with fillets. Spoon reduced liquid over fillets and garnish with basil sprigs. Serves 4.

PAN-GRILLED CHICKEN WITH SUMMER SQUASH

1½ pounds zucchini, yellow squash, and/or baby pattypan squash
½ medium red onion
4 boneless skinless chicken breast halves (about 1½ pounds total)
1 tablespoon olive oil
2 tablespoons dry white wine
1 tablespoon fresh lemon juice
2 teaspoons minced fresh thyme leaves

Cut squash into 1½-inch pieces and cut onion into ½-inch-thick wedges. Pat chicken dry.

In a large heavy nonstick skillet heat oil over moderately high heat until hot but not smoking and sauté chicken, skinned sides down, until golden, about 3 minutes. Turn chicken over and add squash. Cook mixture, covered, over moderate heat 5 minutes, or until chicken is just cooked through.

Transfer chicken to a plate and keep warm. Add onion to squash and sauté over high heat, stirring occasionally, until vegetables begin to brown. Add wine and lemon juice and boil until liquid is evaporated. Stir in thyme and salt and pepper to taste. Serve chicken with squash. Serves 4.

MINTED LAMB BURGERS ☺

1 small head romaine
¼ English cucumber
½ cup plain yogurt
¼ cup chopped fresh mint leaves
1¼ pounds ground lamb
½ teaspoon ground cumin
1 medium eggplant
olive oil for brushing eggplant
4 pita pockets (4 inch rounds)

Prepare grill.

Thinly slice enough romaine to measure 1½ cups. Seed and chop cucumber. In a small bowl stir together cucumber, yogurt, 2 tablespoons mint, and salt and pepper to taste. In a large bowl blend together lamb, cumin, remaining 2 tablespoons mint, and salt and pepper to taste. Form lamb mixture into four 1-inch-thick patties.

Cut eggplant crosswise into eight ¼-inch-thick slices and brush lightly with some oil. Grill eggplant slices on an oiled rack set 5 to 6 inches over glowing coals 5 minutes on each side, or until tender. Transfer slices to a platter and keep warm. Grill lamb patties about 4½ minutes on each side for well-done and transfer to platter. (Alternatively, eggplant and burgers may be cooked in a hot well-seasoned cast-iron skillet or ridged grill pan.) Toast pita and split horizontally.

Transfer burgers to pitas and top with cucumber mixture, eggplant, and romaine. Serves 4.

Photo above

STEAMED VEGETABLES WITH BASIL PECAN PESTO

- 6 medium carrots
- 2 fennel bulbs (sometimes called anise)
- 1½ pounds small red potatoes
- 1½ pounds green beans
- 1¼ cups basil pecan pesto (recipe follows)
- 3 tablespoons hot water plus additional if necessary

Diagonally cut carrots into ⅛-inch-thick slices. Trim fennel stalks flush with bulbs and cut bulbs lengthwise into ⅛-inch-thick slices. Cut potatoes into ¼-inch-thick slices. On a large steamer rack set over boiling water layer carrots, fennel, and potatoes and steam, covered, until potatoes are tender, about 10 minutes. Transfer steamed vegetables to a platter. Trim beans and steam, covered, until just tender, about 10 minutes. Transfer beans to platter.

In a food processor blend pesto with 3 tablespoons hot water, adding more hot water if necessary to reach desired consistency.

Serve vegetables warm or at room temperature with pesto. Serves 6.

Photo opposite

BASIL PECAN PESTO

- ½ cup pecans
- 2 large garlic cloves
- ½ teaspoon salt
- 2 cups packed fresh basil leaves
- ⅔ cup olive oil
- ⅓ cup freshly grated Parmesan

Toast pecans until golden brown and cool. In a food processor purée pecans with remaining ingredients until smooth and season with salt and pepper. Makes about 1¼ cups.

pesto—
tricks of the trade

Whether making pesto the time-honored way, with mortar and pestle, or whizzing it up in a food processor, there's no getting around the fact that the basil will start to break down and turn a murky swamp-green once the leaves are bruised. You can punch up the green by adding parsley (use ½ cup parsley for every 2 cups basil). If you're not serving the pesto immediately, float a thin film of olive oil directly on its surface—as contact with air blackens the pesto, this will keep discoloration to a minimum. Pesto will keep this way, chilled, up to 2 weeks (add olive oil after each use). One *Gourmet* reader passed along an unorthodox tip that also seems to do the trick: He mixes yogurt into his pesto (as little as 1 part yogurt to 8 parts pesto).

To prepare pasta with pesto properly, the pesto should be thinned to the consistency of a sauce with some of the pasta cooking water. Remove a cup or so of the water during the last few minutes of cooking and stir 1 to 2 tablespoons of water per serving into the pesto.

—Jane Daniels Lear

HEIRLOOM TOMATO SALAD

See informational box on page 48 for heirloom tomato varieties.

3 large garlic cloves
½ cup olive oil
3 pounds assorted heirloom tomatoes

Thinly slice garlic and in a heavy saucepan cook in oil over moderately low heat, stirring, until pale golden, about 3 minutes. Remove pan from heat and transfer oil with garlic to a glass measuring cup to cool. (Garlic will continue to brown as it cools.)

Cut tomatoes into wedges and in a serving dish toss together. Season tomatoes with salt and pepper and drizzle with garlic oil. Serves 6.

Photo on page 45

CORN AND OKRA WITH TOMATO ◐

Look for okra that is no longer than 3 inches with bright green, tender pods and a moist stem end. Its green-bean flavor makes it a natural accompaniment to the corn and tomato.

1 medium onion
1 large vine-ripened tomato
   (about 8 ounces)
¾ pound okra
2 large ears corn
1 tablespoon olive oil
¼ cup water
1 teaspoon cider vinegar

Separately chop onion and tomato and cut okra into ½-inch-thick slices. Cut corn from cobs.

In a nonstick skillet heat oil over moderately high heat until hot but not smoking and sauté onion, stirring occasionally, until softened. Add okra and sauté, stirring

occasionally, until okra begins to brown. Add tomato and water and simmer until liquid is evaporated. Add corn and vinegar and cook over moderately high heat, stirring occasionally, until corn is crisp-tender, about 2 minutes. Serves 4.

BULGUR SALAD WITH GREEN BEANS, BELL PEPPER, AND FETA

1 cup bulgur
¾ cup plus 2 tablespoons water
¾ pound green beans
1 red bell pepper
½ red onion
⅓ cup fresh flat-leafed parsley leaves
¼ cup fresh mint leaves
¼ cup extra-virgin olive oil
2 tablespoons fresh lemon juice
1 tablespoon red-wine vinegar
1 cup crumbled feta (about 5 ounces)

In a large bowl stir together bulgur and water. *Let bulgur stand, covered, 1 hour.*

In a saucepan of boiling salted water cook beans until crisp-tender, about 5 minutes. Drain beans in a colander and rinse under cold water to stop cooking. Trim beans and cut into ¼-inch pieces. Cut bell pepper and onion into ¼-inch dice. Chop parsley and mint.

To bulgur add beans, bell pepper, onion, herbs, and remaining ingredients and toss to combine. Season salad with salt and pepper. Serves 4 to 6.

"Succotash" Salad

Succotash traditionally is made with lima beans, corn, and a bit of milk. Our modified version substitutes black-eyed peas for the limas and olive oil for the dairy—and adds cucumbers for good measure. Black-eyed peas are medium-sized, cream-colored beans with a distinctive dark spot. If you cannot find them fresh, buy them frozen.

1	cup shelled fresh or frozen black-eyed peas (about 3 pounds in pod)
2	large ears corn
¼	cup olive oil
1	large cucumber (about ¾ pound)
3	scallions
1	tablespoon white-wine vinegar
1	teaspoon Dijon mustard
½	teaspoon ground cumin
½	teaspoon salt
3	tablespoons chopped fresh chives

In a saucepan bring peas with water to cover by 1 inch to a boil and simmer 20 minutes for fresh peas and 5 minutes for frozen. Drain peas in a colander and rinse under cold water to stop cooking. Cut corn from cobs. In a large nonstick skillet heat 1 tablespoon olive oil over moderately high heat until hot but not smoking and sauté corn, stirring occasionally, until crisp-tender, about 3 minutes. Transfer corn to a plate and cool.

Peel and seed cucumber and cut into ¼-inch dice. Thinly slice scallions.

In a large bowl whisk together vinegar, mustard, cumin, salt, and remaining 3 tablespoons oil until combined well. Add peas, corn, cucumber, scallions, and chives and toss to combine well. Season salad with salt and pepper. Serves 4.

shell beans

 The term refers not to a specific cultivar but rather to any kind of bean that can be shelled and cooked fresh. All beans go through this intermediate stage of growth; if the beans are left on the plant, they will become the dried beans with which we are all familiar. Depending on the variety, fresh shell beans appear from early summer to early fall. A not-uncommon sight at farmers markets during this season are crates piled high with speckled cranberry beans, fat favas (sometimes called broad beans), French *flageolets*, and scarlet runners.

Southerners, transplanted or *in situ*, tend to buy black-eyed peas and limas by the bushel; once you taste the creamy richness of fresh limas still warm from the pot, you'll understand how they came to be called butter beans. When buying shell beans, look for pods that have a soft, leathery texture; you should also be able to feel good-sized beans inside—a sign that they are mature. They can be chilled unshelled for a couple of days or, shelled, overnight. The cooking time is far less than that of dried beans, although it does take some time to actually do the shelling beforehand (and, in the case of favas, peeling them afterward). What better reason, though, to sit on the porch and watch the world go by?

—Jane Daniels Lear

ROASTED PEPPER AND ARUGULA SALAD

2 red bell peppers
2 yellow bell peppers
8 Kalamata or other brine-cured black olives
1 small garlic clove
½ teaspoon fennel seeds
2 tablespoons olive oil
1 tablespoon chopped fresh oregano leaves
4 cups packed arugula leaves
2 teaspoons fresh lemon juice

Roast and peel bell peppers (procedure on page 64).

Pit olives and cut into thin slivers. Finely chop garlic. In a mortar with a pestle or in an electric coffee/spice grinder coarsely grind fennel seeds. Cut bell peppers into 1-inch-wide strips. In a bowl stir together oil, olives, garlic, fennel seeds, and oregano and add peppers, tossing to coat. *Marinate bell peppers at room temperature 20 minutes. Peppers may be made 1 day ahead and chilled, covered. Bring peppers to room temperature before proceeding.*

Discard coarse stems from arugula and tear large leaves in half. To bell peppers add lemon juice and salt and pepper to taste and toss to coat. In a large bowl toss together bell peppers and arugula until combined well. Serves 6.

PINK GOOSEBERRY, PEACH, AND ELDERFLOWER SOUP WITH VANILLA ICE CREAM

Elderflowers, with their subtle, honeyed sweetness, are often paired with gooseberries in English cookery. In this particular recipe pink gooseberries are best; the green ones are too tart.

1   cup pink gooseberries (about 6 ounces)
1¼   cups dry white wine
½   cup water
⅓   cup elderflower concentrate*
½   cup sugar
2   small firm-ripe peaches (preferably white)
6   large fresh basil leaves
1   pint vanilla superpremium ice cream

*available at some specialty foods shops and by mail order from Dean & DeLuca, tel. (800) 999-0306, ext. 269

Pull off tops and tails of gooseberries and halve berries lengthwise. Transfer berries to a 1-quart heatproof jar or a heatproof bowl. In a small saucepan bring wine, water, elderflower concentrate, and sugar to a boil, stirring until sugar is dissolved, and pour hot syrup over berries. Cool mixture. *Chill mixture, covered, until cold, at least 2 hours, and up to 6.*

Peel peaches and cut into very thin wedges. Gently stir peaches into berry mixture and divide among 6 soup plates. Thinly slice basil and sprinkle over soup. Scoop ice cream into soup. Serves 6.

Photo opposite

Peach Tartes Tatin

- 12 firm-ripe medium peaches
  (about 4 pounds)
- 1 package frozen puff pastry sheets
  (17¼ ounces; thawed according to
  package instructions)
- 1 vanilla bean
- ½ stick (¼ cup) unsalted butter
- 1¼ cups sugar

SPECIAL EQUIPMENT
four 16-ounce soufflé dishes
*(available by mail order from Bridge Kitchenware,
tel. 800-274-3435 or 212-838-1901)*

ACCOMPANIMENT
toasted almond or butter pecan ice cream

Halve peaches lengthwise, discarding pits,
and cut each half into 4 wedges.

On a lightly floured surface unfold pastry
sheets and lightly roll them out just enough
to eliminate fold marks (sheets should not
increase in size by more than 1 inch over-
all). Using an inverted 16-ounce soufflé
dish as a guide, cut out 2 rounds from each
sheet. Transfer rounds to a tray and chill,
covered.

Preheat oven to 375° F.

Halve vanilla bean lengthwise. In a 10-inch
heavy skillet melt butter over moderately
low heat and pour sugar evenly over butter.
Cook sugar mixture, stirring slowly with a
fork (to help sugar melt evenly), until sugar
is dissolved and mixture is pale golden.
With tip of a knife scrape vanilla seeds into
caramel and add pod. Cook caramel without
stirring, swirling skillet, until deep golden.
Remove skillet from heat and discard vanilla
pod. Divide caramel among 4 soufflé dishes,
tilting dishes to coat bottoms evenly.

Arrange peaches decoratively over caramel
(bottom layer will be on top when dessert
is inverted), using 24 wedges in each soufflé
dish and mounding them. Put soufflé dishes
in a shallow baking pan and bake peaches in
middle of oven 40 to 45 minutes, or until
caramel bubbles vigorously.

Cut 2 parallel 1-inch slits in middle of each
pastry round and set 1 round on top of
each soufflé dish. Bake tarts 25 to 30 minutes, or until pastry is deep golden. *Let tarts
stand 1 hour in baking pan on a rack for juices to
thicken. Tarts may be made up to this point 4 hours
ahead and kept, uncovered, at room temperature.*

Carefully tilt each soufflé dish to see if
juices are thick and syrupy. (If juices are
thin, carefully pour a few tablespoons from
each tart into a small saucepan and boil
until thick and syrupy, 3 to 5 minutes.)
Reheat tarts in a 400° F. oven 5 minutes
before unmolding. Invert a rimmed plate
over each soufflé dish and invert soufflé
dish onto plate. Wait 30 seconds before
lifting soufflé dishes off tarts. If syrup was
thickened in pan, drizzle syrup over each
peach tart.

Serve tarts warm with ice cream. Serves 4.

Photo below

Chocolate Chip Zucchini Cupcakes

2 medium zucchini
1 cup walnuts
2 cups all-purpose flour
1 tablespoon cinnamon
2 teaspoons baking soda
1 teaspoon salt
¼ teaspoon baking powder
3 large eggs
2 cups sugar
1 cup vegetable oil
1 tablespoon vanilla
1 cup semisweet chocolate chips

SPECIAL EQUIPMENT
2 muffin pans, each for twelve ⅓-cup muffins

Preheat oven to 350° F. and line muffin cups with paper liners.

Coarsely grate enough zucchini to measure 2 cups loosely packed. Lightly toast walnuts and chop. Into a bowl sift together flour, cinnamon, baking soda, salt, and baking powder. In a large bowl with an electric mixer beat eggs until frothy. Beat in sugar, oil, and vanilla and beat mixture until thick and pale. Stir in zucchini and flour mixture until batter is combined well and fold in walnuts and chocolate chips.

Spoon batter into muffin cups, filling them halfway, and bake in upper and lower thirds of oven, switching position of pans halfway through baking, 15 minutes total, or until a tester comes out clean. Cool cupcakes in muffin pans on racks 5 minutes and turn out onto racks to cool completely. *Cupcakes keep in an airtight container 2 days.* Makes about 24 cupcakes.

Cantaloupe Rum Granita

½ cup sugar
1¼ cups water
¼ cup dark rum
1 cantaloupe (about 2 pounds)
1 tablespoon fresh lemon juice, or to taste

In a saucepan bring sugar, water, and rum to a boil, stirring until sugar is dissolved, and simmer syrup 4 minutes. Cool syrup.

Halve cantaloupe and discard seeds. Remove rind and chop enough fruit to measure about 2½ cups. In a blender or food processor purée cantaloupe until smooth. Add syrup and blend mixture well. Stir in lemon juice and a pinch salt. Transfer mixture to a shallow metal baking pan. Freeze mixture, stirring and crushing lumps with a fork every hour, until mixture is firm but not frozen hard, about 3 to 4 hours. *Granita may be made 2 days ahead and kept frozen, covered.*

Just before serving, scrape *granita* with a fork to lighten texture. Serve *granita* in chilled bowls. Makes about 1 quart.

simple syrup

Simple syrup is a mixture of equal parts sugar and water that has been brought to a boil and cooked, stirring, until the sugar is dissolved. It can be flavored with herbs, spices, extracts, juices, or liqueurs. Some savvy cooks keep a pitcher of simple syrup in the fridge, for its uses are manifold, especially in the long, languid days—or daze, as the case may be—of summer. Aside from making a great sweetener for iced tea (no need for strenuous stirring, and no sweet sludge in the bottom of the glass), simple syrup is also excellent for:

- drizzling over fresh berries and oranges
- poaching fruits such as figs, plums, and apricots
- making sorbets and granitas
- moistening cake layers before frosting them
- sweetening lemonade (try infusing the syrup with mint, basil, or rosemary), cocktails, and other drinks

—Jane Daniels Lear

BLUEBERRY CHAMBORD SAUCE WITH VANILLA ICE CREAM

This sauce is also great over slices of angel food cake or even waffles.

2	tablespoons unsalted butter
¼	cup sugar
2	teaspoons cornstarch
¾	cup cold water
2	teaspoons fresh lemon juice
1	cup picked-over blueberries
1	teaspoon freshly grated orange zest
½	teaspoon cinnamon
1	tablespoon Chambord (black raspberry liqueur)
1	quart vanilla superpremium ice cream

Cut butter into bits and let soften. In a large saucepan whisk together sugar, cornstarch, and a pinch salt until combined well and whisk in cold water and lemon juice. Bring mixture to a boil, whisking constantly, and simmer, whisking, 5 minutes. Add blueberries and zest and simmer 2 minutes, or until half of blueberries have burst. Remove saucepan from heat and add butter, cinnamon, and Chambord, stirring until butter is incorporated.

Serve sauce warm over ice cream. Makes about 2 cups sauce, serving 4 to 6.

SPICE CAKE WITH BERRY AND NECTARINE COMPOTE

FOR SIMPLE SYRUP

1 cup sugar
1 cup water
1 tablespoon fresh lemon juice
2 cinnamon sticks (each 3 inches long)
½ teaspoon whole allspice

FOR CAKE

1 stick (½ cup) unsalted butter, softened
1 cup sugar
4 large eggs
1½ cups all-purpose flour
1½ teaspoons ground cinnamon
1½ teaspoons ground ginger
1 teaspoon ground allspice
1 teaspoon baking powder
¼ teaspoon salt
⅔ cup milk

1 firm-ripe nectarine
3 cups mixed berries such as raspberries, blackberries, and/or blueberries

Make syrup:
In a saucepan bring syrup ingredients to a boil, stirring until sugar is dissolved, and simmer 5 minutes. Remove pan from heat and cool syrup. *Chill syrup, covered, until cold, at least 2 hours, and up to 3 days.*

Make cake:
Preheat oven to 350° F. and butter and flour a 9-inch square baking pan.

In a large bowl with an electric mixer beat together butter and sugar until light and fluffy and beat in eggs 1 at a time, beating well after each addition. Sift flour, spices, baking powder, and salt over egg mixture and add milk. Beat batter 1 minute and pour into baking pan. Bake cake in middle of oven until a tester comes out clean, about 35 minutes. Cool cake completely in pan on a rack.

Pour syrup through a sieve into a bowl. Halve and pit nectarine. Cut nectarine into thin wedges and gently toss with berries and syrup.

Serve cake topped with compote. Serves 8.

FRESH CORN ICE CREAM

6 large ears corn
2 cups heavy cream
1½ cups whole milk
1 cup plus 2 tablespoons sugar
4 large egg yolks

Cut enough corn from cobs to measure 4 cups. In a saucepan bring corn, cream, milk, and sugar to a boil, stirring until sugar is dissolved, and simmer, covered, until corn is very tender, about 30 minutes. In a food processor or in a blender in batches purée mixture (use caution when blending hot liquids). Pour purée through a fine sieve into a clean saucepan, pressing hard on solids, and discard solids.

Bring corn purée to a simmer. In a large bowl whisk yolks until smooth. Add hot corn purée in a slow stream, whisking, and transfer custard to pan. Cook custard over moderately low heat, stirring constantly, until thickened and a thermometer registers 170° F. Remove pan from heat and pour custard through a sieve into a bowl. Cool custard. *Chill custard, its surface covered with wax paper, until cold, at least 3 hours, and up to 1 day.*

Freeze custard in an ice-cream maker. Transfer ice cream to an airtight container and put in freezer to harden. Makes about 5 cups.

RASPBERRY LIMEADE

For brilliant color and sweet flavor, it's best to use red raspberries (rather than the black variety) for this limeade. However, if golden raspberries are available, they can be substituted. The golden berries won't give you that glorious red color, but they are remarkably sweet.

2 cups raspberries
3½ cups water
¾ cup sugar, or to taste
1 cup fresh lime juice

GARNISH
fresh mint sprigs

In a blender or food processor purée 1 cup raspberries with 1 cup water and force purée through a fine sieve into a pitcher. Discard solids. Add remaining cup raspberries, remaining 2½ cups water, sugar, and lime juice and stir until sugar is dissolved.

Serve limeade in ice-filled tall glasses and garnish with mint. Makes about 5 cups.

Photo left

VODKA AND WATERMELON COOLER ◔

Firm yet juicy red flesh indicates a fully ripe watermelon, but precut melon may not be available at your farmers market. When buying a whole watermelon, look for a heavy, firm one that has no soft spots.

a 3-pound piece of watermelon
½ cup vodka
¼ cup triple sec or other orange-flavored liqueur
3 tablespoons fresh lime juice

GARNISH
thin watermelon slices

Remove rind and seeds from watermelon and coarsely chop watermelon. In a blender purée watermelon and pour through a very fine sieve into a pitcher, discarding solids (there should be about 2⅓ cups juice). Stir in vodka, liqueur, and lime juice.

Serve cooler in ice-filled stemmed glasses and garnish with watermelon slices. Makes 6 drinks.

WATERMELON PIMM'S CUP ◔

1 medium cucumber
a 2-pound piece of watermelon
1½ cups Pimm's No. 1 Cup
3 cups ginger ale

Peel and seed cucumber and cut into ¼-inch dice. Cut a lengthwise wedge from watermelon and reserve. Cut remaining watermelon into pieces and discard rind. Cut enough watermelon into ¼-inch dice, discarding seeds, to measure 1 cup and in a 2-quart pitcher stir together with cucumber, Pimm's, and ginger ale.

Cut reserved watermelon into thin spears. Serve drinks in ice-filled tall glasses and garnish with spears. Makes 6 to 8 drinks.

Photo on front jacket

juicing limes

 Pick out firm specimens that are thin-skinned (they will yield to pressure when gently squeezed) and that are heavy for their size. And, because the juiciness of limes varies, it's always a good idea to buy more than you think you'll need. Before juicing limes, roll them back and forth on a work surface, pressing firmly with the palm of your hand; the pressure will break down the membranes inside the fruit and make the juice run more freely. There are many gizmos for squeezing citrus juices, including the simple hand-held wooden reamer and the classic juicer set in its own shallow bowl (the electric version of this is easier on the wrist).

For squeezing lots of limes, though, it's hard to beat a Mexican lime press, which turns a lime half inside out to extract as much juice as possible. This sturdy metal gadget is available at specialty kitchenware shops and by mail order from Williams-Sonoma, tel. (800) 541-2233.

—Jane Daniels Lear

apples BEETS arugula LIMA BEANS broccoli BRUSSELS SPROUTS cauliflower CHILES dates FENNEL grapes ONIONS pears PERSIMMONS pomegranates SALSIFY sweet potatoes PUMPKINS

fall

FALL BRUNCH
FOR TWO

✳ Goat Cheese, Sweet Potato, and Crouton Omelets
✳ Romaine and Radish Salad with Lemon Vinaigrette
✳ Individual Apple Cranberry Cobblers
✳ *Signorello Napa Valley Sémillon 1997*

Goat Cheese, Sweet Potato, and Crouton Omelets

2   tablespoons unsalted butter
1   cup ½-inch cubes country-style bread
1   small sweet potato (about ½ pound)
1   small red onion
2   ounces soft mild goat cheese
1   teaspoon minced fresh rosemary leaves
5   large eggs

Preheat oven to 350° F.

In an 8-inch nonstick skillet melt 1 tablespoon butter over moderate heat and in a bowl toss with bread cubes. On a baking sheet toast bread cubes in middle of oven until pale golden and crisp, about 10 minutes, and transfer to a bowl.

Peel sweet potato and cut into ¼-inch dice. Thinly slice onion. In a steamer set over boiling water steam sweet potato and onion until tender, about 4 minutes, and toss with croutons. Cool mixture. Crumble goat cheese and toss with crouton mixture and rosemary.

In a bowl whisk together eggs and salt and pepper to taste. In skillet heat ½ tablespoon butter over moderately high heat until foam subsides. Pour in half of eggs, tilting skillet to spread evenly over bottom. Cook omelet 1 minute, or until almost set, stirring top layer with back of a fork and shaking skillet, letting any uncooked egg run underneath. Sprinkle half of omelet with half of crouton mixture and cook 1 minute more, or until set. Fold omelet over filling and transfer to a plate. Keep omelet warm while making another omelet in same manner. Serves 2.

Photo opposite

eggs

The quality of freshness is just as important in eggs as it is in fruits and vegetables. A farm-fresh egg—with its plump, orange yolk and rich, full flavor—is light-years away from the pallid, sometimes weeks-old version we usually pick up in the supermarket. Chicken eggs are available pretty much year-round at farmers markets; quail, duck, goose, and pheasant lay eggs more on a seasonal basis, primarily in the spring and summer.

You might have heard that brown eggs are more flavorful than white eggs, but that's not true. The color of an egg is determined simply by the breed of the chicken it comes from. Many small farms have a mix of breeds scratching around out back, and the variety in egg color is astonishing—white, brown, tan, pale-green, pale-blue, speckled. One thing that does have an impact on flavor, though, is what the chickens are fed, which explains the popularity of eggs from free-range and/or organic birds.

Once you get your eggs home from the market, store them in their original carton on a shelf in the fridge, rather than in the compartment in the door. This will prevent them from absorbing refrigerator odors and from being jostled.

—Jane Daniels Lear

ROMAINE AND RADISH SALAD WITH LEMON VINAIGRETTE ◉

¼ teaspoon freshly grated lemon zest
1 teaspoon fresh lemon juice
1 teaspoon white-wine vinegar
2 tablespoons olive oil
1 heart of romaine
4 radishes

In a bowl whisk together zest, juice, vinegar, and salt and pepper to taste and whisk in oil until emulsified. Tear enough romaine into bite-size pieces to measure about 4 cups and cut radishes into julienne strips. Toss romaine and radishes with vinaigrette until combined well. Serves 2.

INDIVIDUAL APPLE CRANBERRY COBBLERS ☺

1 Granny Smith apple
½ cup picked-over fresh cranberries
⅓ cup plus ½ teaspoon sugar
½ teaspoon cornstarch

FOR BISCUIT TOPPING
2½ tablespoons cold unsalted butter
⅓ cup all-purpose flour
½ teaspoon baking powder
⅛ teaspoon freshly grated nutmeg
⅛ teaspoon salt
2½ tablespoons milk

ACCOMPANIMENT
heavy cream

Preheat oven to 400° F. and butter two 1-cup ramekins or custard cups.

Peel and core apple and cut into ¼-inch pieces. Coarsely chop cranberries. In a bowl stir together ⅓ cup sugar and cornstarch and add apple and cranberries, tossing to coat. Divide apple mixture between ramekins or custard cups and cover with foil. Bake apple mixture in middle of oven 10 minutes.

Make topping while apple mixture is baking: Cut butter into bits. Into a small bowl sift together flour, baking powder, nutmeg, and salt and with a pastry blender blend in butter until mixture resembles coarse meal. With a fork stir in milk just until a soft dough forms.

Remove foil from ramekins or cups and drop half of dough onto fruit in each. Sprinkle remaining ½ teaspoon sugar over dough and bake cobblers, uncovered, in middle of oven until biscuit is golden and fruit is bubbling, 15 to 20 minutes.

Serve cobblers warm, topped with cream. Serves 2.

Roasted Racks of Lamb with Artichokes, Red Onions, and Garlic Cloves

Artichokes have 2 growing seasons—a primary spring harvest and a smaller one in the fall. When touched by the first frost they become sweeter.

1 lemon
4 artichokes
1 pound Jerusalem artichokes (sometimes called sunchokes)
4 medium red onions (1½ pounds total)
16 large garlic cloves, unpeeled, plus
1 tablespoon finely chopped garlic
2 tablespoons plus 2 teaspoons extra-virgin olive oil
2 racks of lamb (8 ribs, about 1¼ pounds each), frenched and trimmed of all but a thin layer of fat by butcher
1 teaspoon vegetable oil
3 tablespoons fresh oregano leaves or 2 teaspoons dried oregano, crumbled
1½ teaspoons kosher salt
½ teaspoon freshly ground black pepper
½ cup chicken broth

Quarter lemon and into a bowl of water squeeze juice from 2 quarters, dropping them into water. Break off and discard stem of 1 artichoke. Bend back outer leaves until they snap off close to base and remove several more layers of leaves until pale inner leaves are reached. Trim base and sides of artichoke with a very sharp stainless-steel knife and cut off top 1½ inches. Cut artichoke into quarters and cut away choke and spiky purple-tipped leaves. Rub artichoke quarters all over with a remaining lemon quarter and drop them into bowl of water. Prepare remaining 3 artichokes in same manner, using other lemon quarter if necessary.

Preheat oven to 475° F.

In a saucepan of boiling salted water blanch artichoke quarters 3 minutes and with a slotted spoon transfer to a bowl. Peel Jerusalem artichokes and cut into 1-inch wedges. In boiling salted water blanch Jerusalem artichokes 5 minutes and drain. Peel onions and, leaving enough of root ends attached to keep wedges intact, cut onions into 6 wedges. In a 17- by 11½ by 2-inch flameproof roasting pan toss artichokes, Jerusalem artichokes, onions, and garlic cloves with 2 tablespoons olive oil and salt and pepper to taste. Roast vegetables in middle of oven 20 minutes.

While vegetables are roasting, heat a 12-inch heavy skillet over moderately high heat until hot. While skillet is heating, season lamb with salt and pepper. Add vegetable oil to skillet and brown lamb, meaty sides down, 2 minutes. Turn lamb over and brown 2 minutes more. Transfer lamb to a plate and cool slightly.

In a small bowl stir together chopped garlic, oregano, kosher salt, freshly ground pepper, and remaining 2 teaspoons olive oil and rub all over lamb.

Remove pan from oven and stir vegetables. Arrange lamb, rib sides down, over vegetables and roast 20 minutes, or until an instant-read thermometer inserted in fleshy part registers 130° F. for medium-rare.

Remove 8 garlic cloves from pan and squeeze garlic out of skins into a blender. Add chicken broth and blend until smooth. Transfer remaining vegetables and lamb to a heated platter, reserving juices in pan, and let stand, covered loosely, 10 minutes.

To roasting pan add garlic broth and salt and pepper to taste and on top of stove deglaze over moderately high heat, scraping up brown bits. Boil sauce until slightly thickened and transfer to a sauceboat.

Cut lamb racks in half or into individual chops and serve with vegetables and sauce. Serves 4.

Photo opposite

jerusalem artichokes

Neither native to the city of Jerusalem nor indeed an artichoke at all, the Jerusalem artichoke is a member of the sunflower family. (You may also see it sold under the trademarked name "Sun Choke," which was coined back in the sixties by Frieda Caplan, founder of Frieda's, Inc., a California specialty produce purveyor.)

French explorers first came across Jerusalem artichokes in North America in the early 1600s, and they thought its earthy flavor was similar to that of the globe artichoke. When the plant began to be cultivated in Europe, it became known as a plant that "turns to the sun." "Jerusalem" is generally thought to be an anglicized version of *girasole*, Italian for "sunflower."

The brown tuber resembles a small, knobby potato or, in its more gnarled varieties, fresh gingerroot. It can be eaten sautéed, roasted, boiled and mashed, sliced paper-thin and deep-fried, or cooked in soups. Notwithstanding a reputation for being difficult to digest, Jerusalem artichokes are also delicious raw and provide a welcome, water chestnut–like crunch in salads. They will keep about a week, stored in a plastic bag in the refrigerator.

—Jane Daniels Lear

SWEET AND WHITE POTATO GALETTE WITH ROSEMARY ☉

Sweet potatoes are either moist with bright-orange flesh (often incorrectly called yams) or dry with yellow flesh. The moist varieties—Garnet, Jewel, and Centennial—should be used in our galette for vivid color and sweet flavor. Beauregard, a delicious new variety, would be another good choice.

- 1 large sweet potato
- 1 large baking (russet) potato
- 1½ tablespoons unsalted butter
- 1 tablespoon olive oil
- ½ teaspoon minced fresh rosemary leaves

Preheat oven to 450° F.

Peel both potatoes and with a *mandoline* or other manual slicer slice very thin, about ¹⁄₁₆ inch thick. In a 10-inch heavy skillet (preferably cast-iron) melt butter with oil, swirling skillet to coat bottom, and pour into a small bowl. Arrange potatoes in skillet, overlapping slightly. Drizzle potatoes with butter mixture and season with salt and pepper. Cook potatoes over moderately high heat until underside begins to brown, 3 to 5 minutes.

Roast potatoes in skillet in upper third of oven until tender and golden, about 10 minutes. Sprinkle *galette* with rosemary.

Cut *galette* into 8 wedges and invert wedges onto plates. Serves 4.

RADICCHIO AND FENNEL SLAW

Radicchio, a chicory native to the Veneto region of northern Italy, commonly appears in tight burgundy globes with reddish purple leaves and creamy white ribs. The elongated variety, called Treviso, resembles endive. In this recipe, radicchio's slightly bitter taste plays off the sweetness of refreshing fennel.

- 2 teaspoons red-wine vinegar
- 2 tablespoons extra-virgin olive oil
- 2 large fennel bulbs (sometimes called anise)
- ½ head *radicchio*

In a bowl whisk together vinegar, oil, and salt and pepper to taste. Trim fennel stalks flush with bulbs, discarding stalks, and halve and core bulbs. Thinly slice fennel and *radicchio* and add to dressing, tossing to combine well. *Let slaw stand, covered and chilled, at least 30 minutes and up to 3 hours. Serves 4.*

ORANGE CARAWAY SEED CAKES

- 1 teaspoon caraway seeds
- ¾ cup cake flour (not self-rising)
- ¼ teaspoon baking powder
- ¼ teaspoon baking soda
- ¼ teaspoon salt
- ¾ stick (6 tablespoons) unsalted butter, softened
- ½ cup granulated sugar
- 1 large egg
- 1 teaspoon freshly grated orange zest
- ½ teaspoon vanilla
- ⅓ cup sour cream
  confectioners' sugar for dusting cakes

SPECIAL EQUIPMENT
eight ⅓-cup fluted brioche molds
or eight ½-cup muffin cups

Preheat oven to 325° F. and generously butter brioche molds or muffin cups.

In a dry small heavy skillet toast caraway seeds over moderate heat, shaking skillet occasionally, until a shade darker, 3 to 5

minutes. Cool seeds. Into a bowl sift together flour, baking powder, baking soda, and salt and stir in caraway seeds. In another bowl with an electric mixer beat butter and granulated sugar until light and fluffy and beat in egg until combined well. Beat in zest and vanilla. Add flour mixture alternately with sour cream in batches, beginning and ending with flour mixture and beating after each addition. Divide batter among molds or cups and, if using molds, arrange on a baking sheet.

Bake cakes in middle of oven 25 to 30 minutes, or until a tester comes out clean. Cool cakes in molds or cups 3 minutes and turn out onto a rack to cool completely. *Cakes keep in an airtight container at room temperature 2 days.*

Just before serving, dust cakes with confectioners' sugar. Serves 4 generously.

Photo on page 99

PORT AND HONEY POACHED PEARS WITH LEMON CURD MOUSSE

Unlike most fruits, pears should be picked before they're ripe, otherwise they'll be soft at the core and mealy. Always buy hard pears and allow them to mature at room temperature until they yield slightly near the stem. Here we call for firm ripe Anjou or Bartlett pears, but virtually any firm European variety, such as Comice, Packham, Red Blush, or Winter Nellis, will do.

4 firm-ripe pears (preferably Anjou or Bartlett; about 1½ pounds total)
1 orange
½ cup dry red wine
⅓ cup Ruby Port
¾ cup water
¼ cup sugar
¼ cup honey
2 cloves

ACCOMPANIMENT
lemon curd mousse (recipe follows)

Peel, halve, and core pears. With a vegetable peeler remove three 3-inch strips zest from orange. In a large heavy saucepan simmer wine, Port, and water with sugar, honey, zest, and cloves, stirring, until sugar is dissolved and add pears. Simmer pears, covered, turning occasionally, 10 to 15 minutes, or until tender. With a slotted spoon transfer pears and zest to a shallow bowl and boil poaching liquid until reduced to about ¾ cup. Cool poaching liquid and pour over pears. *Chill pears, covered, until cold, at least 2 hours, and up to 2 days.*

Serve poached pears with mousse. Serves 4.

Photo opposite

LEMON CURD MOUSSE

½ stick (¼ cup) unsalted butter
5 large egg yolks
½ cup plus 2 tablespoons sugar
6 tablespoons fresh lemon juice
1½ teaspoons freshly grated lemon zest
½ cup plus 2 tablespoons well-chilled heavy cream

Cut butter into pieces and soften. In a heavy saucepan whisk together yolks, sugar, juice, and butter and cook over moderately low heat, whisking constantly, 5 to 7 minutes, or until it just reaches a boil (do not let boil). Pour curd through a fine sieve into a bowl and stir in zest. Cool curd, its surface covered with a buttered round of wax paper. *Chill curd until cold, at least 3 hours, and up to 2 days.*

In a bowl with an electric mixer beat cream until it holds stiff peaks. Whisk one fourth cream into curd to lighten and fold in remaining cream gently but thoroughly. Transfer mousse to a serving bowl. *Chill mousse, covered, 1 day.* Makes about 2 cups.

Fall Supper for Four

* Peppered Pears, Blue Cheese, and Fried Sage
* Sautéed Polenta with Sweet Italian Sausage and Broccoli Rabe
* Sherried Portabella and Cremini Mushrooms
* Frisée Salad with Garlic Balsamic Dressing
* Grappa Walnut Cake
* *Silverado Vineyards Napa Valley Sangiovese 1996*

PEPPERED PEARS, BLUE CHEESE, AND FRIED SAGE ◔

Even when ripe and juicy, slender brownish-gold Bosc pears remain crisp. Here, their sweet nutty flavor contrasts with the sharpness of blue cheese and the lemony tartness of fried sage. In our menu this flavorful dish acts as a prelude of things to come, but on another evening it might please cheese-lovers as an intriguing not-too-sweet finale.

2   firm-ripe Bosc pears
1   tablespoon coarse freshly ground
     black pepper
2   tablespoons unsalted butter
1   tablespoon fresh lemon juice
2   ounces blue cheese
     fried sage leaves (recipe follows)

Halve pears lengthwise and core. Cut pears lengthwise into ¼-inch-thick slices and sprinkle pepper on both sides.

In a large nonstick skillet heat 1 tablespoon butter over moderately high heat until foam subsides and sauté half of pear slices until golden brown, about 1½ minutes on each side. With a spatula transfer sautéed pears to a plate and drizzle with ½ tablespoon lemon juice. Sauté and drizzle remaining pear slices in same manner.

Divide pears among 4 plates. Crumble blue cheese over pears. Serve pears with sage leaves. Serves 4.

Photo right

FRIED SAGE LEAVES ◔

     about 3 cups vegetable oil
½   cup loosely packed fresh sage leaves
     kosher salt

In a heavy saucepan heat 1 inch oil until a deep-fat thermometer registers 365° F. Working quickly, fry sage leaves, 5 at a time, 2 seconds, transferring with a slotted spoon to paper towels to drain. Immediately sprinkle sage leaves with kosher salt to taste. Makes about ½ cup.

Sautéed Polenta with Sweet Italian Sausage and Broccoli Rabe

Broccoli rabe (sometimes called rapini) has a bitter taste that adds a lively note to dishes. Its stems, leaves, buds, and flowers are all edible. If you are concerned about the bitterness, blanch broccoli rabe for 1 minute before cooking.

3 cups basic polenta (recipe follows),
   kept warm
2 tablespoons olive oil plus additional
   if necessary
1 pound sweet Italian sausage links
¼ cup water
1 bunch broccoli rabe (about 1 pound)
1 garlic clove
½ teaspoon salt
a 28- to 32-ounce can whole tomatoes
1 cup chicken broth
¼ cup dried currants
2 tablespoons tomato paste

ACCOMPANIMENT
freshly grated Parmesan

On a lightly oiled baking sheet spread warm polenta about ¾ inch thick and cool to room temperature. *Polenta may be made 2 days ahead and chilled, covered.*

In a large nonstick skillet heat 1 tablespoon oil over moderately high heat until hot but not smoking and brown sausage links. Add water and cook sausage, covered, turning occasionally, until cooked through, about 10 minutes. Remove lid and cook mixture until any remaining water is evaporated. Transfer sausage with tongs to a bowl and reserve fat remaining in skillet. Cool sausage slightly and slice diagonally.

Cut polenta into 1½-inch diamonds or squares. In skillet sauté polenta in 2 batches in reserved fat over moderately high heat, turning occasionally, adding oil to skillet if necessary, until golden on both sides. Add polenta as sautéed with a slotted spoon to sausage and keep warm, covered.

Coarsely chop broccoli rabe, discarding tough stems. Chop garlic and mash to a paste with salt. Drain, seed, and chop tomatoes. In skillet heat remaining tablespoon oil over moderately high heat until hot but not smoking and sauté broccoli rabe with salt to taste, stirring, until just wilted. Add garlic paste and sauté, stirring, 1 minute. Stir in tomatoes, broth, currants, and tomato paste and simmer, stirring, until paste is incorporated and sauce is slightly thickened. Add sausage and polenta and cook until heated through.

Serve polenta sprinkled with Parmesan. Serves 4 generously.

Photo on page 100

Basic Polenta

4 cups water
1 teaspoon salt
1 cup cornmeal or instant polenta

In a heavy saucepan bring water and salt to a boil and gradually add cornmeal or instant polenta in a thin stream, whisking. Cook polenta over moderately low heat (it should be barely boiling), stirring constantly, until very thick and pulls away from side of pan, about 15 minutes for instant polenta or about 40 minutes for cornmeal. Remove pan from heat and cover polenta to keep warm (up to about 20 minutes). Stir polenta just before using. Makes about 3 cups.

Sherried Portabella and Cremini Mushrooms ◔

Since portabella and cremini mushrooms are varieties of the cultivated white mushroom, they are available year-round. Creminis have an assertive woodsy flavor; portabellas, 3 to 5 inches across, are mature creminis with a meaty texture.

½   pound portabella mushrooms
½   pound fresh *cremini* mushrooms
1   medium onion
1   tablespoon olive oil
1   tablespoon unsalted butter
2   tablespoons chopped fresh flat-leafed parsley leaves
1   tablespoon medium-dry Sherry

Discard stems from portabella mushrooms and thinly slice all mushrooms. Thinly slice onion and in a 10- to 12-inch heavy skillet cook in oil and butter over moderate heat, stirring occasionally, until golden. Add mushrooms and cook, stirring occasionally, until liquid mushrooms give off is evaporated. Stir in parsley, Sherry, and salt and pepper to taste and cook, stirring, 30 seconds. Serves 4.

Frisée Salad with Garlic Balsamic Dressing ◔

With its white and pale yellow heart and frilly leaves, frisée, a variety of chicory, is a sturdy salad green. Although frisée is less bitter it, too, holds its own with a garlicky vinaigrette.

1   large garlic clove
½   teaspoon kosher salt
2   teaspoons balsamic vinegar
3   tablespoons olive oil
1   head *frisée* (French curly endive)

Mince garlic and mash to a paste with salt. In a bowl whisk together garlic paste, vinegar, oil, and pepper to taste. Separate *frisée* into leaves and toss with dressing. Serves 4.

Grappa Walnut Cake

1¼   cups walnuts
1¾   cups all-purpose flour
2   teaspoons baking powder
½   teaspoon salt
¼   cup grappa (Italian brandy)
¼   cup milk
1   teaspoon vanilla
1¼   sticks (½ cup plus 2 tablespoons) unsalted butter, softened
¾   cup sugar
2   large eggs

ACCOMPANIMENT
grapes and/or sliced fresh fruit such as pears or apples

Preheat oven to 350° F. Butter and flour a 9- by 1½-inch round cake pan, knocking out excess flour.

In a shallow baking pan spread walnuts in one layer and toast in middle of oven until a shade darker, about 6 minutes. Cool walnuts and with your fingers rub off any loose skins. Chop walnuts.

Into a bowl sift together flour, baking powder, and salt. In a small bowl stir together grappa, milk, and vanilla. In a large bowl with an electric mixer beat together butter and sugar until light and fluffy and add eggs 1 at a time, beating well after each addition. Add flour mixture and grappa mixture alternately in batches, beginning and ending with flour mixture and beating well after each addition. Stir in walnuts and turn batter into cake pan, smoothing top.

Bake cake in middle of oven until a tester comes out with a few crumbs adhering, about 35 minutes. Cool cake in pan on a rack 10 minutes. Run a knife around edge of pan and turn cake out onto rack to cool completely.

Serve cake with fruit. Serves 4 with leftovers.

Roasted Red Pepper and
Garlic Dip with Fennel Crudités

The Italians and French have been enjoying fennel for centuries. This strange-looking vegetable (sometimes called anise) consists of a swollen base, celery-like stalks, and feathery fronds. While the leaves and stalks are sometimes used for flavoring, its bulbous base is most prized. Here we enjoy it raw for maximum crunch and licorice flavor.

3   medium fennel bulbs
    (sometimes called anise)

FOR DIP
1   red bell pepper
1   small head garlic
½   teaspoon cumin seeds
½   teaspoon caraway seeds
½   cup sour cream
1   tablespoon olive oil
¾   teaspoon salt, or to taste
a   pinch cayenne, or to taste

Trim fennel stalks flush with bulbs, discarding stalks, and discard any discolored or tough outer layers. Cut bulbs lengthwise into ⅛-inch-thick slices and if desired halve slices lengthwise. Transfer fennel to a bowl of ice and cold water. *Chill fennel until crisp, at least 30 minutes, and up to 3 hours.*

Make dip while fennel is chilling:
Preheat oven to 450° F.

Quarter bell pepper lengthwise and discard stem, seeds, and ribs. In a shallow baking pan arrange quarters skin sides up. Separate garlic cloves, leaving skins intact, and wrap together in foil. Add garlic package to pan with bell pepper and bake in upper third of oven 20 minutes. When cool enough to handle, peel pepper and transfer to a blender. Remove garlic from foil and squeeze pulp into blender.

In a small heavy skillet toast cumin and caraway seeds over moderate heat, stirring, until fragrant and a few shades darker, about 1 minute, being careful not to burn them. In an electric coffee/spice grinder grind seeds to a powder and add to pepper mixture. Add remaining dip ingredients and purée until smooth. *Dip may be made 5 days ahead and chilled, covered.*

Drain fennel in a colander and pat dry. Serve dip with fennel. Serves 6.

Photo opposite

PROVENÇAL CHICKEN STEW

1 large onion
2 large garlic cloves
2 red bell peppers
4 large zucchini (about 1¾ pounds total)
1 pound fresh plum tomatoes or a
  28-ounce can whole plum tomatoes
12 chicken pieces such as thighs,
  drumsticks, and breast halves
2 tablespoons olive oil
½ cup dry red wine
2 cups water
1¾ cups chicken broth (about a 14½-ounce can)
3 tablespoons unsalted butter, softened
2 tablespoons all-purpose flour
1 cup Niçoise olives
  fresh lemon juice to taste

ACCOMPANIMENT
lemon and thyme couscous (recipe follows)

Chop onion and finely chop garlic. Cut bell peppers into ½-inch-wide strips and cut zucchini into 1-inch pieces. Seed fresh tomatoes or drain canned tomatoes. Chop tomatoes.

Pat chicken dry and season with salt and pepper. In a 7-quart heavy kettle heat oil over moderately high heat until hot but not smoking and brown chicken in batches, transferring to a bowl. Pour off all but about 1 tablespoon fat from kettle and in remaining fat cook onion and garlic over moderate heat, stirring, until softened.

Add wine and deglaze kettle, scraping up brown bits. Stir in water, broth, tomatoes, and chicken. Simmer mixture, covered, until breast halves are just cooked through, about 18 minutes, and with tongs transfer breast halves to a large bowl. Simmer mixture, covered, until thighs and drumsticks are cooked through, 10 to 12 minutes more,

and with tongs transfer chicken to bowl. Add bell peppers and zucchini to sauce and simmer, uncovered, stirring occasionally, until tender, 8 to 10 minutes. With a slotted spoon transfer vegetables to bowl and boil sauce until reduced to about 4 cups.

While sauce is boiling, in a small bowl with your fingertips blend together butter and flour. Whisk butter mixture, a little at a time, into reduced sauce and simmer, whisking, until slightly thickened, about 2 minutes. Stir in olives, chicken, and vegetables and season with lemon juice, salt, and pepper.

Serve chicken over couscous. Serves 6.

LEMON AND THYME COUSCOUS ◐

1½ cups water
1 cup chicken broth
1 tablespoon fresh thyme leaves
1 teaspoon freshly grated lemon zest
1¾ cups couscous (about a ¾-pound box)
1 tablespoon extra-virgin olive oil

In a 2- to 2½-quart heavy saucepan bring water, broth, thyme, and zest to a boil and stir in couscous. Cover pan and immediately remove from heat. Let couscous stand, covered, 5 minutes. Fluff couscous with a fork and stir in oil and salt and pepper to taste. Serves 6.

Braised Basil- and Garlic-Stuffed Eggplants

6 small eggplants (about 1 to
   1½ pounds total)
3 vine ripened tomatoes
1 cup packed fresh basil leaves
   plus 3 large basil sprigs
4 garlic cloves
1 onion
½ cup olive oil

GARNISH
fresh basil sprigs

With a sharp small knife trim stems of eggplants and make five or six ½-inch-deep
lengthwise incisions in each eggplant, beginning and ending about ½ inch from top
and bottom. *In a large bowl of salted water soak
eggplants 2 hours.*

Peel and seed tomatoes (procedure on page
109) and chop enough to measure 1½ cups.
Finely chop basil leaves and mince garlic.
Mince basil leaves with garlic and season
with salt and pepper. Rinse and drain eggplants and pat dry. Stuff some basil mixture
into each incision, being careful not to
break eggplants.

Mince onion and in a skillet large enough
to hold eggplants in one layer cook onion
in oil over moderately low heat, stirring,
until softened. Add eggplants and cook
over moderate heat, turning occasionally,
until lightly browned. Stir in tomatoes,
3 basil sprigs, and salt and pepper to taste.
Bring mixture to a boil and simmer, covered, 30 to 40 minutes, or until eggplants
are tender.

Serve eggplants hot or at room temperature
and garnish with basil sprigs. Serves 6.

Photo right

To Peel and Seed Tomatoes ☉

Cut a small shallow X in bottom end of tomatoes. In a kettle of boiling salted water blanch tomatoes 10 seconds, or until skin starts to curl at X. With a slotted spoon transfer tomatoes to a bowl of ice water and let stand until cool enough to handle. Remove skin. Halve tomatoes crosswise and with a small spoon scoop out seeds.

Anise Hyssop Ice Cream ☉+

Anise hyssop, a member of the mint family, is a pretty perennial herb with lilac-colored flowers. Here we use the leaves to infuse a licorice flavor into a custard ice cream base.

1 cup whole milk
½ cup fresh anise hyssop leaves or
  1½ teaspoons ground anise seeds
⅔ cup sugar
2 teaspoons cornstarch
2 large egg yolks
¾ teaspoon vanilla
2 cups chilled heavy cream

In a 2- to 2½-quart heavy saucepan bring milk and anise hyssop or ground anise just to a boil and remove pan from heat. If using anise hyssop, steep mixture 10 minutes and pour through a sieve into a bowl, pressing hard on leaves. If using anise seeds, do not steep.

In a bowl stir together sugar and cornstarch and stir in yolks until combined well. Whisk in infused milk and transfer to saucepan. Bring mixture to a boil, whisking, and simmer 1 minute, whisking. Stir in vanilla and cool custard. *Chill custard, covered, until cold, about 3 hours.*

Stir cream into custard and freeze in an ice-cream maker. Transfer ice cream to an airtight container and put in freezer to harden. Makes about 1 quart.

Pistachio Cookies

½ cup salted shelled roasted pistachios
1 stick (½ cup) unsalted butter, softened
½ cup granulated sugar
¼ cup packed light brown sugar
1 large egg
½ teaspoon vanilla
1¼ cups all-purpose flour
½ teaspoon baking powder

Preheat oven to 350° F.

Finely chop pistachios. In a bowl with an electric mixer beat together butter and sugars until light and fluffy and beat in egg and vanilla. Into egg mixture sift together flour, baking powder, and a pinch salt and beat until just combined. Stir in pistachios.

Drop level teaspoons of dough 2 inches apart onto baking sheets and bake in middle of oven until pale golden, 10 to 12 minutes. Cool cookies on sheets on racks 1 minute and transfer to racks to cool completely. *Cookies keep in airtight containers 5 days.* Makes about 75 cookies.

fall recipes

GARLIC POTATO PURÉE WITH SHIITAKE RAGOUT AND POTATO CRISPS

Although shiitake mushrooms can be found in the wild, they also are cultivated for year-round availability. These firm mushrooms are coveted for their meaty, smoky flavor, but the stems are tough and should be removed. You may want to freeze the stems for later use—they add earthiness when simmered in meat broths.

FOR CRISPS
2 tablespoons vegetable oil
1 large russet (baking) potato

FOR PURÉE
2 pounds russet (baking) potatoes
1 large head garlic (about 22 cloves)
¾ stick (6 tablespoons) unsalted butter
¾ cup milk

FOR RAGOUT
3 garlic cloves
1 pound fresh *shiitake* mushrooms
2 tablespoons olive oil
1 cup medium-dry Sherry
1 cup chicken broth
3 tablespoons soy sauce such as Kikkoman
2 teaspoons cornstarch
1 tablespoon cold water
3 tablespoons minced fresh parsley leaves

Make crisps:
Preheat oven to 400° F. and generously brush a baking sheet with some oil.

Scrub potato (don't peel). Cut one end of potato on the diagonal to facilitate slicing. In a food processor fitted with 2-millimeter slicing disk or with a *mandoline* or other manual slicer thinly slice potato on the diagonal. Immediately arrange slices in one layer on baking sheet. Brush slices with remaining oil and season with salt. Bake slices in middle of oven 12 to 15 minutes, or until golden brown. With a metal spatula transfer crisps while still warm to a rack and cool. *Crisps keep in a sealable plastic bag at room temperature 2 days.*

Make purée:
Peel potatoes and cut potatoes into 1-inch pieces. Peel garlic cloves. In a steamer set over boiling water steam potatoes and garlic cloves, covered, 12 to 15 minutes, or until potatoes are very tender. While mixture is steaming, cut butter into bits and let soften. In a small saucepan bring milk just to a boil and remove pan from heat. Force garlic and potatoes through a ricer or a food mill fitted with medium disk into a large bowl and stir in butter, milk, and salt and pepper to taste. *Purée may be made 1 day ahead and chilled, covered. Reheat purée before serving.* Keep purée warm, covered.

Make ragout:
Mince garlic. Discard mushroom stems and quarter caps. In a large heavy skillet heat oil over moderately high heat until hot but not smoking and sauté garlic and mushrooms with salt and pepper to taste 5 minutes, or until liquid mushrooms give off is evaporated. Add Sherry and boil until almost all liquid is evaporated. Add broth and soy sauce and bring to a boil. In a cup stir together cornstarch and cold water until cornstarch is dissolved and stir into sauce. Simmer ragout, stirring occasionally, 2 minutes and stir in parsley. *Ragout may be made 1 day ahead and chilled, covered. Reheat ragout before serving.*

Divide purée among 8 heated small plates, mounding it, and arrange 3 crisps decoratively in each mound. Spoon ragout over and around purée. Serves 8 as a first course.

Photo opposite

SQUASH AND SHRIMP BISQUE

4 small squash such as golden nugget or
  mini pumpkin (about 1 pound each)
2½ tablespoons unsalted butter, softened
½ pound small shrimp (about 28)
2 large leeks (white and pale green parts only)
1 large garlic clove
3 cups water
½ cup heavy cream
2 teaspoons finely chopped fresh chervil
  sprigs or a pinch ground anise
a pinch cayenne, or to taste

Preheat oven to 375° F.

With a sharp knife cut about 1 inch off top
of each squash, reserving tops. Scrape out
seeds and membranes and discard. Brush
flesh sides of squash, including tops, with
1½ tablespoons butter and season with salt
and pepper. In a shallow baking pan arrange
squash, including tops, flesh sides up, and
add enough water to just cover bottom of
pan. Bake squash in middle of oven until
very tender, 55 minutes to 1 hour. *Squash
may be baked 1 day ahead and chilled, covered.* With
a small spoon carefully scoop out pulp from
squash, including tops (leave about an ⅛-
inch-thick bottom shell if using squash as
serving bowls) and transfer pulp to a bowl.

Shell and devein shrimp. Chill shrimp,
covered. Halve leeks lengthwise and cut
crosswise into ¼-inch pieces. In a large
bowl of cold water wash leeks well and lift
from water into a colander to drain. Mince
garlic. In a 2- to 2½-quart heavy saucepan
cook leeks and garlic in remaining tablespoon butter over moderately low heat,
stirring occasionally, until softened. Add
squash pulp, 2½ cups water, and cream
and simmer mixture until squash begins
to fall apart, 3 to 5 minutes. In a blender
purée squash mixture with chervil or anise
in 2 batches until smooth (use caution
when blending hot liquids), transferring
to another saucepan.

Add shrimp to bisque and simmer until
just cooked through, 1 to 2 minutes. Season
bisque with cayenne and salt to taste and stir
in enough of remaining ½ cup water to thin
to desired consistency.

Serve bisque in squash shells if desired. Makes
about 6 cups, serving 4 as a first course.

BROCCOLI POTATO SOUP WITH PARMESAN CROUTONS ⊙

1¾ pounds boiling potatoes
2 garlic cloves
7 cups water
2 cups ½-inch cubes country-style bread
2 tablespoons extra-virgin olive oil
¼ cup freshly grated Parmesan
1 pound broccoli (about 1 bunch)

Preheat oven to 375° F.

Peel potatoes and cut into 1-inch pieces.
Mince garlic. In a 4-quart saucepan boil
potatoes, garlic, and water, skimming
froth, until potatoes are very tender,
about 15 minutes.

While potatoes are boiling, in a shallow
baking pan toast bread in middle of oven,
stirring occasionally, until pale golden, 6
to 8 minutes. In a bowl drizzle bread with
oil. Season bread with salt and toss to coat
with oil. In baking pan arrange bread in
one layer as close together as possible and
sprinkle with half of Parmesan. Toast bread
in middle of oven until Parmesan is melted,
3 to 5 minutes.

Discard coarse stems from broccoli and cut
broccoli into 1-inch florets. Peel remaining stems and thinly slice. Transfer potatoes
with a slotted spoon to a bowl, reserving
cooking water in pan, and with a potato
masher coarsely mash. Stir potatoes and
broccoli into reserved cooking water and
simmer, partially covered, stirring occasionally, until broccoli is tender, about 5 minutes. Stir in remaining Parmesan and salt
and pepper to taste.

Serve soup with croutons. Makes about
8 cups, serving 4.

HERBED GOAT CHEESE TOASTS WITH GRAPE SALSA

3 ounces soft mild goat cheese
½ teaspoon finely chopped fresh rosemary leaves
½ teaspoon finely chopped fresh thyme leaves
3 tablespoons extra-virgin olive oil

FOR TOASTS
5 or 6 slices country-style bread (¼ inch thick)
1½ tablespoons olive oil

FOR GRAPE SALSA
1 cup seedless green or red grapes
1 small red onion
1 small fresh hot green or red chile
1 tablespoon fresh lime juice
¼ teaspoon salt, or to taste

Coat goat cheese with herbs, pressing to adhere, and transfer to a small airtight container. Pour oil over cheese. *Marinate cheese in airtight container, chilled, at least 1 day and up to 3.*

Make toasts:
Preheat oven to 375° F.

Brush bread slices on one side with oil and cut into 28 rectangular pieces, each about 2- by 1½-inches. On a baking sheet toast bread in middle of oven until golden, 8 to 10 minutes, and cool. *Toasts may be made 1 day ahead and kept in an airtight container at cool room temperature.*

Make salsa:
Halve grapes lengthwise and thinly slice lengthwise. Mince enough onion to measure 3 tablespoons and, wearing protective gloves, mince chile (including some seeds for a hotter salsa). In a bowl toss together grapes, minced onion, chile, lime juice, and salt. *Salsa may be made 1 day ahead and chilled, covered.*

Spread toasts with goat cheese, including some oil, and top with grape salsa. Serves 4 to 6 as an hors d' oeuvre.

artisanal cheeses

 Small farms are using artisanal, or traditional, methods to produce Cheddar, Camembert, feta, and a wide range of goat cheeses, and many farmers markets offer a nice selection. Pick up some fruit and a loaf of the very best bread you can find—a crusty baguette, an honest multigrain, a walnut-studded whole-wheat. One last stop at the wine shop, and you've the makings for a simple, sublime meal.

To learn more about this country's hand-made cheeses, contact The American Cheese Society at (414) 728-4458 or online at www. cheesesociety.org. Another source of information is the lively, passionately written *Cheese Primer* by Steven Jenkins. His section on "American Treasures"—the finest artisanal cheeses in the States— includes a list of cheesemakers, many of whom ship.

—Jane Daniels Lear

COLCANNON-STUFFED BRUSSELS SPROUTS ◐

If you've only seen Brussels sprouts at the supermarket, you'd never guess how they grow—20 to 40 are attached to a thick stalk up to 3 feet long. At farmers markets you can buy them this way for ultimately fresh, sweet sprouts. Refrigerate them on the stalk and use them quickly.

½   pound red potatoes
3   bacon slices
6   Brussels sprouts
1   tablespoon unsalted butter
½   teaspoon salt, or to taste

Peel potatoes. In a saucepan cover potatoes with cold water by 2 inches and simmer, covered, until very tender but not falling apart, about 20 minutes.

Preheat oven to 350° F. and butter a shallow baking dish.

While potatoes are cooking, cook bacon until crisp and crumble it. Trim Brussels sprouts. With a paring knife cut 4 firm cup-shaped leaves from stem end of each sprout and reserve. Quarter rest of each sprout and slice thin.

With a slotted spoon transfer potatoes to a colander to drain, reserving cooking water in pan, and transfer potatoes to a bowl. Add butter, salt, and pepper to taste and with an electric mixer beat potatoes until smooth.

Have ready a bowl of ice and cold water and bring reserved cooking water to a boil. Gently stir in reserved sprout leaves and blanch 5 seconds. Working quickly, with a skimmer or slotted spoon transfer leaves to bowl of ice water. Blanch shredded sprouts 30 seconds and drain in a sieve. Beat shredded sprouts into potato purée.

Transfer leaves to paper towels to drain upside down. Transfer purée to a pastry bag fitted with a ½-inch plain tip and pipe into upturned leaf cups. Arrange filled leaf cups in baking dish. *Hors d'oeuvres may be prepared 3 hours ahead and chilled, covered.* Sprinkle tops of hors d'oeuvres with bacon and heat in middle of oven 3 minutes, or until heated through. Makes 24 hors d'oeuvres.

Photo left

TURKEY, SQUASH, AND LIMA BEAN POTPIE WITH CHEDDAR BACON CRUST

In the fall, farmers markets abound with winter squash varieties. Turban, calabaza, or kabocha can be substituted for butternut squash here; you'll need only about 3 cups of cubed squash.

1   small butternut squash
1   cup shelled fresh or thawed frozen baby lima beans
5   ounces pearl onions (about 15)
3   tablespoons unsalted butter
3   tablespoons all-purpose flour
1   cup chicken broth
2   tablespoons minced fresh sage leaves
3   cups ¾-inch cubes cooked turkey

FOR CRUST
4   bacon slices
2   tablespoons cold unsalted butter
1¼ cups all-purpose flour
1½ teaspoons baking powder
½   teaspoon salt
5   ounces grated extra-sharp Cheddar (about 1½ cups)
½   to ⅔ cup milk

GARNISH
fresh sage sprig

Have ready a bowl of ice and cold water. Peel, seed, and cut squash into ¾-inch cubes. In a saucepan bring 3 cups salted water to a boil and cook squash 6 to 8 minutes, or until just tender. With a slotted spoon transfer squash to ice water to stop cooking. Cook lima beans in boiling water 3 minutes, or until just tender, and with slotted spoon transfer to ice water to stop cooking. Blanch pearl onions in boiling water 2 minutes. Reserve 1 cup cooking water and drain onions. When cool enough to handle, peel onions.

In a large saucepan melt butter over moderate heat. Add flour and cook *roux*, whisking, 3 minutes. Add broth and reserved cooking water in a stream, whisking, and add sage and salt and pepper to taste. Simmer sauce, stirring occasionally, 10 minutes. Drain squash and lima beans and stir into sauce with onions and turkey. Pour mixture into a 1½-quart shallow baking dish. *Potpie may be prepared up to this point 1 day ahead and chilled, covered.* Bring mixture to room temperature before proceeding.

Preheat oven to 425° F.

Make crust:
Cook bacon until crisp and crumble it. Cut butter into bits. Into a bowl sift together flour, baking powder, and salt. Add butter and with your fingertips or a pastry blender blend until mixture resembles meal. Stir in Cheddar and bacon and stir in enough milk to form a soft, sticky dough. Transfer dough to a pastry bag fitted with a ¾-inch star tip and pipe it around edge of turkey mixture. (Alternatively, dough may be dropped by rounded tablespoons onto turkey mixture.)

Bake potpie in lower third of oven 20 to 25 minutes, or until crust is golden.

Garnish potpie with sage sprig. Serves 4 to 6.

Photo right

STEWED DUCK IN LOUISIANA SAUCE PIQUANTE

When cooking a cajun-style roux don't be tempted to raise the heat to cook it faster—it may scorch.

a   5- to 6-pound Long Island duck (also called Pekin), thawed if frozen
2   onions
1   green bell pepper
2   celery ribs
2   large garlic cloves
1   tablespoon vegetable oil
⅔   cup all-purpose flour
¼   cup tomato paste
8   cups water
a   14- to 16-ounce can whole plum tomatoes
1   teaspoon cayenne
4   scallions
1   tablespoon Worcestershire sauce

ACCOMPANIMENT
cooked rice

Reserve duck giblets for another use and cut duck into serving pieces, discarding excess neck skin and fat. Chop onions, bell pepper, and celery and mince garlic.

Pat duck dry and season with salt and pepper. In a heavy skillet heat oil over moderately high heat until hot but not smoking and brown duck in batches, transferring to a 7- to 8-quart kettle. Pour off all but ⅓ cup fat from skillet and whisk in flour. Cook *roux* over moderately low heat, whisking constantly, until color of peanut butter, 15 to 20 minutes. Whisk in tomato paste until smooth. Add chopped vegetables and garlic and cook, stirring occasionally, until softened. Stir in 2 cups water until combined well.

Pour *roux* mixture over duck and add remaining 6 cups water, tomatoes including juice, and cayenne. Bring *sauce piquante* to a boil, breaking up tomatoes with a wooden spoon, and simmer, covered, 1 hour, or until duck is very tender.

While duck is simmering, thinly slice scallions. Transfer duck pieces with tongs to a bowl and gently boil sauce until reduced to about 7 cups. Stir in scallions, Worcestershire sauce, and salt to taste and add duck.

Serve duck and sauce over rice. Serves 4.

BRAISED PORK WITH FUYU PERSIMMONS

Unlike Hachiya persimmons, which must be allowed to soften before eating, the squat, round Fuyu variety are best enjoyed when firm. They have a subtle taste and a texture reminiscent of melon. Hachiyas (see page 130) aren't suitable here.

a   3-pound piece trimmed pork shoulder
1   onion
1   green bell pepper
1   celery rib
1   large garlic clove
a   14- to 16-ounce can whole plum tomatoes
3   tablespoons vegetable oil
1   tablespoon ground coriander seeds
2   teaspoons ground cumin
1   teaspoon turmeric
⅛   teaspoon cayenne
2   cups chicken broth
2   cups water
3   Fuyu persimmons
4   scallions (green parts only)

ACCOMPANIMENT
cooked egg noodles or rice

Cut pork into 1½-inch pieces. Chop onion, bell pepper, and celery and mince garlic. Drain tomatoes and discard liquid.

Pat pork dry and season with salt. In a 6-quart heavy kettle heat half of oil over moderately high heat until hot but not smoking and brown pork in batches, transferring with a slotted spoon to a bowl and adding remaining oil as necessary. In oil remaining in kettle cook onion, bell pepper, celery, and garlic over moderate heat, stirring occasionally, until softened. Add spices and cook over moderate heat, stirring, 1 minute. Stir in tomatoes, broth, water, and pork with any juices and simmer, partially covered, until pork is very tender, about 1½ hours.

While pork is braising, peel persimmons and cut into ¼-inch-thick wedges. Stir persimmons into braised pork and simmer, partially covered, 10 minutes. Thinly slice scallion greens and stir into pork with salt to taste.

Serve braised pork over noodles or rice. Serves 6 to 8.

RABBIT WITH MUSTARD SAUCE

1	medium onion
a	3-pound rabbit, cut into 8 pieces
2	tablespoons vegetable oil
2	tablespoons unsalted butter
1¼	cups dry white wine
1¾	cups chicken broth
¼	cup Dijon mustard
1	teaspoon cornstarch
1	tablespoon cold water
2	tablespoons chopped fresh parsley leaves

Finely chop onion. Pat rabbit pieces dry and season with salt and pepper. In a deep large heavy skillet heat oil over moderate heat until hot but not smoking and brown rabbit pieces in 2 batches on all sides. Transfer rabbit as browned to a large bowl.

To oil remaining in skillet add 1 tablespoon butter and cook onion over moderately low heat, stirring, until softened. Add wine and boil until liquid is reduced by about half. Return rabbit to skillet and add broth. Simmer rabbit, covered, until tender, about 40 minutes.

Transfer rabbit to cleaned large bowl and boil sauce until reduced to about 2 cups. In a small bowl whisk together ¼ cup sauce and mustard and whisk mixture into sauce. In another small bowl stir together cornstarch and 1 tablespoon cold water until cornstarch is dissolved and whisk into sauce. Simmer sauce, whisking, 3 minutes, or until thickened. Whisk in remaining tablespoon butter, parsley, and salt and pepper to taste. Return rabbit to skillet and cook over moderately low heat, turning rabbit to coat with sauce, until heated through. Serves 4 to 6.

Photo right

Mu Shu Beef and Broccoli

Look for bright emerald-green broccoli without any hint of yellow. Although only the florets are used here, don't throw out the crunchy, mild-flavored broccoli stalks; they can be peeled and sliced before being steamed or served raw with a dip.

a 1-pound piece boneless sirloin steak
2 teaspoons cornstarch
¼ cup plus 1 teaspoon soy sauce such as Kikkoman
6 tablespoons medium-dry Sherry
½ teaspoon sugar
4 large eggs
1 large bunch broccoli
6 scallions
8 flour tortillas (6 to 7 inches)
6 tablespoons vegetable oil

Trim fat from sirloin steak and cut meat into ¼-inch-thick strips. In a bowl stir together cornstarch, 2 tablespoons soy sauce, 2 tablespoons Sherry, and sugar until cornstarch is dissolved and add beef, tossing until coated well. *Marinate beef, covered, at room temperature 20 to 30 minutes.*

Preheat oven to 350° F.

In a bowl whisk together eggs and 1 teaspoon soy sauce. Cut enough broccoli into 1-inch florets to measure about 4 cups, reserving remainder for another use. Cut scallions crosswise into 1½-inch pieces and halve white pieces lengthwise.

Wrap tortillas in a sheet of foil and heat in oven until hot, about 8 minutes.

While tortillas are heating, heat a wok or 10- to 12-inch heavy skillet over moderately high heat until a bead of water dropped on cooking surface evaporates immediately and add 2 tablespoons oil, swirling wok or skillet to coat evenly. Heat oil until it just begins to smoke and stir-fry eggs until just cooked through but not browned, about 10 seconds. Transfer eggs to a bowl and break into bite-size pieces.

Carefully wipe out wok or skillet with paper towels. In wok or skillet heat 2 tablespoons oil until hot but not smoking and stir-fry broccoli 2 minutes. Add 2 tablespoons Sherry and scallions and stir-fry 30 seconds, or until broccoli is crisp-tender. Add vegetables to eggs. Add remaining 2 tablespoons oil to wok or skillet and heat until hot and just begins to smoke. Stir-fry beef with marinade 2 minutes, or until no longer pink. Add vegetable mixture with remaining 2 tablespoons soy sauce and 2 tablespoons Sherry and stir-fry until heated through.

Serve beef mixture with tortillas for wrapping. Serves 4.

PECAN WAFFLES WITH ASIAN PEAR AND POMEGRANATE COMPOTE

Asian pears combine the crisp snap of apples with the juiciness of pears and, as you'll see, they retain their crunch even when cooked. Although we used a Belgian waffle iron, a standard waffle iron will also work. The batter yields eight 4-inch-square Belgian waffles or sixteen 4-inch-square standard waffles.

FOR COMPOTE
1   pomegranate
1   cup sugar
¾   cup water
1   large Asian pear (about ¾ pound)

FOR WAFFLES
½   cup pecans
2   tablespoons sugar
1   cup all-purpose flour
4   teaspoons baking powder
½   teaspoon salt
½   stick (¼ cup) unsalted butter
2   large eggs
1½ cups very fresh seltzer or club soda
    vegetable-oil cooking spray

ACCOMPANIMENT
softened unsalted butter

Make compote:
Cut pomegranate in half and with a manual citrus juicer squeeze juice from one half, pressing sides against center of juicer and pressing on any whole seeds in juicer with thumbs. In a saucepan bring pomegranate juice, sugar, water, and a pinch salt to a boil, stirring until sugar is dissolved, and boil until thickened, 5 to 8 minutes. Cool syrup to warm. *Syrup may be made 1 day ahead and chilled, covered. Reheat syrup before proceeding.*

With your hands gently break remaining pomegranate half in 2 pieces. Bend back rind and dislodge seeds from membranes. Peel and core Asian pear and cut into ¼-inch dice. Stir pomegranate seeds and pear into warm syrup.

Make waffles:
In a food processor finely grind pecans with sugar. Into a bowl sift together flour, baking powder, and salt and stir in pecan mixture. Melt butter and cool slightly. In a small bowl whisk together eggs and butter and stir into flour mixture with seltzer until batter is just combined.

Preheat oven to 250° F. Coat an unheated well-seasoned or nonstick Belgian waffle iron with cooking spray and preheat iron.

Using a 1-cup measure of batter for two 4-inch-square Belgian waffles pour batter into waffle iron, spreading evenly, and cook according to manufacturer's instructions. Transfer waffles to a baking sheet and keep warm, uncovered, in middle of oven. Make more waffles in same manner (don't respray iron).

Serve waffles with butter and warm compote. Serves 4.

PEAR AND VANILLA UPSIDE-DOWN PANCAKE

     1 vanilla bean
    ¼ cup sugar
    ⅔ cup all-purpose flour
     1 teaspoon baking powder
    ½ teaspoon baking soda
    ¼ teaspoon salt
    ½ stick (¼ cup) unsalted butter
    ½ cup well-shaken buttermilk
     2 large eggs
  1½ firm-ripe Bosc or Barlett pears
       (about ¾ pound)
     1 tablespoon fresh lemon juice

ACCOMPANIMENT
warm pure maple syrup

Preheat oven to 400° F.

Split vanilla bean lengthwise and with tip of a knife scrape seeds into a small bowl. Add sugar and rub together with seeds to separate seeds.

Into a bowl sift together flour, baking powder, baking soda, salt, and 1 tablespoon vanilla sugar. In a well-seasoned 10-inch cast-iron skillet melt butter over moderately low heat and remove skillet from heat. In a bowl whisk together buttermilk, eggs, and 1 tablespoon melted butter, leaving remaining butter in skillet, and whisk buttermilk mixture into flour mixture until just combined. Let batter stand 15 minutes.

Peel and core pears and cut lengthwise into ¼-inch-thick wedges. Add pears with lemon juice to remaining vanilla sugar, tossing to coat. Arrange pears decoratively in butter remaining in skillet. Sprinkle any remaining sugar mixture over pears and cook over moderate heat until barely tender and sugar begins to caramelize, about 8 minutes.

Pour batter evenly over pears and bake in middle of oven 15 minutes. Reduce temperature to 350° F. and bake 15 minutes more, or until top is golden and center is firm to the touch.

Immediately run a thin knife around edge of skillet. Invert a plate over skillet and keeping plate and skillet firmly pressed together, invert pancake onto plate. Carefully lift skillet off pancake and replace any fruit that is stuck to bottom of skillet.

Serve pancake with syrup. Serves 2.

Photo opposite

BAKED CHEDDAR GRITS WITH CARAMELIZED ONIONS

     1 pound onions (about 3 medium)
  2½ tablespoons unsalted butter
  2¼ cups water
    ¾ teaspoon salt
    ½ cup old-fashioned white hominy grits
       (not quick-cooking) such as Quaker's
     3 ounces grated sharp Cheddar
       (about 1 cup)
     1 large egg

Thinly slice onions and in an 8- to 10-inch heavy skillet cook in 1½ tablespoons butter over moderately low heat, stirring occasionally, until caramelized, 25 to 30 minutes. Season onions with salt and pepper.

Preheat oven to 350° F. and butter an 8-inch square baking dish (2-quart capacity).

In a 2- to 2½-quart heavy saucepan bring water with salt to a boil and add grits in a slow stream, stirring. Cook grits over very low heat, covered, stirring occasionally, 15 to 20 minutes, or until thickened. Remove pan from heat and stir in remaining tablespoon butter, Cheddar, and salt and pepper to taste until Cheddar is melted. In a small bowl whisk egg and whisk into grits until combined well. Spread grits in baking dish and scatter onions evenly over top. *Grits may be prepared up to this point 1 day ahead and chilled, covered.*

Bake grits in middle of oven 30 minutes, or until slightly puffed. Serves 4 to 6.

ANAHEIM CHILE WHOLE-WHEAT STRATA

1 loaf whole-wheat bread (1 pound)
1 pound fresh green Anaheim chiles (about 9)
1 medium onion
2 garlic cloves
4 scallions
2 tablespoons unsalted butter
1 tablespoon ground cumin
9 large eggs
2¾ cups milk
2 tablespoons Creole or Dijon mustard
½ teaspoon cayenne
¾ pound grated Monterey Jack cheese (about 4 cups)

Butter a 13- by 9- by 2-inch baking dish (4-quart capacity).

Cut enough bread into 1-inch cubes to measure 8 cups, reserving remainder for another use. Wearing protective gloves, halve chiles, discarding seeds, and chop. Chop onion. Mince garlic and thinly slice scallions. In a large heavy skillet cook onion and garlic in butter over moderate heat, stirring occasionally, until golden. Stir in chiles and cook over moderately low heat, stirring occasionally, until chiles are tender. Stir in scallions, ground cumin, and salt and pepper to taste.

In a bowl whisk together eggs and whisk in milk, mustard, cayenne, and salt to taste. In baking dish arrange half of bread in one layer and top evenly with chile mixture. Sprinkle chile mixture with half of cheese and top with remaining bread. Sprinkle bread with remaining cheese and pour egg mixture evenly over top. *Chill strata, covered, at least 8 hours and up to 1 day.*

Preheat oven to 350° F. and let *strata* stand at room temperature while oven is heating.

Bake *strata* in middle of oven until puffed and golden, 50 minutes to 1 hour.
Serves 6.

ROASTED ONION TARTS

7 medium red onions (about 3 inches in diameter)
7 medium yellow onions (about 3 inches in diameter)
1½ tablespoons olive oil plus additional if desired
1½ tablespoons heavy cream
1 package frozen puff pastry sheets (17¼ ounces; thawed according to package instructions)

Preheat oven to 425° F. and lightly grease a large baking sheet.

Slice enough of red and yellow onions to measure 2½ cups each and in a large skillet cook in 1½ tablespoons oil with salt and pepper to taste, covered, over moderate heat, stirring occasionally, until golden and tender, about 15 minutes. Stir in cream and cool.

Cut remaining onions lengthwise into sixths, keeping wedges intact, and arrange, narrow sides up, ½ inch apart on baking sheet. Season onion wedges with salt and pepper and roast in middle of oven 20 minutes, or until tender. Cool wedges.

On a lightly floured surface with a lightly floured rolling pin roll out 1 pastry sheet into a 13-inch square. Using an inverted 6-inch plate as a guide, cut out four 6-inch rounds, discarding scraps. Make 4 more rounds in same manner.

Transfer rounds to 2 ungreased baking sheets and chill until firm, about 10 minutes. Fold in edge of each pastry round to form a ¼-inch-wide border and top each round evenly with a scant ¼ cup sliced onion mixture. Arrange roasted onions on their sides decoratively (alternating yellow and red) on top of tarts and season with salt and pepper.

Bake tarts in middle and lower third of oven, switching position of sheets halfway through baking, 20 to 25 minutes, or until bottoms are golden brown and roasted onions are very tender. Transfer tarts to racks to cool. *Tarts may be made 1 day ahead and chilled, covered loosely with plastic wrap. Bring tarts to room temperature before serving or reheat in a preheated 350° F. oven.*

Brush tarts with additional oil and serve whole or halved. Makes 8 individual tarts.

Photo right, top

BUTTERNUT SQUASH AND RED PEPPER CASSEROLE

3½	pounds butternut squash
1	large red bell pepper
2	large garlic cloves
3	tablespoons olive oil
3	tablespoons minced fresh parsley leaves
1½	teaspoons minced fresh rosemary leaves
½	cup freshly grated Parmesan (about 2 ounces)

Preheat oven to 400° F.

With a sharp knife cut squash crosswise into 2-inch-thick slices. Working with 1 slice at a time, a cut side down, cut away peel and seeds and cut enough squash into 1-inch cubes to measure about 9 cups. Cut bell pepper into 1-inch pieces and mince garlic.

In a large bowl stir together squash cubes, bell pepper, garlic, oil, herbs, and salt and pepper to taste. Transfer mixture to a 2- to 2½-quart gratin dish or other shallow baking dish and sprinkle evenly with Parmesan. Bake casserole in middle of oven until squash is tender and top is golden, about 1 hour. Serves 6 as a side dish.

Photo right, bottom

SPICY PICKLED BEETS

1½ pounds beets without greens
(about 6 medium)
1 medium onion
2 hot fresh red or green chiles such as
cayenne or jalapeño (each 3 to 4 inches)
1⅓ cups red-wine vinegar
1 tablespoon salt
6 tablespoons sugar
4 black peppercorns
3 whole allspice
1 whole clove

SPECIAL EQUIPMENT
a sterilized 1-quart Mason-type jar
(procedure follows) if keeping longer
than 1 week

Trim beets, leaving 1½ inches of stems
attached. In a 4-quart saucepan generously
cover beets with cold water and bring to a
boil. Simmer beets, partially covered, until
tender, 30 to 40 minutes. While beets are
cooking, thinly slice onion and, wearing
protective gloves, chop chiles (including
some seeds for spicier beets).

Drain beets and, when cool enough to handle, slip off skins and stems. Cut beets into
½-inch wedges. In a bowl toss beets with
onion, chiles, and remaining ingredients.
*Marinate beets in an airtight container, covered and
chilled, at least 3 days and up to 1 week. Alternatively,
pickled beets keep, covered and chilled, in a sterilized jar
2 months.* Makes about 4 cups.

TO STERILIZE JARS AND LIDS ◑

Wash jars thoroughly in hot suds and rinse
well. Put jars and lids in a kettle and cover
completely with hot water. Bring water to
a boil, covered, and boil jars and lids
15 minutes from time that steam emerges
from kettle. Turn off heat and let jars and
lids stand in hot water. Just before they
are filled, invert jars and lids onto kitchen
towels to dry. (Jars should be filled and
sealed while still hot.)

APPLE CIDER, ONION, AND RAISIN CHUTNEY

*There's nothing quite like fresh-pressed sweet cider,
a staple of most fall farmers markets and farm stands.
Fresh cider is perfectly safe to use in this recipe because
the chutney is boiled. When using cider in an uncooked
recipe, look for the pasteurized product.*

1¼ pounds pearl onions
6 cups apple cider
½ cup cider vinegar
¾ cup raisins
¼ cup packed light brown sugar
a pinch ground cloves

In a large saucepan of boiling water blanch
pearl onions 1 minute and drain. When
cool enough to handle, peel onions. In
saucepan stir together onions, remaining
ingredients, and salt and pepper to taste
and boil, stirring occasionally, 30 to 35
minutes, or until liquid is reduced to a
syrupy consistency. *Chutney keeps in an airtight
container, covered and chilled, 1 week.*

Serve chutney with roasted meats or
poultry. Makes about 2 cups.

Photo below

APPLE GINGER CHUTNEY

4   large Granny Smith apples
2   large onions
1   red bell pepper
1   piece fresh gingerroot (about 4 inches)
1½ cups cider vinegar
1½ cups packed dark brown sugar
1   cup golden raisins
¾ teaspoon dry mustard
¾ teaspoon salt
½ teaspoon dried hot red pepper flakes

SPECIAL EQUIPMENT
sterilized Mason-type jars (procedure on page 124) if keeping longer than 1 week

Peel, core, and chop apples. Mince enough onion to measure 2 cups and mince bell pepper. Peel gingerroot and mince enough gingerroot to measure ¼ cup. In a large saucepan bring apples, onions, bell pepper, gingerroot, and remaining ingredients to a boil, stirring, and simmer, stirring occasionally, 40 minutes, or until thickened. *Chutney keeps in an airtight container, covered and chilled, 1 week. Alternatively, chutney keeps, covered and chilled, in sterilized jars 1 month.* Makes about 6 cups.

Photo on page 130

CRANBERRY HAZELNUT CORN-BREAD STUFFING

This recipe makes enough stuffing for a 14-pound turkey. If cooking the stuffing in the bird, cool it completely beforehand and don't moisten it with the final cup of broth.

¾ cup hazelnuts
1   cup yellow cornmeal
½ cup all-purpose flour
1   teaspoon salt
2¼ teaspoons baking powder
1   large egg
¾ cup milk
1   large onion
1   large green bell pepper
¾ cup fresh cranberries
1   cup packed fresh parsley leaves
2   cups chicken broth

Preheat oven to 350° F.

In a baking pan toast nuts in one layer in middle of oven until colored lightly and skins are blistered, 7 to 10 minutes. Wrap nuts in a kitchen towel and let steam 1 minute. Rub nuts in towel to remove loose skins (don't worry about skins that don't come off) and cool completely. In a food processor finely grind ½ cup nuts, reserving remainder.

Increase temperature to 425° F. and oil an 8-inch square (2-quart) baking pan.

Heat baking pan in oven until very hot, about 12 minutes. While pan is heating, in a bowl whisk together ground hazelnuts, cornmeal, flour, salt, and baking powder. In another bowl whisk together egg and milk and add to cornmeal mixture, whisking until just combined. Pour batter into hot pan, spreading evenly, and bake in middle of oven 8 to 10 minutes, or until a tester inserted in center comes out clean. Run a knife around edge of pan and invert corn bread onto a rack to cool.

Lower temperature to 325° F. and lightly butter a shallow baking dish.

Thinly slice enough onion to measure 1 cup and chop enough bell pepper to measure ¾ cup. Coarsely chop cranberries and mince enough parsley to measure ⅓ cup. Chop reserved ¼ cup toasted hazelnuts.

In a skillet bring sliced onion, chopped bell pepper, and 1 cup broth to a boil and simmer, covered, 5 minutes, or until vegetables are just tender. Into a large bowl coarsely crumble corn bread and add cranberries, parsley, onion mixture, hazelnuts, and salt and pepper to taste, stirring until combined.

Spoon stuffing into baking dish and drizzle with remaining cup broth. Bake stuffing, covered, in middle of oven 1½ hours. Uncover stuffing and bake 20 to 30 minutes more, or until lightly browned. Serves 8.

SAUTÉED SALSIFY WITH GARLIC

Salsify and scorzonera are closely related European root vegetables that can be found in some farmers markets and Spanish, Italian, or Greek markets. Both resemble long, skinny carrots, however salsify is beige and scorzonera is black. Both are creamy-beige when peeled and taste like delicate asparagus.

1¾ pounds salsify (sometimes called oyster plant) or scorzonera
⅓   cup fresh lemon juice
1   garlic clove
1   tablespoon unsalted butter
1½ teaspoons olive oil

In a 4-quart kettle bring 3 quarts water to a boil for salsify.

In a bowl combine 3 cups cold water and lemon juice and peel salsify, transferring to lemon water to keep from browning. Diagonally cut salsify into ¼-inch-thick slices and cook in boiling water until tender, about 20 minutes. Drain salsify in a colander. Mince garlic. In a large nonstick skillet heat butter and olive oil over moderately high heat until foam subsides and sauté garlic, stirring, until pale golden, about 30 seconds. Add salsify and salt and pepper to taste and sauté, stirring, until heated through. Serves 4.

SWISS CHARD WITH BACON AND SHALLOTS ◉

Delicately flavored shallots are one of the prizes of the onion family. They're quite sweet, even when raw, and retain their mellowness when cooked.

4   bacon slices
3   shallots
1¼ pounds red or green Swiss chard (1 to 2 bunches)
¼   cup water

Chop bacon and thinly slice shallots. Thinly slice chard stems and chop leaves.

In a 4-quart heavy saucepan cook bacon and shallots over moderate heat, stirring, until bacon is crisp and shallots are golden and with a slotted spoon transfer to paper towels to drain. In fat remaining in skillet cook chard stems over moderately low heat, stirring, until softened. Stir in chard leaves and water and cook, covered, over moderately high heat, stirring occasionally, until chard is tender, 6 to 8 minutes. Season chard with salt and pepper and sprinkle with bacon and shallots. Serves 4.

ROASTED CAULIFLOWER WITH GARLIC AND PARMESAN ◉

A fresh head of cauliflower has a cream-colored curd that hasn't yet opened into flowers, surrounded by layers of pale green leaves. Purple and green varieties may be available and are worth a try.

1   head cauliflower
1½ tablespoons olive oil
1   large garlic clove
2   tablespoons freshly grated Parmesan

Preheat oven to 400° F.

Cut cauliflower into 1½-inch florets and in a bowl toss with oil and salt and pepper to taste. In a shallow baking pan roast cauliflower in middle of oven, stirring occasionally, until just tender, 12 to 15 minutes. While cauliflower is roasting, mince garlic. Sprinkle garlic over cauliflower and roast 1 minute more. Sprinkle cauliflower with Parmesan. Serves 4.

WILD RICE, HICKORY NUT, AND CURRANT PILAF

Wild rice, with its nutty flavor and chewy texture, is native to the Great Lakes region and can be found in many farmers markets there. The seed of a marsh grass that can grow as tall as 8 feet, it's traditionally hand-harvested in canoes. Today, most commercial wild rice is grown from hybrid seeds, cultivated in man-made paddies, and mechanically harvested.

½   cup hickory nuts* or pecans
1   small onion
1   cup wild rice (about 6 ounces)
2   tablespoons unsalted butter
¼   cup dried currants
1½   cups water
1   cup chicken or vegetable broth

available by mail order from American Spoon Foods, tel. (888) 735-6700 or (616) 347-9030

Separately chop nuts and onion. In a bowl rinse rice well in several changes of water and drain well in a sieve. In a 2- to 2½-quart heavy saucepan cook nuts in 1 tablespoon butter with salt to taste over moderate heat, stirring, until nuts are fragrant and begin to turn golden, about 3 minutes, and transfer to a bowl. In saucepan cook onion in remaining tablespoon butter over moderately low heat, stirring, until softened. Stir in rice and cook, stirring, 1 minute. Stir in currants, water, and broth and bring liquid to a boil. Cook rice, covered, over low heat 1 hour, or until rice is tender and liquid is absorbed. Fluff rice with a fork and stir in nuts and pepper to taste. Serves 4 to 6.

heirlooms

Webster's defines *heirloom* as something having special value that is handed on from one generation to another. When referring to fruits or vegetables, the term more specifically applies to varieties that are open-pollinated (meaning that they will produce identical plants from seed the following year, unlike hybrids) and that are known to be at least 50 years old.

Cherished seeds were planted as staple or ceremonial crops by Native Americans, or they were sewn into dress hems or suitcase linings and brought to America by immigrants—from those on the *Mayflower* to more recent ones from Laos and Vietnam. Hundreds of heirlooms, however, have gradually disappeared because farmers couldn't produce them on a large commercial scale—they didn't grow uniformly, or yield enough, or survive long-distance shipping. Over the past 20 years, though, an heirloom movement has been forged by backyard gardeners and many restaurant chefs, as well as preservation networks such as the Seed Savers Exchange, in Decorah, Iowa (319-382-5990). But perhaps it's the spread of farmers markets that has made the most difference—there people are standing in line for an authentic taste of the past.

—Jane Daniels Lear

ALSATIAN-STYLE APPLE AND CREAM TART

1 recipe pastry dough (recipe follows)
  pie weights or raw rice for weighting shell
4 Granny Smith apples (about 2 pounds)
2 tablespoons fresh lemon juice
6 tablespoons sugar
3 large egg yolks
1 cup heavy cream
1 teaspoon vanilla
⅓ cup golden raisins
a pinch cinnamon

On a lightly floured surface with a floured rolling pin roll out dough ⅛ inch thick (about a 12-inch round). Fit dough into a 9-inch tart pan with a removable bottom and trim edge flush with rim of pan. With a fork prick bottom of shell all over. *Chill shell 30 minutes, or until firm.*

Preheat oven to 425° F.

Line shell with foil and fill with pie weights or raw rice. Bake shell in lower third of oven 15 minutes. Carefully remove weights or rice and foil and bake shell 10 minutes more, or until pale golden. Cool shell in pan on a rack.

Lower temperature to 375° F.

Peel and core apples. Cut apples into 8 wedges and in a bowl toss with lemon juice and 2 tablespoons sugar until coated well. In a large bowl whisk together yolks, cream, 2½ tablespoons sugar, a pinch salt, and vanilla and stir in raisins. Arrange apples decoratively in shell. Pour cream mixture over apples and sprinkle top with remaining 1½ tablespoons sugar and cinnamon.

Bake tart in middle of oven 1 hour and 10 minutes, or until apples are tender when pierced with tip of a knife. Cool tart in pan on rack. Serves 6 to 8.

Photo opposite, front

PASTRY DOUGH ☉+

The amount of water necessary to make pastry dough is likely to change slightly from time to time, depending on variables such as humidity and the moisture content of butter and flour. This recipe may be doubled if necessary. If doubled, form dough into 2 disks and wrap separately in plastic wrap.

¾ stick (6 tablespoons) cold unsalted butter
1¼ cups all-purpose flour
2 tablespoons cold vegetable shortening
¼ teaspoon salt
2 to 4 tablespoons ice water

To blend by hand:
Cut butter into ½-inch cubes. In a bowl with your fingertips or a pastry blender blend together flour, butter, shortening, and salt until most of mixture resembles coarse meal with remainder in small (roughly pea-size) lumps. Drizzle 2 tablespoons ice water evenly over mixture and gently stir with a fork until incorporated. Test mixture by gently squeezing a small handful: When it has proper texture it should hold together without crumbling apart. If necessary add enough remaining water, 1 tablespoon at a time, stirring until incorporated and testing, to give mixture proper texture. (If you overwork mixture or add too much water, pastry will be tough.)

To blend in a food processor:
Cut butter into pieces. In a food processor pulse together flour, butter, shortening, and salt until most of mixture resembles coarse meal with remainder in small (roughly pea-size) lumps. Add 2 tablespoons ice water and pulse 2 or 3 times, or just until incorporated. Test mixture by gently squeezing a small handful: When it has proper texture it should hold together without crumbling apart. If necessary, add enough remaining water, 1 tablespoon at a time, pulsing 2 or 3 times after each addition until incorporated and testing, to give mixture proper texture. (If you over-process mixture or add too much water, pastry will be tough.)

To form dough after blending by either method:
Turn mixture out onto a work surface and divide into 4 portions. With heel of your hand smear each portion once in a forward motion to help distribute fat. Gather dough together and form it, rotating it on work surface, into a disk. *Chill dough, wrapped in plastic wrap, until firm, at least 1 hour, and up to 1 day.* Makes enough dough for a single-crust 9-inch pie or an 11-inch tart.

APPLESAUCE CAKE WITH PENUCHE FROSTING

FOR CAKE LAYERS
¾ cup raisins
2 cups plus 1 tablespoon all-purpose flour
1 stick (½ cup) unsalted butter, softened
½ cup granulated sugar
½ cup packed light brown sugar
1¾ cups pink applesauce (recipe on page 130) or bottled unsweetened applesauce
1 large egg
2 teaspoons baking soda
1 teaspoon cinnamon
½ teaspoon freshly grated nutmeg
¼ teaspoon ground cloves
1 teaspoon vanilla
¼ cup old-fashioned rolled oats

FOR FROSTING
3 cups packed light brown sugar
1½ sticks (¾ cup) unsalted butter, softened
¾ cup milk

SPECIAL EQUIPMENT
candy or digital thermometer

Make cake:
Preheat oven to 350° F. and generously butter two 8-inch round cake pans.

Chop raisins and in a small bowl toss with 1 tablespoon flour to coat. In a large bowl with an electric mixer beat together butter and sugars until light and fluffy and beat in applesauce and egg. Into mixture sift together remaining 2 cups flour, baking soda, and spices and stir until combined. Stir in coated raisins, vanilla, and oats

and stir until cake batter is combined well. Divide batter between cake pans and bake in middle of oven 25 to 30 minutes, or until a tester comes out clean. Turn layers out onto racks to cool completely.

Make frosting:
In a heavy saucepan bring brown sugar, butter, milk, and a pinch salt to a boil over moderate heat, stirring until sugar is dissolved. Boil mixture, without stirring, until thermometer registers 234° F. Cool mixture to room temperature and beat until thickened, lightened in color, and beginning to lose its sheen.

Working quickly, frost top of 1 cake layer and top with other layer. Frost top and side of cake. (If frosting becomes too hard to spread, reheat it over low heat, stirring, until it reaches spreading consistency and cool.) *Cake keeps, loosely covered, at room temperature 1 day.* Serves 8 to 10.

Photo below, back

PINK APPLESAUCE ◯

Of the nearly 7,000 apple varieties grown in the United States, fewer than a dozen are cultivated commercially. Fortunately, farmers markets are encouraging the revival of heirlooms (see box on page 127) and other unusual apples. Any tart variety, such as Cortland, Fameuse or Snow, Jonathan, Macoun, or Winesap, can be used for our applesauce.

   3   pounds McIntosh apples (about 8)
½   cup water
½   cup fresh lemon juice
½   cup sugar

Core and quarter apples (do not peel). In a large heavy saucepan bring apples and remaining ingredients to a boil and simmer, stirring occasionally, 25 minutes, or until apples are very tender. Force mixture through a food mill fitted with the fine disk into a bowl.

Serve applesauce warm or chilled. Makes about 4 cups.

Photo above

PERSIMMON BREAD PUDDING

Ripe deep-orange acorn-shaped Hachiya persimmons have sweet, almost jellied flesh. Underripe persimmons, however, are tannic and mouth-puckeringly astringent. Speed up ripening by placing them in a paper bag with a banana or apple. When ripe, they will yield to a gentle touch. Fuyu persimmons (page 116) aren't suitable here.

   1   pound very ripe Hachiya persimmons
       (about 4 medium)
½   cup walnuts
   3   large eggs
¾   cup packed dark brown sugar
   2   cups whole milk
   1   teaspoon vanilla
   8   slices firm white sandwich bread
⅓   cup raisins
   2   tablespoons unsalted butter

ACCOMPANIMENT
heavy cream

Preheat oven to 375° F. and butter a 2-quart shallow baking dish.

Remove hard stems from persimmons and force pulp through a fine sieve, scraping with a rubber spatula and pressing hard on solids. Measure 1⅓ cups persimmon purée and reserve remainder for another use. Coarsely chop walnuts and in a shallow baking pan toast in middle of oven until a shade darker, 4 to 6 minutes.

In a large bowl whisk together eggs, brown sugar, milk, persimmon purée, vanilla, and a pinch salt. Tear bread into bite-size pieces, dropping them into persimmon mixture, and add walnuts and raisins. Toss mixture until combined well and turn into baking dish. Let pudding mixture stand, covered, at room temperature 15 minutes.

Cut butter into bits. Dot pudding with butter and bake in middle of oven until puffed and set, 35 to 40 minutes. Cool pudding slightly on a rack.

Serve bread pudding warm with heavy cream. Serves 6 to 8.

BURNT-SUGAR PECAN PUMPKIN PIE

1 recipe pastry dough (page 128)
2 tablespoons unsalted butter
⅓ cup sugar
1 cup light corn syrup
2 tablespoons dark rum
3 large eggs
1 teaspoon vanilla
⅔ cup fresh pumpkin purée (recipe follows)
  or canned solid-pack pumpkin
1 teaspoon ground ginger
1 cup pecan halves

ACCOMPANIMENT
sweetened whipped cream

On a lightly floured surface with a floured rolling pin roll out dough into a 12-inch round. Fit dough into a 9-inch pie plate and trim edge. Crimp edge decoratively. *Chill shell 30 minutes, or until firm.*

Preheat oven to 350° F.

Cut butter into bits. In a dry small heavy saucepan cook sugar over moderately low heat, stirring slowly with a fork (to help sugar melt evenly), until a pale golden caramel. Continue to cook caramel without stirring, gently swirling pan, until golden. Remove pan from heat and add corn syrup (caramel will bubble up and steam), stirring until combined well. Add rum and butter and simmer, stirring, 1 minute. Cool mixture until it stops bubbling.

In a bowl whisk together eggs, vanilla, and a pinch salt and add caramel mixture in a stream, whisking. In another bowl whisk together pumpkin and ginger and whisk in 1¼ cups egg mixture. Pour pumpkin mixture into shell and decoratively arrange pecan halves on mixture. Spoon remaining egg mixture over pecans (pecans will float).

Bake pie in middle of oven 45 to 50 minutes, or until filling is set and crust is pale golden. Cool pie on a rack.

Serve pie with whipped cream. Serves 8.

Photo right

FRESH PUMPKIN PURÉE

1½ tablespoons unsalted butter
1 pumpkin (8 pounds; preferably a sugar pumpkin)

Preheat oven to 375° F.

Melt butter and cut off stem end of pumpkin 2½ inches from top, reserving it. Scrape out seeds and membranes, reserving seeds for toasting if desired (procedure on page 133), and brush inside of pumpkin with butter. Top pumpkin with reserved stem end and bake pumpkin in a shallow baking pan in middle of oven 1½ hours, or until pulp is tender. Cool pumpkin in pan. When pumpkin is cool enough to handle, discard any liquid that may have accumulated in pumpkin and scoop out pulp. In a blender purée pulp in batches, transferring to a large sieve or colander lined with overlapping large coffee filters and set over a large bowl. Cover surface of purée with a round of wax paper. *Drain purée, chilled, 8 hours. Purée keeps, frozen, in airtight containers 3 months.* Makes about 4 cups.

DATE PECAN MOLASSES CAKE

FOR CAKE

1 cup pecans
1 cup pitted dates (about 6 ounces)
2¼ cups all-purpose flour
½ teaspoon salt
1½ teaspoons baking soda
¾ cup hot water
1 large egg
½ cup vegetable oil
1 cup unsulfured molasses or cane syrup

FOR FROSTING

4 ounces cream cheese, softened
2 tablespoons unsalted butter, softened
1 cup confectioners' sugar
½ teaspoon cinnamon
1 tablespoon unsulfured molasses or cane syrup

Make cake:
Preheat oven to 350° F. Butter and flour a 9- by 2-inch square baking pan, knocking out excess flour.

In a shallow baking pan spread pecans evenly and toast in middle of oven until a shade darker, 3 to 5 minutes. Cool pecans and chop. With a lightly oiled knife chop dates. Into a bowl sift together flour and salt. In a small bowl stir together baking soda and hot water until dissolved. In a large bowl whisk together egg, oil, and molasses or cane syrup and stir in flour mixture alternately with soda mixture in batches, beginning and ending with flour mixture and beating until just combined. Stir in pecans and dates and turn batter into baking pan, spreading evenly. Bake cake in middle of oven until a tester comes out clean, 18 to 20 minutes. Cool cake in pan on a rack.

Make frosting:
In a bowl with an electric mixer beat together frosting ingredients until smooth.

Spread frosting on top of cake in pan. *Cake keeps, covered, at room temperature 3 days. Serves 8 to 10.*

PEAR ROSEMARY UPSIDE-DOWN CAKE

Although rosemary is usually added to savory dishes, it also enhances sweet pears with a warm, herbal note. (In Provençal kitchens, rosemary perfumes apple desserts and honey.) Use the larger quantity of herbs for distinctive rosemary flavor, the smaller amount for a subtle hint.

3 tablespoons unsalted butter
½ cup packed brown sugar
1 tablespoon dark rum
3 firm-ripe Bosc pears (about 1½ pounds)

FOR CAKE BATTER

1½ cups all-purpose flour
1½ teaspoons baking powder
¼ teaspoon salt
1 to 1½ teaspoons minced fresh rosemary leaves
¾ stick (6 tablespoons) unsalted butter, softened
¾ cup granulated sugar
1 whole large egg
1 large egg yolk
¾ teaspoon vanilla
⅔ cup whole milk

ACCOMPANIMENT
sweetened whipped cream

Preheat oven to 375° F. and butter a 9- by 2-inch round cake pan.

In a small saucepan melt butter with brown sugar over moderate heat, stirring, and stir in rum. Pour sugar mixture into cake pan, spreading evenly. Peel, quarter, and core pears. Cut pears lengthwise into ¼-inch-thick slices and decoratively arrange enough pears in one layer to cover sugar mixture, reserving remainder for another use.

Make batter:

Into a small bowl sift together flour, baking powder, and salt and stir in rosemary. In a large bowl with an electric mixer beat together butter and sugar until light and fluffy and beat in whole egg, yolk, and vanilla. Add flour mixture alternately with milk in batches, beating after each addition until just combined.

Turn batter into cake pan, spreading evenly, and bake in middle of oven until a tester comes out clean, 25 to 30 minutes. Cool cake in pan on a rack 5 minutes. Invert a plate over cake pan and, holding pan and plate together with both hands, invert cake onto plate.

Serve cake warm with whipped cream. Serves 8 to 10.

TOASTED PUMPKIN SEEDS ◌+

½ cup fresh pumpkin seeds, unrinsed
1 tablespoon vegetable oil

Preheat oven to 250° F.

In a bowl toss seeds with oil and salt to taste and transfer to an ungreased shallow baking pan. Bake seeds in middle of oven, stirring occasionally, 1 to 1¼ hours, or until golden and crisp. Makes ½ cup.

nuts

The pecan is perhaps the most commonly seen nut at farmers markets and roadside stands, as it is grown in at least 12 states (principally Georgia, Texas, Oklahoma, and North Carolina), but you'll also find walnuts and almonds in California and filberts (hazelnuts) in both Washington and Oregon.

When buying nuts in the shell, look for clean ones that are heavy for their size, with shiny, well-formed shells—a good indicator of fresh, meaty kernels. Pecans, because of their fat content of more than 70 percent, start to turn rancid very easily. It's always a good idea to shop for them in peak season—autumn. An added advantage to buying them at a farmers market is that you can usually sample them on the spot—they should have a rich, mellow flavor but leave a clean feeling on the palate.

To keep pecans and other nuts as fresh as possible, you can refrigerate them in an airtight container for about 3 months or keep them frozen for up to 6 months. Don't even think about making that "perfect" pecan pie with the nuts you squirreled away in the fridge last year. You might be able to coat those pecans in a spicy mixture and roast them for cocktail nibbles, but for desserts you want the buttery sweetness of fresh-from-the-grove pecans.

—Jane Daniels Lear

cabbage CARROTS celery root CRANBERRIES grapefruit LIMES
BLOOD ORANGES lemons BEET GREENS chard COLLARD GREENS
kale LEEKS parsnips POTATOES quince RUTABAGAS turnips

winter

SAUSAGE-STUFFED MUSHROOMS ◌

8 medium mushrooms (about 6 ounces)
1 garlic clove
1 scallion (green part only)
1 Italian sausage link (about 3 ounces)
½ teaspoon olive oil
1 large egg white
1 tablespoon dry bread crumbs
2 tablespoons freshly grated Parmesan

Remove stems from mushrooms and finely chop stems, reserving caps. Mince garlic and finely chop enough scallion green to measure 2 tablespoons. Discard casing from sausage and break up sausage into a bowl.

Preheat oven to 400° F. and lightly grease a small shallow baking pan.

In a small skillet heat oil over moderate heat until hot but not smoking and cook mushroom stems, garlic, and chopped scallion, stirring, until softened. Increase heat to moderately high. Add sausage and sauté, stirring and breaking up lumps, until sausage is no longer pink. Remove skillet from heat and cool mixture slightly. Stir in egg white, bread crumbs, 1 tablespoon Parmesan, and salt and pepper to taste. Arrange mushroom caps, cut sides up, in baking pan and fill with sausage mixture, mounding it. (Discard any leftover filling.) Sprinkle stuffed mushrooms with remaining tablespoon Parmesan and bake in middle of oven until tops are golden brown, about 12 minutes. Makes 8 hors d'oeuvres.

FISH CHOWDER WITH HERBED OYSTER CRACKERS ◌

Carrots offer sweet flavor to soups, stews, and stocks. Look for firm dry carrots, and to avoid bitterness, choose those without green shoulders (this indicates premature harvesting).

4 bacon slices
1 small onion
1 carrot
1 celery rib
1 tablespoon unsalted butter
2 teaspoons all-purpose flour
½ teaspoon paprika
8 ounces bottled clam juice
1 cup water
½ cup heavy cream
1 russet (baking) potato (about ½ pound)
¾ pound firm white fish fillet
  such as halibut or cod
2 tablespoons minced fresh parsley leaves

ACCOMPANIMENT
herbed oyster crackers (recipe on page 138)

Coarsely chop bacon. Finely chop onion, carrot, and celery. In a heavy saucepan cook bacon over moderate heat, stirring, until crisp and transfer with a slotted spoon to paper towels to drain. Pour off fat and in saucepan cook onion, carrot, and celery in butter over moderately low heat, stirring occasionally, until softened. Sprinkle flour over mixture and cook, stirring, 3 minutes. Stir in paprika and cook, stirring, 30 seconds. Add clam juice, water, and cream and bring to a boil, stirring occasionally.

While mixture is heating, peel potato and cut into ¼-inch dice. Add potato to mixture and simmer chowder, uncovered, 12 minutes. Discard fish skin and cut fish into 1-inch pieces. Stir fish into chowder and simmer, stirring occasionally, until just cooked through, about 5 minutes. Stir in parsley, bacon, and salt and pepper to taste.

Serve chowder with oyster crackers. Serves 2.

Photo opposite

HERBED OYSTER CRACKERS

1½ tablespoons unsalted butter
¼ teaspoon dried rosemary, crumbled
¼ teaspoon dried thyme, crumbled
1½ cups packaged oyster crackers

Preheat oven to 350° F.

In a small saucepan melt butter with rosemary, thyme, and salt and pepper to taste over moderate heat, stirring. Add crackers, tossing to coat, and on a baking sheet arrange in one layer. Bake crackers in middle of oven until deep golden, about 10 minutes. Makes 1½ cups.

ROMAINE WITH ORANGE CUMIN DRESSING

½ head romaine
1 orange
a scant ¼ teaspoon cumin seeds
1 teaspoon white-wine vinegar
2 tablespoons olive oil

Tear enough romaine into bite-size pieces to measure 1 quart. Grate enough zest from orange to measure ¼ teaspoon and squeeze enough juice to measure 1 teaspoon. In a dry small heavy skillet toast cumin seeds over moderate heat, stirring, until fragrant, about 30 seconds. In a bowl whisk together zest, juice, cumin seeds, vinegar, and salt and pepper to taste and add oil in a stream, whisking until emulsified. Add romaine pieces and toss to coat. Serves 2.

Photo on page 136

CHEESE WITH QUINCE, GINGER, AND PECAN CONSERVE

Also known as the "golden apple," quince is greenish-yellow and pear-shaped. Its butter-colored, astringent flesh is unpalatable and grainy when raw, but after long slow cooking in sugar, it turns pinkish-orange and develops a delicate flavor and aroma.

½ cup pecans
3 medium quinces (about 1½ pounds total)
1 piece fresh gingerroot (about 1 inch)
1¾ cups sugar
3 cups water
1 teaspoon mustard seeds
¼ teaspoon dried hot red pepper flakes
1 teaspoon white-wine vinegar
½ teaspoon salt

ACCOMPANIMENT
farmers market cheese such as goat cheese

Preheat oven to 350° F.

In a shallow baking pan toast pecans in one layer in middle of oven until golden, about 10 minutes. Cool nuts and coarsely chop. Peel, quarter, and core quinces. Cut quarters lengthwise into ⅛-inch-thick slices and cut each slice crosswise into 6 pieces. Peel gingerroot and cut into thin julienne strips.

In a 3-quart heavy saucepan bring quinces, gingerroot, and all remaining ingredients except pecans to a boil. Simmer mixture, covered, stirring occasionally, 2½ hours (quinces will be deep pinkish orange). *Let mixture stand in pan, covered, at room temperature at least 8 hours and up to 1 day.*

Simmer mixture, stirring occasionally, 15 minutes more. Stir in pecans and transfer conserve to a bowl to cool completely. *Conserve keeps, covered and chilled, 1 month.*

Serve conserve with cheese. Serves 2 with leftovers.

Photo opposite

QUINCES

CREAM OF CAULIFLOWER SOUP WITH TOASTED CUMIN ◎

1 teaspoon cumin seeds
1 medium head cauliflower
  (about 2½ pounds)
4 cups water
1½ teaspoons salt
½ cup heavy cream

In a dry small heavy skillet toast cumin seeds over moderate heat, stirring, until fragrant, about 2 minutes.

Cut cauliflower into 2-inch pieces. In a 4-quart heavy saucepan bring water and salt to a boil and simmer cauliflower, covered, until very tender, about 10 minutes. In a blender purée mixture with cumin in batches (use caution when blending hot liquids), transferring to another saucepan. Stir in cream and salt and pepper to taste. *Soup may be made 1 day ahead and chilled, covered.* Heat soup over moderate heat, stirring occasionally, until heated through. Makes about 6 cups, serving 4.

HAM STEAK WITH CIDER RAISIN SAUCE ◎

2 small onions
3 cups filtered apple cider
¼ cup cider vinegar
2 teaspoons mustard seeds
2 teaspoons Dijon mustard
1½ tablespoons olive oil
2 fully cooked bone-in ham steaks
  (1 pound each; about ½ inch thick)
2 teaspoons grated peeled fresh gingerroot
½ stick (¼ cup) unsalted butter
½ cup raisins
2 tablespoons minced fresh flat-leafed
  parsley leaves

Finely chop onions. In a bowl stir together cider, vinegar, mustard seeds, and Dijon mustard.

In a large heavy skillet heat oil over moderately high heat until hot but not smoking and sauté ham steaks until golden and heated through, about 4 minutes on each side. Transfer ham to a platter and keep warm, covered.

In fat remaining in skillet cook onions over moderate heat, stirring occasionally, until golden, about 5 minutes. Add gingerroot and cook, stirring, 1 minute. Stir cider mixture into onion mixture and boil sauce, stirring occasionally, until reduced to about 1⅓ cups, about 7 minutes. Cut butter into ½-inch pieces. Add raisins to sauce and whisk in butter and parsley until butter is incorporated.

Pour sauce over ham. Serves 4 generously.

Photo opposite

ROSEMARY-ROASTED
SWEET-POTATO WEDGES ☺

Sweet potatoes, a favorite winter storage vegetable,
usually appear in sweet side dishes and desserts. Here
they are paired with rosemary for savory roasted "french
fries" that are remarkably quick and easy to prepare.

6   medium sweet potatoes
    (about 2 pounds total)
½   stick (¼ cup) unsalted butter
2   teaspoons minced fresh rosemary leaves

Preheat oven to 400° F.

Cut potatoes lengthwise into ¾-inch-thick
slices. In a large shallow baking pan heat
butter in oven until melted, about 2 minutes.
Add potatoes, tossing to coat, and sprinkle
with rosemary and salt and pepper to taste.
Roast potatoes in middle of oven, gently
turning with a metal spatula halfway through
roasting, 30 minutes total, or until tender.
Serves 4.

Photo on page 140

CHICORY AND ENDIVE SALAD WITH
SPICY BUTTER-TOASTED WALNUTS ☺

Chicory and Belgian endive come from the same botani-
cal family and, to confuse matters, often share names.
Chicory has bitter, deep green curly leaves in a loosely
packed head; while Belgian endive has milder, white to
pale green, elongated oval leaves in a cylindrical head.

1   cup chopped walnuts
2   tablespoons unsalted butter
⅛   teaspoon cayenne, or to taste
2   small Belgian endives
1   head chicory (curly endive)
3   tablespoons fresh lemon juice
2   tablespoons extra-virgin olive oil

In a skillet toast walnuts in butter over
moderate heat, stirring occasionally, until
golden and sprinkle with cayenne and salt
to taste. Cool nuts slightly.

Thinly slice endives crosswise and chop
enough chicory to measure 2 quarts.
In a large bowl toss greens with spiced
nuts, lemon juice, oil, and salt and
pepper to taste. Serves 4.

Photo on page 140

ORANGE TAPIOCA AND
CRANBERRY PARFAITS

3½   cups whole milk
 2   large eggs
 1   teaspoon finely grated fresh orange zest
 ¼   cup quick-cooking tapioca
 ¾   cup plus 2 tablespoons sugar
 ½   teaspoon vanilla
 1   cup picked-over fresh cranberries

In a 3-quart saucepan whisk together milk,
eggs, zest, tapioca, and ¼ cup plus 2 tablespoons sugar until eggs are incorporated
and let stand 5 minutes. Bring tapioca
mixture to a full boil over moderate heat,
stirring constantly. Remove pan from
heat and stir in vanilla. *Cool tapioca mixture,*
uncovered, 20 minutes and chill until cold.

In a food processor pulse cranberries until
finely chopped and transfer to a small saucepan. Add remaining ½ cup sugar and cook
over moderate heat, stirring, until sugar is
completely dissolved. *Cool cranberry mixture,*
uncovered, 15 minutes and chill until cold.

Reserve 2 tablespoons cranberry mixture for
garnish. Beginning with cranberry mixture
and ending with tapioca mixture, alternately
layer mixtures in each of 4 parfait glasses.
Parfaits may be made 1 day ahead and chilled, covered.
Garnish parfaits with reserved cranberry
mixture. Serves 4.

Photo opposite

Casual Winter Dinner for Four

* Warm Beet and Carrot Salad with Caraway Dressing
* Lemon-Rubbed Chicken Legs with Garlic and Rosemary
* Maple Butternut Squash Purée
* Red Potatoes and Wilted Greens
* Chocolate Brownie Cake with Raspberry Jam
* *Grgich Hills Napa Valley Fumé Blanc 1997*

WARM BEET AND CARROT SALAD WITH CARAWAY DRESSING ☺

Beets come in many different colors (red, white, golden, and multicolored), shapes, and sizes. While the red varieties generally are the most flavorful, all are worth a try. If using red beets, be sure to keep them from touching the carrots, or you'll have pink carrots!

4   beets (about 2 pounds total)
6   medium carrots
1   teaspoon caraway seeds
2   tablespoons white-wine vinegar
2   tablespoons extra-virgin olive oil

Peel beets and halve lengthwise. Cut beets into ⅛-inch-thick slices and arrange on one side of a large steamer. Diagonally cut carrots into ⅛-inch-thick slices. Arrange carrots on other side of steamer and steam vegetables over boiling water, covered, until tender, 6 to 8 minutes.

While vegetables are steaming, in a dry small heavy skillet toast caraway seeds over moderate heat, shaking skillet, until fragrant, about 1 minute. In a large bowl whisk together caraway seeds, vinegar, oil, and salt and pepper to taste until emulsified. Add hot vegetables and toss to combine. Serves 4.

Photo opposite

LEMON-RUBBED CHICKEN LEGS WITH GARLIC AND ROSEMARY

4   whole chicken legs (about 2 pounds total)
2   large lemons
4   teaspoons minced fresh rosemary leaves
2   tablespoons olive oil
3   garlic cloves

Pat chicken dry. Halve lemons and rub 2 lemon halves all over chicken. Season chicken with salt and pepper and sprinkle with 2 teaspoons rosemary. In a 5-quart heavy kettle heat 1 tablespoon oil over moderately high heat until hot but not smoking and brown 2 chicken legs, skin sides down, about 5 minutes. Transfer browned chicken to a plate. In kettle heat remaining tablespoon oil and sauté remaining chicken in same manner. Return browned chicken, skin sides up, with any juices that have accumulated on plate to kettle and squeeze juice from remaining lemon halves over chicken. Cook chicken, covered, over moderately low heat until cooked through, about 30 minutes more. Mince garlic.

Transfer chicken to a platter and keep warm. In fat remaining in kettle sauté garlic with remaining 2 teaspoons rosemary over moderately high heat, stirring, until just golden, about 2 minutes. Drizzle sauce over chicken. Serves 4.

Photo on page 146

MAPLE BUTTERNUT SQUASH PURÉE

3   pounds butternut squash (about 1 medium)
2   tablespoons unsalted butter
½   teaspoon grated peeled fresh gingerroot
3   tablespoons pure maple syrup, or to taste

Preheat oven to 400° F. and lightly oil a shallow baking pan.

Halve squash lengthwise and discard seeds. Arrange squash, cut sides down, in baking pan and roast in middle of oven until very tender, about 45 minutes. Cool squash, cut sides up, in baking pan on a rack until cool enough to handle, about 10 minutes. Scoop flesh from squash into a food processor, discarding skins, and purée with remaining ingredients and salt and pepper to taste. *Purée may be made 2 days ahead and cooled completely before being chilled, covered. Reheat squash before serving.* Serves 4.

RED POTATOES AND WILTED GREENS ◔

Beet greens and Swiss chard are mild-tasting with earthy flavor, while mustard greens, particularly the larger, older leaves, have a hot peppery punch. Choose greens with slender stems that will be tender enough to cook along with the leaves.

1½ pounds small red potatoes
2   small garlic cloves
2   quarts packed beet greens, mustard greens, or Swiss chard (about 12 ounces)
2   tablespoons unsalted butter
1   tablespoon olive oil

In a saucepan cover potatoes with salted water by ½ inch and simmer 15 minutes, or until tender. While potatoes are simmering, mince garlic and discard tough stems from greens.

Drain potatoes in a colander and, when cool enough to handle, cut each potato in half. In a large heavy skillet heat butter and oil over moderate heat until foam subsides and cook potatoes, cut sides down, until golden, about 5 minutes. With a metal spatula loosen potatoes from bottom of skillet. Add garlic and cook, stirring, until garlic is pale golden. Add greens and cook, covered, 3 minutes, or until greens are wilted. Season vegetables with salt and pepper and stir until combined well. Serves 4.

Photo opposite

CHOCOLATE BROWNIE CAKE WITH RASPBERRY JAM

Most farmers markets have homemade goods for sale, and preserves are always a favorite. We've paired raspberry jam with this chocolatey cake, but almost any other berry jam will work equally well.

FOR CAKE
4   ounces fine-quality bittersweet chocolate (not unsweetened)
1   stick (½ cup) unsalted butter
¾   cup granulated sugar

3   large eggs
¼   cup all-purpose flour
¼   cup Dutch-process unsweetened cocoa powder
6   tablespoons raspberry jam

FOR CINNAMON WHIPPED CREAM
1   cup well-chilled heavy cream
2   tablespoons confectioners' sugar
½   teaspoon cinnamon

Make cake:
Preheat oven to 350° F. Butter a 9- by 5- by 3-inch loaf pan and line bottom with wax paper. Butter paper.

Finely chop chocolate. In a double boiler or a metal bowl set over a saucepan of barely simmering water melt chocolate with butter, stirring until smooth. Remove top of double boiler or bowl from heat and whisk in sugar. Add eggs 1 at a time, whisking well after each addition. Sift flour and cocoa powder over mixture and whisk until just combined. Pour batter into loaf pan and bake in middle of oven 50 minutes, or until top is puffed and has a thin crust (it will crack slightly). Cool cake in pan on a rack 5 minutes. Invert cake onto rack and cool completely.

Transfer cake to a cutting board and with a long serrated knife horizontally cut cake into 3 layers. On a plate arrange bottom third of cake, cut side up, and spread top with 3 tablespoons jam. Top jam layer with middle cake layer and spread top with remaining 3 tablespoons jam. Put remaining cake layer, cut side down, on top. *Cake may be made 2 days ahead and chilled in an airtight container. Bring cake to room temperature before serving.*

Make whipped cream:
In a bowl with an electric mixer beat cream with confectioners' sugar and cinnamon until it just holds soft peaks. *Whipped cream may be made 1 hour ahead and chilled, covered.*

Serve cake with whipped cream. Serves 4 with leftovers.

WINTER BRUNCH
for Six

* Broiled Grapefruit with Vanilla Ginger Sugar
* Corned Beef Hash with Fried Eggs
* Cheddar Sage Scones
* *Amaretto Mimosas* or *Eberle Paso Robles Cunoise Rosé 1997*

BROILED GRAPEFRUIT WITH VANILLA GINGER SUGAR ◌

Although Florida leads the nation in grapefruit produc-
tion, Arizona, California, and Texas also are major
producers. Grapefruit is an excellent source of vitamin
C, but only the pink variety contains vitamin A. While
many think that pink grapefruit is sweeter than white, it
really isn't—flavor and degree of sweetness vary with
weather conditions.

⅔ cup sugar
3 tablespoons chopped crystallized ginger
¾ teaspoon vanilla
6 large pink grapefruits

Preheat broiler.

In an electric coffee/spice grinder finely
grind sugar, ginger, and vanilla.

Halve each grapefruit crosswise and run a
knife around each section to loosen it from
membranes. Arrange grapefruits, cut sides
up, in a flameproof baking dish or baking
pan just large enough to hold them in one
layer and sprinkle with sugar mixture. Broil
grapefruits about 1½ inches from heat until
sugar is melted and tops begin to brown, 10
to 15 minutes.

Serve grapefruits at room temperature.
Serves 6.

Photo opposite

citrus know-how

Zesting—The tangy zest of citrus fruits can make a world of
difference to savory dishes as
well as to sweet ones. When
zesting lemons, for example,
it's always a good idea to use fruit that's fresh,
cold, dry, and firm enough to peel or grate
easily. *To take off zest in strips*, use a vegetable
peeler and remove the colored part of the rind
only, without any of the bitter white pith. The
pieces of zest may be used as is, cut into julienne strips, or chopped. *To grate zest*, we rec-
ommend working in one direction only, using
quick, sharp motions—preferably on the
smallest teardrop-shaped holes found on
many four-sided graters or the panel with the
tiny (infernally sharp) holes. We like to avoid
the practice of grating citrus fruits on a grater
covered with a thin layer of plastic wrap as
tiny shreds of plastic can end up in the zest.
When you've finished zesting, be sure to glean
every rasping from both the outside and the
inside of the grater with a pastry brush.

Sectioning—With a freshly sharpened knife cut
a slice from the top and bottom of each piece
of fruit to expose the pulp, and, cutting from
top to bottom, remove all the peel and pith.
Working over a bowl to catch the juices, free
each section of fruit by cutting it away from the
membrane on both sides. Lift out the section
and discard the seeds.

—Jane Daniels Lear

CORNED BEEF HASH WITH FRIED EGGS

2 russet (baking) potatoes (about 1 pound)
1 large onion
1 large garlic clove
1 green bell pepper
a 1-pound piece cooked corned beef
2 tablespoons unsalted butter
2 tablespoons olive oil
1 tablespoon all-purpose flour
¾ cup beef broth
2 tablespoons drained bottled horseradish
  (preferably in beet juice)
1 tablespoon Worcestershire sauce

ACCOMPANIMENT
fried eggs

Fill a large saucepan three fourths full with salted water and bring to a boil for potatoes. Peel potatoes and cut into ½-inch cubes. Cook potatoes in boiling water 5 minutes, or until just tender, and drain in a colander.

Coarsely chop onion and mince garlic. Coarsely chop separately bell pepper and corned beef. In a large nonstick skillet heat butter and oil until foam subsides and cook onion over moderate heat, stirring, until golden. Add garlic and cook 1 minute. Add bell pepper and cook, stirring, 4 minutes. Sprinkle flour over mixture and cook, stirring, 2 minutes. Stir in broth, horseradish, and Worcestershire sauce and simmer, stirring, 1½ minutes. Add corned beef, potatoes, and salt and pepper to taste and cook, turning hash occasionally, until browned and crisp in spots, about 15 minutes.

Serve hash topped with fried eggs. Serves 6.

Photo left

CHEDDAR SAGE SCONES ◌

Cheddar cheese, made with fresh cow's milk, is one of the artisanal cheeses offered at some farmers markets (see cheese box on page 113). Most Cheddars are aged for 1 year; sharp Cheddars are aged for at least 2 years. Ask for a taste before you buy.

```
  2   cups all-purpose flour
2½    teaspoons baking powder
  2   teaspoons sugar
  1   teaspoon salt
  a   generous pinch cayenne
  1   tablespoon minced fresh sage leaves
 ¾    stick (6 tablespoons) cold unsalted butter
1¾    cups coarsely grated sharp Cheddar
  2   large eggs
 ¾    cup heavy cream
```

Preheat oven to 425° F. and lightly grease a baking sheet.

In a bowl whisk together flour, baking powder, sugar, salt, cayenne, and sage. Cut butter into bits and with your fingertips or a pastry blender blend butter into flour mixture until mixture resembles coarse meal. Stir in 1½ cups Cheddar until just combined. Separate eggs into 2 bowls and whisk cream into yolks. With a fork stir yolk mixture into flour mixture just until a soft dough forms. Turn dough out onto a lightly floured surface and gently knead 8 to 10 times. Halve dough and pat each piece into a 6-inch round. With a sharp knife cut each round into 6 wedges. Lightly beat egg whites.

On baking sheet arrange scones about 2 inches apart and brush tops lightly with some egg white. Sprinkle scones evenly with remaining ¼ cup cheese and bake in middle of oven 15 to 17 minutes, or until golden and cooked through. Makes 12 scones.

AMARETTO MIMOSAS ◌

```
  3   cups fresh orange juice
 ¼    cup almond-flavored liqueur such as
      Di Saronno Amaretto, or to taste
  1   bottle chilled sparkling wine such as
      Freixenet (750 ml)
```

Pour orange juice through a fine sieve into a pitcher and stir in liqueur. Fill 6 Champagne flutes halfway with juice mixture and top off with sparkling wine. Makes about 12 drinks.

Photo on page 148

WINTER DINNER FOR SIX

* Sweet Potato Chips with Blue Cheese and Spiced Pecans
* Chicken Stew with Sausage, Hominy, and Crispy Onions
* Parsley Spätzle
* Fresh Apple Cake with Chile de Árbol Caramel Glaze
* *Columbia Winery Yakima Valley Washington State Syrah 1996*

Sweet Potato Chips with Blue Cheese and Spiced Pecans

*When time is tight, feel free to substitute store-bought
sweet potato chips for the fresh fried ones in this recipe.*

1   tablespoon unsalted butter
½   teaspoon chili powder
½   teaspoon cayenne
1   cup pecan halves
1   large sweet potato (about ½ pound)
3   cups vegetable oil
¼   pound blue cheese or soft goat cheese
    at room temperature

Preheat oven to 350° F.

In a small saucepan melt butter with spices
over moderately low heat. In a shallow baking
pan drizzle butter over pecans with salt and
pepper to taste and toss to coat. Bake nuts in
middle of oven, stirring occasionally, until one
shade darker, about 10 minutes. Cool nuts.

Peel sweet potato and, with a *mandoline* or
other manual slicer, cut potato crosswise
into twenty-four ⅛-inch-thick slices.

In a 3-quart heavy saucepan heat oil over
moderately high heat until a deep-fat thermometer registers 365° F. and fry potato
slices in 2 batches, stirring frequently, until
golden brown on edges (chips will be marble-
ized with orange and brown), 1 to 2 minutes.
Transfer chips as fried with a slotted spoon
to paper towels to drain and season with salt.

Top each chip with about 1 teaspoon cheese
and a spiced pecan. Makes 24 hors d'oeuvres.

CHICKEN STEW WITH SAUSAGE, HOMINY, AND CRISPY ONIONS

2   teaspoons sweet paprika
1   teaspoon dry mustard
1   teaspoon fresh marjoram leaves
½   teaspoon cayenne, or to taste
a   pinch ground cloves
1   teaspoon black pepper
¾   teaspoon salt
a   3-pound chicken, cut into 8 pieces
1   pound good-quality smoked sausage links
4   large onions
1   carrot
1   green bell pepper
2   mild fresh green chiles such as Anaheim
2   cups canned whole tomatoes
3   tablespoons olive oil
1   tablespoon finely chopped garlic
1   cup chicken broth
1   can golden hominy including liquid
     (1 pound)
½   pound green beans

In a large bowl stir together paprika, mustard, marjoram, cayenne, cloves, pepper, and ½ teaspoon salt and add chicken, tossing to coat. *Marinate chicken, covered and chilled, 1 hour.*

Cut sausage into ¼-inch-thick slices and thinly slice enough onions to measure 4 cups. Finely chop carrot and chop bell pepper. Wearing protective gloves, seed chiles and chop. Drain, seed, and chop tomatoes. In a heavy kettle heat 1 tablespoon oil over moderately high heat until hot but not smoking and brown sausage, transferring it with a slotted spoon to paper towels to drain. In kettle brown chicken pieces on both sides and transfer to a plate. Pour off all but 2 tablespoons fat from kettle and cook carrot and 2 cups onions, covered, over moderate heat, stirring occasionally and scraping up any brown bits,

until softened. Add bell pepper, chiles, and garlic and cook, stirring, 2 minutes. Add tomatoes, broth, and hominy with liquid and bring mixture to a boil. Add sausage and chicken with any juices that have accumulated on plate and simmer stew, covered, 40 to 45 minutes, or until chicken is just tender.

While stew is simmering, in a large skillet heat remaining 2 tablespoons oil over moderate heat until hot but not smoking and cook remaining 2 cups onions with remaining ¼ teaspoon salt, covered, stirring occasionally, 15 to 17 minutes, or until onions just begin to turn golden. Cook onions, uncovered, stirring occasionally, 15 minutes, or until crisp and golden brown, and transfer to paper towels to drain.

Cut beans into 2-inch pieces. Add beans to stew and cook over moderate heat 7 to 10 minutes, or until beans are just tender.

Serve stew garnished with crispy onions. Serves 6.

Photo opposite

PARSLEY SPÄTZLE

These small, tender German dumplings are made by forcing a smooth, batterlike dough through holes of a Spätzle-maker or a colander into boiling water. Spätzle-makers may be ordered by mail from Schaller and Weber, tel. (212) 879-3047.

2½ cups all-purpose flour
1½ teaspoons salt
¾ cup plus 1 tablespoon whole milk
2 cups packed fresh flat-leafed parsley leaves
3 large eggs
½ cup water
½ stick (¼ cup) unsalted butter

In a 6-quart kettle bring 5 quarts salted water to a boil for *Spätzle*.

In a large bowl whisk together flour and salt. In a small heavy saucepan bring milk just to a simmer. Put parsley in a blender and with motor running add milk in a stream (use caution when blending hot liquids), blending until mixture is very green. In a large bowl whisk together eggs and water and add milk mixture in a slow stream, whisking constantly. Add egg mixture to flour mixture, whisking until a smooth, batterlike dough forms.

Preheat oven to 375° F.

Force dough through a *Spätzle*-maker or holes of a colander into boiling water and stir gently to separate. Cook *Spätzle* 5 minutes, or until just tender, and drain in a large colander. Rinse *Spätzle* well under cold water and drain well. Transfer *Spätzle* to a large baking dish.

Melt butter and drizzle over *Spätzle*, tossing to coat. Season *Spätzle* with salt and pepper. *Spätzle may be prepared up to this point 1 day ahead and chilled, covered.*

Bake *Spätzle*, covered, in middle of oven 20 minutes, or until heated through. Serves 6.

FRESH APPLE CAKE WITH CHILE DE ÁRBOL CARAMEL GLAZE

1 cup pecans
3 cups all-purpose flour
2 teaspoons cinnamon
1½ teaspoons freshly grated nutmeg
1 teaspoon baking soda
¼ teaspoon salt
3 large apples such as Braeburn, Jonathan, Winesap, or Gala (about 1½ pounds)
1½ cups vegetable oil
1¾ cups sugar
3 large eggs
1 tablespoon vanilla
   chile de árbol caramel glaze (recipe follows)

SPECIAL EQUIPMENT
10-cup bundt pan

Preheat oven to 325° F. and butter and flour bundt pan, knocking out excess flour.

In a shallow baking pan toast pecans in one layer in middle of oven 7 minutes, or until fragrant. Cool nuts and finely chop. (Leave oven on.)

Into a bowl sift together flour, cinnamon, nutmeg, baking soda, and salt. Peel and core apples and dice enough to measure 3 cups. In a large bowl with an electric mixer beat together oil and sugar until combined well and add eggs 1 at a time, beating well after each addition. Stir in vanilla, flour mixture, diced apples, and pecans until just combined.

Spoon batter into bundt pan and bake in middle of oven 1 hour and 20 minutes, or until a tester comes out clean. Cool cake in pan on a rack 10 minutes and invert onto rack. While cake is still warm, brush with glaze several times and cool. *Glaze will remain shiny for 8 hours. Cake keeps, covered loosely with plastic wrap or under a cake dome, at room temperature 5 days.* Serves 6 with leftovers.

Photo opposite

CHILE DE ÁRBOL CARAMEL GLAZE

The "de Árbol" chile is a narrow, 2- to 3-inch-long, pointed variety from Mexico that adds considerable heat to dishes. The mature pods are dark red, but they turn lighter when dried. Dried cayenne chiles are a good substitute.

2	dried *árbol* chiles*
¾	stick (6 tablespoons) unsalted butter
⅓	cup granulated sugar
⅓	cup packed dark brown sugar
⅓	cup heavy cream
2	teaspoons vanilla

available by mail order from Chile Today—Hot Tamale, tel. (800) 468-7377

Wearing protective gloves, chop chiles including seeds. In a saucepan bring all ingredients except vanilla to a boil, stirring until sugar is dissolved, and remove pan from heat. Stir in vanilla and keep glaze warm, covered. Makes about 1½ cups.

winter recipes

SHERRIED PARSNIP SOUP WITH HAZELNUT PESTO

Subtly sweet, earthy parsnips resemble carrots, but have slightly wider shoulders tapering to thinner tips. For freshness, choose the palest cream-colored parsnips you can find. If the central core is woody or tough, it should be trimmed away, since it won't soften with cooking.

1	pound parsnips (about 6 medium)
5	large shallots
3	leeks (white and pale green parts only)
1	celery rib
5	tablespoons unsalted butter
¼	cup plus 1 tablespoon dry Sherry
4½	cups water
3	tablespoons heavy cream, or to taste (optional)
¾	cup hazelnut pesto (recipe follows)

GARNISH
chopped toasted hazelnuts

Peel and chop parsnips. Finely chop shallots. Finely chop leeks and wash well. Chop celery. In a 4-quart heavy kettle sauté parsnips, shallots, leeks, and celery with salt and pepper to taste in butter over moderately high heat, stirring, until browned, about 10 minutes. Add ¼ cup Sherry and boil until liquid is evaporated. Stir in water and simmer, covered, about 20 minutes, or until vegetables are very soft.

In a blender purée mixture in batches (use caution when blending hot liquids), transferring to a large saucepan. Stir in remaining tablespoon Sherry, cream, and salt and pepper to taste and cook over moderately high heat, stirring occasionally, until heated through.

Serve soup topped with a dollop of hazelnut pesto and garnished with toasted hazelnuts. Makes about 6 cups, serving 4 to 6.

Photo opposite

HAZELNUT PESTO ◔

This pesto—created for the parsnip soup—would also be great on pasta (use about ¾ cup for 1 pound pasta, thinning the pesto with some of the pasta cooking water), grilled fish and meats, or vegetables.

1	cup hazelnuts (about 4½ ounces)
2	cups packed fresh flat-leafed parsley leaves (about 1 large bunch)
2	large garlic cloves
¾	cup olive oil
2	tablespoons hazelnut oil* (optional)

*available by mail order from Dean & DeLuca, tel. (800) 221-7714

Preheat oven to 350° F.

In a baking pan toast hazelnuts in one layer in middle of oven 10 to 15 minutes, or until colored lightly and skins are blistered. Wrap nuts in a kitchen towel and let steam 1 minute. Rub nuts in towel to remove loose skins (don't worry about skins that don't come off) and cool completely.

In a food processor grind nuts with remaining ingredients and salt and pepper to taste until smooth. *Pesto keeps, covered and chilled, 1 week, or frozen 1 month.* Makes about 1½ cups.

MINESTRONE

Blue-green kale is the most common variety, but there are plenty of other edible ones that taste like strong spring greens. Tuscan kale (called lacinata, dinosaur kale, or cavolo nero), with dark green stalks and nearly black leaves, is popular at many farmers markets. Like collards, kale sweetens after the first frost.

½ pound dried white beans such as
Great Northern (about 1¼ cups)

½ teaspoon salt

¼ pound *pancetta* (Italian unsmoked
cured bacon) or sliced lean bacon

1 medium onion

1 large carrot

1 celery rib

2 medium zucchini

3 garlic cloves

¼ pound green beans

½ pound boiling potatoes

1 medium head green cabbage
(preferably Savoy)

½ pound kale

1 can whole tomatoes (28 ounces)

⅓ cup olive oil

4½ cups chicken broth

ACCOMPANIMENTS
freshly grated Parmesan
garlic *bruschetta* (page 161)
dry-cured sausages

Pick over white beans and rinse. *In a large bowl soak beans in water to cover by 2 inches for 8 hours and drain, or quick-soak beans (procedure follows).* In a saucepan cover beans with water by 2 inches. Simmer beans, uncovered, adding more water if necessary to keep barely covered, 45 to 60 minutes, or until tender. Add salt and simmer beans 5 minutes more. Remove pan from heat and let beans stand, uncovered.

Chop bacon and chop onion. Separately cut carrot, celery, and zucchini into ½-inch cubes. Finely chop garlic. Cut green beans into ½-inch pieces. Peel potatoes and cut into ¾-inch cubes, transferring to a bowl of cold water. Thinly slice enough cabbage to measure 4 cups. Discard stems from kale and chop leaves. Drain tomatoes and coarsely chop. In a heavy kettle cook bacon in oil over moderate heat, stirring, until crisp and pale golden. Add onion and cook, stirring, until onion is softened. Add carrot, celery, and garlic and cook, stirring, 4 minutes. Drain potatoes and add to onion mixture with zucchini and green beans. Cook mixture, stirring, 4 minutes. Add cabbage and kale and cook, stirring, until cabbage is wilted. Add tomatoes and broth and simmer soup, covered, 1 hour.

In a large sieve set over a bowl drain white beans, reserving cooking liquid, and in a blender or food processor purée half of beans with 1 cup of reserved liquid. Stir purée and whole beans into soup and simmer, uncovered, 15 minutes. Thin soup to desired consistency with remaining reserved bean liquid and season with salt and pepper. *Soup may be made 3 days ahead and chilled, covered. Reheat soup, thinning with water if necessary.*

Serve soup with Parmesan, *bruschetta*, and sausages. Makes about 10 cups, serving 6 to 8 as a main course.

Photo opposite

To Quick-Soak Dried Beans ◌+

Pick over beans and in a saucepan cover with cold water by 2 inches. Bring water to a boil and boil beans 2 minutes. Remove pan from heat. *Soak beans 1 hour.* Drain beans in a sieve.

Garlic Bruschetta ◌

8 slices crusty peasant bread (¾-inch-thick; preferably from a large round loaf)
3 garlic cloves
6 tablespoons extra-virgin olive oil

Preheat broiler.

On a baking sheet toast bread slices in batches under broiler about 3 inches from heat until golden, about 1 minute on each side, transferring to a work surface. Halve garlic cloves crosswise and rub one side of each toast with cut side of a garlic clove. Brush toasts with oil and season with salt. Serves 8.

GUMBO WITH MIXED GREENS AND RED BEANS

Leafy green carrot tops needn't be thrown away. They're a tasty green to add to this gumbo along with a host of assorted greens. Just remember to twist the tops off the carrots as soon as you get home, since they pull moisture from the vegetables.

2 large onions
1 large green bell pepper
3 celery ribs
⅓ cup vegetable oil
½ cup bread flour
7 quarts water
5 bunches assorted greens such as collards, beet greens, Swiss chard, kale, mustard greens, turnip greens, and/or spinach (7 to 8 quarts total)
1 bunch carrot tops (about 5 cups packed)
1 pound picked-over dried red kidney beans (about 2½ cups)
6 large garlic cloves

ACCOMPANIMENT
Cajun-style white rice (recipe follows)

Chop onions, bell pepper, and celery. In a heavy skillet (preferably cast-iron) cook oil and flour over moderately low heat, stirring constantly with a flat-edged metal or wooden spatula, until *roux* is a dark reddish-brown, about 45 minutes. *Roux may be made 1 week ahead, cooled completely, and chilled, covered, in a glass or stainless-steel bowl. Reheat roux in skillet over moderately low heat, stirring, before proceeding.* Stir chopped vegetables into *roux* and cook, stirring occasionally, until vegetables are softened.

In a 10- to 12-quart heavy kettle bring 4 quarts water to a boil for greens.

Discard tough stems from carrot tops and other greens and simmer, stirring occasionally, until just tender, about 15 minutes. With tongs transfer greens to a large shallow baking dish, letting excess cooking liquid drip into kettle and reserving all cooking liquid. Cool greens until they can be handled and coarsely chop.

Stir kidney beans and remaining 3 quarts water into reserved liquid and simmer, partially covered, until beans are tender, about 1 hour. (Older beans may take longer to cook.) Mince garlic. Add *roux* mixture to beans by large spoonfuls, stirring well after each addition, and stir in greens, garlic, and salt and pepper to taste. Simmer gumbo, partially covered, stirring occasionally, 30 minutes. *Gumbo may be made 2 days ahead and cooled completely, uncovered, before being chilled, covered.*

Serve gumbo ladled over rice in large soup plates. Makes about 24 cups, serving 10 to 12 as a main course.

Photo opposite

CAJUN-STYLE WHITE RICE ◔

2 cups white rice
3 cups water
½ teaspoon salt

In a 3-quart heavy saucepan wash rice in several changes of water, pouring off water carefully, until water is almost clear. Drain rice in a sieve and return to pan. Add 3 cups water and salt and bring to a boil, uncovered, without stirring. Boil mixture until surface of rice is covered with steam holes and grains on top appear dry, 8 to 10 minutes. Reduce heat to low and cook rice, covered, without stirring, 15 minutes. Remove pan from heat and let rice stand, covered, 5 minutes. Fluff rice with a fork. Makes about 6 cups.

collard greens

The word collard is a corruption of "colewort," the name given to members of the Brassica, or cabbage, family that do not form a head. Collard greens are English in origin, but the custom of stewing them down to "low gravy" is an African-American one.

Collards grow throughout the South. Like mustard greens and kale, they are eaten all year long, although they are at their best after the first frost (summer collards are tougher and take much longer to "tenderize"). They are often cooked with a smoked hog jowl or ham hock.

This enduring dietary staple is celebrated in annual festivals in Gaston, South Carolina, and Ayden, North Carolina. In 1984 the Ayden festival committee put together *Leaves of Greens: The Collard Poems* after holding a collard poetry contest. More than 500 entries were submitted from poets in 32 states and 3 European countries.

—Jane Daniels Lear

leeks

You'll see leeks at the farmers market with the roots and most of the stiff, dark-green leaves attached. The leaves should look fresh, and the white shank, or stem, should be firm. Leeks keep best if left untrimmed until just before using. Wrapped in a damp towel and stored in a plastic bag, small leeks will keep several days and larger, more mature specimens will last a little longer.

Because of the way that leeks grow, you'll often find sand or grit trapped between the leaves. If a recipe calls for chopping leeks or cutting them into julienne strips, it's best to wash them after chopping or cutting. Rinse the cut pieces thoroughly in a large bowl of cold water, swishing them around with your hand to ensure that no sand or grit is left clinging to them. After the dirt has settled to the bottom of the bowl, lift the leeks from the water with your hands and transfer them to a sieve to drain. (Don't pour the leeks with the water into the sieve, or the dirt will end up back on the leeks.)

If cooking your leeks halved, wash the halves under cold running water, taking pains to sluice water between each and every leaf. Gently bend the leaves back and rub each leaf between your fingers to remove the soil. This method also works with whole leeks; before washing, trim them and slit them lengthwise, beginning about 2 inches from the root end.

—Jane Daniels Lear

LEEK SOUP

9 medium leeks (white and pale green parts only)
2 tablespoons unsalted butter
1½ cups chicken broth
2½ cups water
½ cup packed fresh flat-leafed parsley leaves
¼ cup heavy cream

Cut leeks crosswise into ¼-inch-thick rounds and wash well in a large bowl of cold water. Lift leeks from water into a colander and drain. In a large saucepan cook leeks in butter over moderate heat, stirring occasionally, until softened, about 15 minutes. Add broth and water and simmer until leeks are very tender, 10 to 15 minutes.

In a blender purée about two thirds leek mixture with parsley (use caution when blending hot liquids) and add to remaining leek mixture. Stir in cream and bring soup to a boil. Season soup with salt and pepper. Makes about 6 cups, serving 4 to 6.

BEET SOUP WITH RED WINE

1¾ pounds beets without greens
1 medium onion
1 tablespoon olive oil
1½ cups beef broth
3 cups water
½ cup dry red wine
1½ tablespoons balsamic vinegar

Peel beets and cut into ½-inch pieces. Halve onion through root end and cut crosswise into ¼-inch-thick slices. In a large saucepan cook onion in oil over moderate heat, stirring occasionally, until softened. Add beets, broth, and water and simmer until beets are just tender, about 15 minutes. Stir in wine and vinegar and bring soup just to a boil. Season soup with salt. Makes about 7 cups, serving 4 to 6.

ROOT VEGETABLE AND ARUGULA RISOTTO

Firm, knobby celery root makes a savory addition to a root vegetable mixture. To prepare it, cut off a good amount from both ends and then peel off a thick layer of skin with a paring knife. The firm, white vegetable revealed underneath tastes strongly of parsley and subtly of artichokes, and has an herbal aroma.

1½	pounds mixed root vegetables such as carrots, celery root, parsnips, turnips, fennel bulb, and/or leeks (white and pale green parts only)
1	large red onion
3	tablespoons unsalted butter
1	teaspoon salt
4	cups chicken broth
2	cups water
1	bunch arugula
1½	cups Arborio rice
¼	cup dry white wine
⅓	cup freshly grated Parmesan (about 1 ounce)

Peel root vegetables if necessary and cut into ½-inch pieces. (If using leeks, wash pieces well and drain.) Chop onion. In a 2- to 3-quart heavy saucepan melt 1½ tablespoons butter over moderate heat and add root vegetables, half of onion, and salt, stirring to coat with butter. Cook vegetables, covered, stirring occasionally, until tender and slightly caramelized, about 15 minutes.

While vegetables are cooking, in another 2- to 3-quart saucepan bring broth and water to a simmer and keep at a bare simmer. Discard tough stems from arugula and coarsely chop leaves. In a 4-quart heavy kettle cook remaining onion in remaining 1½ tablespoons butter over moderately low heat, stirring, until softened. Add rice and cook, stirring, 2 minutes. Add wine and cook, stirring, until wine is absorbed, about 1 minute. Stir in ½ cup simmering broth and cook over moderate heat, stirring constantly and keeping at a strong simmer throughout, until absorbed. Continue simmering and adding broth, about ½ cup at a time, stirring constantly and letting each addition be absorbed before adding next, until rice is tender and creamy-looking but still *al dente*, about 18 minutes total. (There will be some broth left over.)

Stir in caramelized vegetables, arugula, Parmesan, salt and pepper to taste, and enough remaining broth to thin risotto to a thick, souplike consistency, and cook, stirring, until arugula is wilted, about 2 minutes. Serve risotto immediately. Serves 4 as a main course.

CELERY ROOT

ROAST COD WITH POTATOES, ONIONS, AND OLIVES

1 pound onions (about 3 medium)
3 large garlic cloves
¾ cup Kalamata or other brine-cured black olives
¼ cup olive oil
1 pound boiling potatoes (about 2 large)
⅓ cup vegetable oil
½ teaspoon dried rosemary, crumbled
¼ cup minced fresh parsley leaves
a 2-pound piece center-cut cod fillet

Preheat oven to 450° F.

Cut onions into ½-inch-thick slices and mince garlic. Pit and quarter olives. In a large skillet cook onions and garlic in olive oil over moderate heat, stirring occasionally, until pale golden.

While onions are cooking, peel potatoes and cut into ¼-inch-thick slices. In another large skillet heat vegetable oil over moderately high heat until hot but not smoking and sauté potatoes in batches, turning them, 5 to 8 minutes, or until pale golden, transferring to a bowl.

Add onions to potatoes with olives, rosemary, parsley, and salt and pepper to taste and toss gently to combine. Arrange cod in center of a large shallow baking dish and season with salt and pepper. Scatter potato mixture around cod and roast in middle of oven 20 to 25 minutes, or until fish is just cooked through. Serves 4.

Photo left

Roasted Chicken with Carrots, Turnips, and Zucchini

Roasted chicken makes a warming supper when prepared with winter vegetables, like white turnips with purple collars. Buy firm turnips with their peppery-flavored greens still attached—they'll be crisper and more delicate.

3 medium garlic cloves
1 teaspoon ground coriander seeds
2 teaspoons ground cumin
1½ teaspoons kosher salt
⅓ cup finely chopped fresh cilantro sprigs
3½ to 4½ tablespoons unsalted butter, softened
a 4-pound chicken
1 pound carrots (about 5 large)
1 pound turnips (about 4 medium)
1 pound zucchini (about 2 medium)
1 cup chicken broth
½ cup water
½ tablespoon all-purpose flour

Preheat oven to 425° F. and oil a large flameproof roasting pan.

Finely chop garlic and in a small bowl stir together with spices, kosher salt, and cilantro. Transfer 3 tablespoons spice mixture to another small bowl and into remainder stir 3 tablespoons butter.

Reserve giblets for another use and rinse chicken inside and out. Remove any excess fat from opening of body cavity and pat chicken dry. Put chicken in center of roasting pan. With your fingers loosen skin from breast at both ends and push half of seasoned butter under skin, spreading over breastbone to each side of breast. Massage skin from outside to spread butter evenly over breast. Put remaining seasoned butter in body cavity and with small metal or wooden skewers completely close body cavity and neck cavity. Tie drumsticks together with kitchen string and season chicken lightly with salt. Roast chicken in middle of oven 20 minutes.

While chicken is roasting, cut carrots diagonally into 1-inch-thick pieces. Peel turnips and cut into 1-inch wedges. Scatter carrots and turnips around chicken and toss with fat in pan (if chicken is very lean, add 1 tablespoon butter and toss with vegetables). Roast chicken and vegetables 30 minutes. Halve zucchini lengthwise and cut diagonally into 1-inch pieces. Scatter zucchini around chicken and sprinkle vegetables with 2 tablespoons spice mixture, tossing to coat. Roast chicken and vegetables 30 minutes, or until an instant-read thermometer inserted in fleshy part of a thigh registers 170° F.

Remove string and skewers from chicken and pour any juices from inside chicken into pan. Transfer chicken to a platter and with a slotted spoon arrange vegetables around chicken. Keep chicken and vegetables warm, covered loosely.

Skim fat from juices in roasting pan. To pan add broth, water, and remaining tablespoon spice mixture and on top of stove deglaze over moderately high heat, scraping up brown bits. Boil sauce until reduced by about half. While sauce is boiling, in a small bowl with your fingers knead together ½ tablespoon butter and flour until combined. Stir butter mixture into sauce and boil, stirring, about 2 minutes, or until slightly thickened. Transfer sauce to a sauceboat.

Serve chicken and vegetables with sauce. Serves 4.

GEMELLI WITH SWISS CHARD, ANCHOVIES, AND RED PEPPER

Although we call for Swiss chard, with shiny, dark green leaves and white veins and ribs, any other chard will do. You may find red chard (sometimes called rhubarb chard), with crimson-veined green leaves and dark red ribs, or ruby chard, with reddish leaves and ribs. The thick, firm ribs take longer to cook than the leaves, so they should be cooked separately.

½ pound *gemelli, rotini,* or *fusilli*
1   pound Swiss chard
4   garlic cloves
1   red bell pepper
3   tablespoons olive oil
a   2-ounce can flat anchovy fillets
2   tablespoons toasted pine nuts

ACCOMPANIMENT
freshly grated Parmesan

Fill a 5-quart kettle three fourths full with salted water and bring to a boil for pasta.

Cut ribs from chard leaves and finely chop enough ribs to measure 1 cup. Coarsely chop leaves. Finely chop garlic. Cut bell pepper into julienne strips.

Cook pasta in boiling water until *al dente.* Reserve ½ cup pasta cooking water and drain pasta in a colander.

While pasta is cooking, in a 12-inch nonstick skillet cook garlic in oil over moderate heat, stirring, until fragrant, about 2 minutes. Drain anchovies and pat dry. Add anchovies to garlic and mash with back of a spoon to a paste. Stir in bell pepper and chopped chard ribs and cook, covered, stirring occasionally, until tender, about 4 minutes. Remove skillet from heat and add chard leaves, tossing with tongs to combine. Add pasta and ¼ cup reserved cooking water and cook over moderately low heat, tossing and adding more cooking water if mixture is too dry, until chard leaves are wilted.

Sprinkle pasta with pine nuts and serve with Parmesan. Serves 4.

CORNED BEEF COLESLAW WITH RYE CROUTONS ◔

4   slices rye bread
1   small onion
1   small green bell pepper
¾ cup mayonnaise
¼ cup bottled chili sauce
1   tablespoon minced drained bottled pimiento
1   teaspoon drained bottled horseradish, or to taste
1   large head green cabbage (about 2¼ pounds)
½ pound sliced trimmed cooked corned beef

Preheat oven to 350° F.

Discard crusts and cut bread into ½-inch cubes. On a baking sheet toast bread cubes in middle of oven, stirring occasionally, 10 to 15 minutes, or until a shade darker. Cool croutons.

Mince enough onion to measure 2 tablespoons and enough bell pepper to measure ¼ cup and in a large bowl whisk together with mayonnaise, chili sauce, pimiento, horseradish, and salt and black pepper to taste.

Shred enough cabbage to measure 2½ quarts and cut corned beef into very thin strips. Add shredded cabbage and corned beef to dressing and toss until combined well. Top coleslaw with croutons. Serves 4 as a light main course.

Photo opposite, back

WARM COLESLAW WITH KIELBASA AND BACON

1 small red onion
1 garlic clove
1 large head red cabbage (about 2¼ pounds)
½ pound *kielbasa* or other fully cooked smoked sausage
6 lean bacon slices
1 large Granny Smith apple
⅔ cup cider vinegar
⅔ cup dry white wine
a pinch ground cloves
¼ teaspoon caraway seeds

Mince red onion and garlic. Finely shred enough cabbage to measure 10 cups. Halve sausage lengthwise and thinly slice crosswise. Cut bacon crosswise into thin strips and in a large kettle cook over moderate heat, stirring, until crisp. With a slotted spoon transfer bacon to paper towels to drain and pour off all but about ¼ cup fat. In fat remaining in kettle cook onion and garlic over moderately low heat, stirring, until softened. Finely chop apple (do not peel). Add apple, vinegar, wine, cloves, and caraway seeds to onion mixture and simmer, stirring occasionally, 3 minutes, or until apple is softened. Stir in shredded cabbage, sausage, and salt and pepper to taste and cook, stirring, 3 minutes, or until cabbage is slightly wilted.

Serve coleslaw topped with bacon. Serves 4 as a light main course.

Photo opposite, front

cabbage

Over the past 3,000 years, farmers throughout Europe have cultivated astounding permutations of one vegetable family, Brassica, which includes Savoy cabbage and the more common green, white, and red cabbages, as well as broccoli, cauliflower, turnips, kohlrabi, rutabagas, kale, collards, bok choy, and Brussels sprouts.

The Savoy—distinguished by crinkled deep-green outer leaves that often are tinged with blue—forms loose, showy heads fancied by generations of still-life painters and ceramicists and takes pride of place in many a backyard cabbage patch. One of the hardiest and most frost-resistant varieties, the Savoy is harvested from October to March.

Unfortunately, cabbage is closely associated in many people's minds with overcooking (and the accompanying rank odor); stodgy meals; and, as the late culinary authority Jane Grigson put it, "a nasty history of being good for you." It is, in fact, loaded with vitamins B and C, iron, potassium, and calcium. One way to preserve the nutrients and flavor is to eat it raw in salads or slaws or to cook it briefly—if you're adding it to soups or stews, cook it until the leaves are softened, not limp. Savoy cabbage, because it's tender and sweet, particularly benefits from quick cooking; try it sautéed or in a stir-fry.

—Jane Daniels Lear

MOLASSES CHEDDAR MUFFINS

½ stick (¼ cup) unsalted butter
8 ounces extra-sharp Cheddar
2 cups all-purpose flour
1 tablespoon baking powder
¼ teaspoon baking soda
1 teaspoon ground cinnamon
¼ teaspoon ground ginger
¼ teaspoon ground allspice
¼ teaspoon freshly grated nutmeg
1 teaspoon salt
1 tablespoon sugar
1 large egg
½ cup milk
½ cup unsulfured dark molasses

Preheat oven to 425° F. and butter twelve ⅓-cup muffin cups.

Melt butter and cool. Grate enough Cheddar to measure 1¾ cups. Into a large bowl sift together flour, baking powder, baking soda, spices, salt, and sugar. In a small bowl lightly beat egg and whisk in milk and molasses. Stir egg mixture into flour mixture until just combined and stir in butter and grated cheese.

Spoon batter into muffin cups and bake in middle of oven 15 minutes, or until a tester comes out with crumbs adhering. Turn muffins out onto a rack. Serve muffins warm or at room temperature. Makes 12 muffins.

CORN BREAD WITH CRANBERRIES

1 cup picked-over fresh cranberries
1 cup all-purpose flour
1 tablespoon baking powder
¾ teaspoon salt
1 cup cornmeal
½ cup sugar
½ cup milk
1 large egg
1 stick (½ cup) unsalted butter, softened

Preheat oven to 400° F. and butter a 9- by 5- by 3-inch loaf pan.

In a food processor pulse cranberries until coarsely chopped. Into a large bowl sift together flour, baking powder, and salt and whisk in cornmeal and sugar until combined well. In a bowl whisk together milk and egg until just combined. Add butter to flour mixture and with an electric mixer beat until mixture resembles coarse meal. Beat in egg mixture until just combined and stir in cranberries.

Pour batter into loaf pan and bake in middle of oven until golden and a tester comes out clean, about 40 minutes. Cool corn bread in pan on a rack 20 minutes and turn out onto rack to cool completely. *Corn bread keeps in an airtight container at cool room temperature 2 days or frozen 2 weeks.* Makes 1 loaf.

SPICED ONION PITAS

3 medium onions
1 teaspoon curry powder
1½ tablespoons olive oil
4 pitas (6- to 7-inches each; preferably pocketless)

Preheat oven to 450° F.

Halve onions through root ends and cut halves crosswise into ¼-inch-thick slices. In a large nonstick skillet cook onions with curry powder and salt to taste in oil over moderate heat, stirring occasionally, until tender and golden.

Brush pita tops with oil from skillet. Divide onion mixture among pitas and season with salt. With a metal spatula transfer pitas to middle rack in oven and bake until crisp on the outside but still soft inside, about 5 minutes.

Serve pitas cut into quarters. Serves 4.

TOASTED HAZELNUTS

TOASTED HAZELNUT SALAD WITH DRIED CRANBERRIES AND HAZELNUT VINAIGRETTE

2   large shallots
3   tablespoons olive oil
½   cup dried cranberries (about 2 ounces)
4   tablespoons Sherry vinegar*, or to taste
3   tablespoons water
1   tablespoon sugar
½   cup hazelnuts (about 2 ounces)
½   teaspoon Dijon mustard
1   tablespoon hazelnut oil* (optional)
3   medium heads baby Bibb lettuce
2   ounces *frisée* (French curly endive)
2   ounces baby spinach or *tatsoi*
    (thick, spoon-shaped Asian greens;
    about 2 cups)

*available by mail order from Dean & DeLuca,
tel. (800) 221-7714*

Preheat oven to 350° F.

Finely chop shallots. In a small saucepan heat 2 teaspoons olive oil over moderate heat until hot but not smoking and cook shallots, stirring, until golden brown. Stir in cranberries, 3 tablespoons vinegar, water, and sugar and simmer, stirring occasionally, until syrupy, about 4 minutes. Transfer mixture to a bowl and cool to room temperature.

In a shallow baking pan toast hazelnuts in middle of oven 10 to 15 minutes, or until colored lightly and skins are blistered. Wrap nuts in a kitchen towel and let steam 1 minute. Rub nuts in towel to remove loose skins (don't worry about skins that don't come off). In a small skillet cook nuts with salt and pepper to taste in 1 teaspoon olive oil over moderate heat, stirring, until golden brown, about 3 minutes. Transfer nuts to a plate and cool.

In a small bowl whisk together mustard, remaining tablespoon vinegar, and salt and pepper to taste. Add hazelnut oil and remaining 2 tablespoons olive oil in a stream, whisking until emulsified.

Separate Bibb lettuce into leaves and tear *frisée* into bite-size pieces. In a large bowl toss all greens with just enough vinaigrette to coat and divide among 6 plates. Drizzle salads with cranberry mixture and sprinkle with nuts. Serves 6.

Photo on page 158

SWISS CHARD WITH ROASTED PEPPER

1   red bell pepper
2½ pounds Swiss chard
2   tablespoons extra-virgin olive oil

Roast and peel bell pepper (procedure on page 64) and coarsely chop. Cut coarse stems from chard and separately chop stems and leaves. In a kettle cook chard stems in ½ cup water, covered, over high heat 5 minutes. Add chard leaves and cook, covered, stirring occasionally, 5 minutes. Drain chard well and in a bowl toss with roasted pepper, oil, and salt and pepper to taste. Serves 6.

Photo on page 166

BRAISED RED CABBAGE WITH PEAR AND WALNUTS ◔

1 head red cabbage (about 2 pounds)
2 medium onions
3 tablespoons olive oil
½ cup apple juice
1 firm-ripe pear
½ cup walnuts
1 tablespoon red-wine vinegar

Halve cabbage through core and cut crosswise into ¼-inch-thick slices, discarding core. Halve onions through root ends and cut crosswise into ¼-inch-thick slices. In a large heavy skillet heat 2 tablespoons oil until hot but not smoking and sauté onions, stirring, until softened and golden. Add cabbage, tossing to coat with oil, and salt to taste and stir in apple juice. Cook cabbage over moderate heat, covered, until just tender, about 10 minutes.

While cabbage is cooking, cut pear into ½-inch pieces and coarsely chop walnuts. In a small heavy skillet cook walnuts with salt to taste in remaining tablespoon oil over moderately high heat, stirring, until fragrant and golden and with a slotted spoon transfer nuts to a bowl. In oil remaining in skillet sauté pear, stirring, until just tender and add to nuts.

Remove lid from cabbage and stir in vinegar. Cook cabbage over moderately high heat, stirring occasionally, until most of liquid is evaporated, about 5 minutes. Season cabbage with salt and pepper and add walnuts and pear, tossing until combined. Serves 6.

ROASTED CELERY ROOT, RED ONIONS, MUSHROOMS, AND SAGE

3 pounds celery root (sometimes called celeriac)
5 tablespoons olive oil
2 teaspoons coarse salt
3 medium red onions (about 1½ pounds total)
1 pound small white mushrooms
½ pound assorted fresh exotic mushrooms such as chanterelles and portabellas
3 tablespoons chopped fresh sage leaves

Preheat oven to 400° F.

With a sharp knife peel celery root and cut into 2- by ½-inch sticks. Divide celery root between 2 large roasting pans and toss each half with 1 tablespoon oil and 1 teaspoon salt. Roast celery root in upper and lower thirds of oven, stirring occasionally and switching position of pans halfway through roasting, 25 minutes total.

Cut onions into 1-inch pieces. Halve mushrooms or quarter if large and in a bowl toss mushrooms and onions with sage, remaining 3 tablespoons oil, and salt and pepper to taste. Divide mushroom mixture between pans, tossing with roasted celery root. Roast vegetables, stirring occasionally and switching position of pans halfway through roasting, about 30 minutes total, or until all vegetables are tender and golden.

Season vegetables with salt and pepper. Serves 6.

Photo opposite

GOAT CHEESE MASHED-POTATO GRATIN

Yukon Gold, Yellow Finn, and Bintje are a few of the yellow-fleshed potato varieties to look for at the farmers market. Yellow-fleshed potatoes are the ultimate for mashing—they look and taste rich and buttery even before any butter, cream, or goat cheese is added.

2	pounds yellow-fleshed potatoes or russet (baking) potatoes
6	garlic cloves, unpeeled
⅓	cup heavy cream
1	stick (½ cup) unsalted butter
⅓	cup soft mild goat cheese (about 3½ ounces)
¼	cup minced scallion

Peel potatoes and cut into ½-inch pieces. In a large saucepan cover potatoes and garlic cloves with salted cold water by ½ inch and simmer, covered, 15 to 25 minutes, or until potatoes are tender but not falling apart. While potatoes are simmering, in a small saucepan heat cream, butter, goat cheese, and salt and pepper to taste over moderately low heat, stirring, until butter and cheese are just melted and smooth and keep warm.

Drain potatoes and garlic and force through a food mill fitted with medium disk or a ricer into a bowl. With an electric mixer beat in butter mixture, scallion, and salt and pepper to taste just until potatoes are fluffy and smooth (do not overbeat) and transfer mixture to a 1-quart shallow flame-proof baking dish. *Potatoes may be prepared up to this point 2 days ahead and chilled, covered. Reheat potatoes in a preheated 400° F. oven 20 minutes, or until heated through, before broiling.*

Preheat broiler.

Broil potatoes about 4 inches from heat 3 to 5 minutes, or until top is golden. Serves 4 to 6.

Photo right

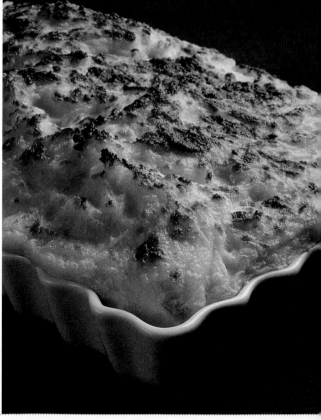

Wheat Berry Salad with Tangelos, Pomegranates, and Currants

Bright orange tangelos (also called honeybells or Minneola tangelos) are a cross between a tangerine and a grapefruit. The fruit is sweet and very juicy and it separates easily into segments.

1	cup wheat berries
3	tablespoons vegetable oil
½	cup sliced almonds
2	tangelos or mandarin oranges
½	pomegranate
1	cup packed fresh flat-leafed parsley leaves
½	cup dried currants
1	tablespoon white-wine vinegar

In a large saucepan simmer wheat berries in 6 cups water until tender, about 50 minutes, and drain.

In a small skillet heat oil over moderate heat until hot but not smoking and cook almonds, stirring, until golden and fragrant. In a bowl stir together wheat berries, almonds, and oil from skillet.

Finely grate zest from tangelos or oranges and add to wheat berries. With a sharp knife cut remaining peel from tangelos or oranges, including all white pith, and working over wheat berries to catch any juice, cut sections free from membranes, dropping them into bowl. With your hands gently break pomegranate half in two. Bend back rind and dislodge seeds from membrane, adding to wheat berry mixture. Chop parsley and add to mixture with currants, vinegar, and salt and pepper to taste, tossing until combined. Serves 6.

wheat berries

Wheat berries are the hulled whole kernels of wheat from which flour is milled. Both hard-wheat (high-protein) and soft-wheat (low-protein) varieties are available and they can be used interchangeably in recipes. Nutritious, virtually fat-free, and with a nutty sweetness and pleasant chewiness, wheat berries can be a wonderful alternative to rice or pasta in salads, casseroles, stews, and stuffings.

Tip: Because salt prevents uncooked wheat berries from absorbing liquid properly, wait until after cooking to salt them.

Like many other whole grains, wheat berries are at their best when recently harvested. Look for them at your local farmers market (many markets have at least one vendor that sells grains and flours) or a natural foods store that has a brisk turnover. Or you can order them from a reputable mail-order source such as Walnut Acres, (800) 433-3998. If possible, buy organic—a good indication of high quality.

—Jane Daniels Lear

LEMON TEA CAKE

This lovely tea cake has a dense, pound-cake-like texture, so be sure to serve it in thin slices. Try Meyer lemons for a sweeter lemony flavor.

5 lemons
3 cups all-purpose flour
2 teaspoons baking powder
¾ teaspoon salt
2 sticks (1 cup) unsalted butter, softened
2½ cups sugar
5 large eggs
¾ cup sour cream

SPECIAL EQUIPMENT
12-cup bundt pan

Preheat oven to 350° F. Butter and flour bundt pan, knocking out excess flour.

Grate enough zest from lemons to measure 2 tablespoons and squeeze enough juice to measure ½ cup plus ⅓ cup. In a bowl stir together flour, baking powder, and salt. In a large bowl with an electric mixer beat together butter and 2 cups sugar until light and fluffy and add eggs 1 at a time, beating well after each addition. Add flour mixture and sour cream, beating until combined well. Stir in grated zest and ½ cup juice and pour batter into bundt pan, smoothing top.

Bake cake in middle of oven until a tester comes out clean, about 1 hour. While cake is baking, in a small saucepan simmer remaining ⅓ cup lemon juice with remaining ½ cup sugar, stirring until sugar is dissolved, and remove pan from heat.

Cool cake in pan on a rack 15 minutes and invert cake onto a rack set over a large plate. Brush warm cake with lemon syrup and cool cake to room temperature. *Tea cake keeps in an airtight container at cool room temperature 2 days.* Serves 16 to 20.

CITRUS COMPOTE WITH STAR ANISE ◐+

Pomegranates, ranging in color from pale pink to dark red, are prized for their ruby-red, sweet-tart seeds. A few surface cracks on the leathery exterior indicate that the fruit was fully ripe when picked and the seeds are juicy and beginning to burst.

½ cup sugar
½ cup water
4 whole star anise
4 grapefruits (preferably 2 pink and 2 white)
2 tangelos or mandarin oranges
1 lime
½ pomegranate

In a small saucepan simmer sugar, water, and star anise, stirring until sugar is dissolved, 5 minutes and cool to room temperature.

With a sharp knife cut peel, including all white pith, from citrus fruits and, working over a bowl to catch any juice, cut sections free from membranes, letting them drop into bowl. With your hands gently break pomegranate half in two. Bend back rind and dislodge seeds from membrane, adding them to citrus sections. Add cooled syrup and toss until combined. *Compote may be made 1 day ahead and chilled, covered.* Serve compote chilled or at room temperature. Serves 6.

APPLE CHEDDAR BREAD PUDDING

If you enjoy a slice of Cheddar with your apple pie, you'll love this homey dish. Try it for brunch—it's buttery, but not too sweet.

14 slices firm white sandwich bread
    (about 1 pound)
 1 stick (½ cup) unsalted butter,
    softened
 ¾ cup granulated sugar
1½ teaspoons cinnamon
 ½ teaspoon freshly grated nutmeg
 3 pounds Granny Smith apples
    (about 6)
1½ tablespoons fresh lemon juice
 ½ cup packed light brown sugar
 ¼ cup water
 4 ounces extra-sharp Cheddar
 4 large eggs
2¾ cups milk
 ¼ teaspoon salt

Preheat oven to 350° F. and butter a 9-cup oval gratin dish or a 13- by 9- by 2-inch shallow baking dish (about 3 quarts).

Spread one side of bread slices thinly with ½ stick butter. In a small bowl stir together ¼ cup granulated sugar, cinnamon, and nutmeg and sprinkle evenly over buttered sides of bread. Arrange bread, buttered sides up, on baking sheets and toast in batches in middle of oven until just golden, about 15 minutes. Cool cinnamon toast on racks and quarter each slice into triangles.

Peel, quarter, and core apples. Cut apples lengthwise into thin slices and in a bowl toss with lemon juice. In a large heavy skillet melt remaining ½ stick butter with brown sugar over moderately high heat, stirring, and add apples and water. Cook mixture, covered, over moderate heat, stirring occasionally, 10 minutes. Remove lid and cook mixture until apples are just tender and most liquid is evaporated, about 5 minutes more.

Coarsely grate enough Cheddar to measure 1 cup. Arrange one layer of cinnamon toasts in gratin dish or baking dish, breaking triangles to fit. Spoon half of apple mixture evenly over toasts in dish and sprinkle evenly with ½ cup cheese. Reserve 24 toasts for top and top cheese layer with another layer of cinnamon toasts and remaining apple mixture. Arrange reserved toasts, sugared sides up, overlapping slightly, in a ring around edge of dish.

In a bowl whisk together eggs, remaining ½ cup granulated sugar, milk, and salt and pour slowly and evenly over apples. *Chill pudding, covered, at least 1 hour and up to 1 day.*

Preheat oven to 350° F.

Bake pudding in middle of oven 30 minutes. Sprinkle remaining ½ cup cheese evenly over top and bake pudding 15 minutes more. Serves 8 to 10.

Photo below

chestnuts

During the holidays, there's nothing like a sack of hot, roasted chestnuts from a New York City pushcart vendor, but if you find yourself far from Rockefeller Center or Museum Mile, it's still possible to indulge your fancy for this snack.

When faced with the prospect of roasting and peeling chestnuts, *Gourmet's* food editors like the following method. Cut an X on the rounded side of the chestnuts with a freshly sharpened small knife or a chestnut knife (its scythe-shaped blade won't gouge the meat of the nut). Roast the chestnuts, cut sides up and covered, in a shallow baking pan in the middle of a preheated 425° F. oven, uncovering them and sprinkling them with a scant ¼ cup water every 15 minutes, for 1 hour.

Die-hard romantics, however, will want to use the fireplace method. Put the chestnuts in a chestnut skillet—a long-handled skillet with holes in the bottom. (You've always wondered what that wedding present was. *Now you know.*) Prop the skillet up over (not on) hot coals, shaking it occasionally, for about 1 hour.

When making the candied chestnuts for the recipe at right, that toasted flavor isn't necessary; we simply boil the nuts briefly to facilitate peeling. In all cases, shell and peel the nuts as soon as they are cool enough to handle.

—Jane Daniels Lear

CHOCOLATE FONDUE WITH WINTER FRUITS AND CANDIED CHESTNUTS AND ORANGE PEEL

FOR CANDIED CHESTNUTS
1 pound fresh chestnuts
1 cup water
1 cup granulated sugar

FOR CANDIED ORANGE PEEL
4 navel oranges
½ cup water
1 cup granulated sugar
1 cup superfine granulated sugar

FOR CHOCOLATE FONDUE
12 ounces fine-quality bittersweet chocolate (not unsweetened)
1¼ sticks (½ cup plus 2 tablespoons) unsalted butter
3 tablespoons brandy, or to taste

1 cup fresh kumquats
1 pound seedless grapes

SPECIAL EQUIPMENT
a 2-cup chocolate fondue pot with candle stand (*available by mail order from Zabar's, tel. 800-697-6301 or 212-787-2000*)

Make candied chestnuts:
With a sharp knife cut a strip of shell from a thin side of each chestnut. In a saucepan cover chestnuts with water by 1 inch and simmer until just tender, about 25 minutes. Pour off a little hot water from pan and replace with same amount of cold water to reduce temperature slightly. With a slotted spoon remove chestnuts 1 at a time and, when just cool enough to handle, carefully peel off shell and thin skin. (If skins become too hard to peel add some very hot water to pan.) *Chestnuts may be peeled 1 day ahead and chilled in a sealable plastic bag.*

Have ready a large sheet of parchment or wax paper on a rack.

In a 3-quart heavy saucepan bring 1 cup water and sugar to a boil, stirring until sugar is dissolved, and boil 1 minute.

Add peeled chestnuts and boil, carefully stirring occasionally, until most of syrup is absorbed by chestnuts, 8 to 10 minutes. Turn out chestnuts onto paper, spreading evenly, and cool on rack. Loosen chestnuts from paper and transfer to a clean sheet of paper. *Dry candied chestnuts, uncovered, at room temperature 1 day. Candied chestnuts keep, covered and chilled, 3 days.*

Make candied orange peel:
With a sharp knife cut peel, including white pith, from oranges in lengthwise strips 2 to 3 inches long and ¾ inch wide and reserve oranges for another use. Cut strips lengthwise in half. Fill a 3-quart saucepan three fourths full with cold water and add peel. Bring water slowly to a boil over moderate heat and drain peel. Repeat procedure 4 more times to remove bitterness from peel.

Have ready a large sheet of parchment or wax paper on a rack.

In a large heavy skillet bring ½ cup water and granulated sugar to a boil, stirring until sugar is dissolved. Add peel and boil, stirring, until most of syrup is absorbed by peel. Turn out peel onto paper, spreading evenly, and cool on rack. Loosen peel from paper and transfer to a clean sheet of paper. *Dry candied peel, uncovered, at room temperature 1 day.* In a shallow bowl toss candied peel, a few pieces at a time, in superfine sugar, shaking off excess. *Candied peel keeps, chilled in a plastic bag, 2 weeks.*

Make chocolate fondue:
Chop chocolate and cut butter into pieces. In a metal bowl set over a saucepan of barely simmering water melt chocolate and butter, stirring until smooth. Stir in brandy and transfer mixture to fondue pot set over a lit candle.

Cut candied chestnuts in half and quarter kumquats lengthwise. Separate grapes into small bunches. Arrange chestnuts, kumquats, grapes, and candied orange peel on a platter around fondue and serve with wooden picks. Serves 8 to 10.

BLOOD ORANGE GRAND MARNIER GELÉE

Depending on the weather, the flesh of a blood orange may be crimson, or pale with dark red streaks (hot days and cool nights produce the most intense color). In any case, you'll never be able to determine flesh color from the orange's skin.

1 lemon
4 pounds blood oranges (about 15)
3¼ teaspoons unflavored gelatin
   (one ¼-ounce envelope plus 1 teaspoon)
¼ cup cold water
⅔ cup sugar
¼ cup Grand Marnier

GARNISH
sections from 1 blood orange

Grate zest from lemon, reserving lemon for another use, and grate zest from 3 oranges. Squeeze enough juice from oranges to measure 3 cups. In a cup sprinkle gelatin over cold water and let stand about 1 minute to soften.

In a saucepan heat 1½ cups orange juice with zests and sugar over moderate heat, stirring, until sugar is dissolved. Add gelatin mixture, stirring until gelatin is completely dissolved. Remove pan from heat and stir in remaining 1½ cups orange juice and Grand Marnier. Pour mixture through a sieve into a nonreactive 1-quart mold and discard zests. *Chill mixture, covered, until firm, at least 4 hours, and up to 2 days.*

Run a thin knife around *gelée* and dip bottom of mold into a large pan of very hot water 3 seconds to loosen. Invert a serving plate over mold and invert *gelée* onto plate, shaking mold to loosen *gelée*.

Garnish *gelée* with blood orange sections. Serves 6.

farmers markets

By early morning, New York City's popular Union Square Greenmarket is in full swing. Neighbors, chefs, and curious tourists mingle, sampling freshly baked muffins and chatting with local farmers. A few *Gourmet* food editors may be there as well, picking up some choice items on their way to work. Last spring, when we began to develop recipes for this book, Shelley went looking for the first rhubarb—she came back with several pounds of crisp, crimson stalks, as well as fava beans and chanterelles. In midsummer, Liz and Katy filled their shopping bags with fresh basil, early corn, and fragrant local peaches. Each week brought something new: multicolored "Easter egg" beets, salsify (a root vegetable), "heirloom" Newtown Pippin apples, fresh goat cheese, organically grown ruby chard...

Farmers markets are one of the few remaining places where you can buy exclusively regional fruits and vegetables. (It's hard to believe, but over 90% of all supermarket produce sold throughout America comes from California.) One of the basic tenets of farmers markets requires that all items sold—whether fruits, vegetables, eggs, cheese, even beeswax candles—must be produced by the seller. There's no doubt about it, buying directly from a farmer (or his relative or employee), who picked lettuce the day before and drove to the market that morning, guarantees a tastier, more nutritious salad. Just as importantly, these venues support the efforts of local growers and food artisans and help to preserve small farms and the green-belts around our cities.

While "direct community" farmers markets sell to individuals, wholesale markets primarily serve restaurants, caterers, and retail markets. Other "public" markets offer a host of goods for sale by middlemen who buy from national or inter-national sources as well as from regional growers.

If bananas, for instance, are for sale, it's likely that local farmers aren't exclusively represented (unless you happen to live in Hawaii). Although good produce buys can be found in any type of market, to support local growers, seek out locations where farmers sell direct.

Traditional farmers markets range from warm weather open-air gatherings in parking lots or plazas to permanent structures that house year-round marketplaces. Some markets sell only produce, but most have at least a few stands of homemade prepared foods and baked goods. Larger markets display seemingly endless bounties of produce, cheese, grains, fish, poultry, meat, and home preserves and condiments. Some farmers grow specialty items—like baby bok choy, pea shoots, or pink gooseberries—for chefs and sell their extras to the public. Many others have been instrumental in reviving "heirloom" fruits and vegetables, produce grown from seeds that have been handed down, in some cases, for hundreds of years. If you're concerned about additives and spraying, find out which growers are committed to organic farming—that is, cultivating crops without using synthetic pesticides or fertilizers. Organically raised poultry and meats, and eggs from organically fed chickens also can be found for sale at many markets.

Perhaps the most rewarding aspect of shopping at your local farmers market is rediscovering the seasons. All of a sudden, the eternal question, "what should I make for dinner?" becomes obvious. There's a precious window of opportunity to enjoy the best of each season and you'll want to make the most of it.

farmers market shopping tips

Early shoppers have the pick of the market, while end-of-the-day buyers usually find plenty of bargains on perishable produce.

A quick walk through the market allows you to compose your menu and compare quality and prices before buying.

Tote along plenty of sturdy canvas bags or string mesh bags.

Handle produce gently and if you're not sure what's ripe, ask the farmer to choose for you.

If you see an unfamiliar item, ask what it is— and ask for some tips on preparing it.

To keep foods fresh, select hardy vegetables and baked goods first, then more delicate produce, and finally meats and dairy products.

Since you'll be paying for items separately, carry small bills and change. Ideally, wear a money belt to leave your hands free.

If you're coming by car, bring an ice cooler to keep food fresh.

Limit the amount of perishable goods that you buy. After all, cooking with fresh ingredients is what it's all about!

Below is a sampling of farmers markets across America. It is, by no means, a comprehensive list. The best way to find farmers markets near you is to contact the Farmers Market State Representative from your state, also listed below. The United States Department of Agriculture offers a National Directory of Farmers Markets (for a free copy call 800-384-8704 or go online: www.ams.usda.gov).

alabama

George Paris
Alabama Dept. of Agriculture
Phone: (334) 240-7250

Jefferson County Truck Growers Assoc.
414 West Finley Avenue
Birmingham, AL 35204
Danny Jones, (205) 251-8737
YEAR-ROUND - Mon.-Sat.

Montgomery State Farmers Market
1655 Federal Drive
Montgomery, AL 36109
Benny Hitch, (334) 242-5350
YEAR-ROUND - Mon.-Sat.

alaska

Doug Warner
Alaska Dept. of Agriculture
Phone: (907) 745-7200

Saturday Farmers Market
700 6th Avenue, Suite 206
Anchorage, AK 99501
Javier Robinson
(800) 770-2227, Fax (907) 279-5073
OPEN-AIR/SEASONAL - Sat.

Tanana Valley Farmers Market
P.O. Box 85138
Fairbanks, AK 99708
Ester, (907) 456-3276 (Tel. & Fax)
OPEN-AIR/SEASONAL - Wed./Fri./Sat.

arizona

Dee Logan
Arizona Dept. of Agriculture
Phone: (623) 848-1234

Phoenix Farmers Markets
P.O. Box 14188
Phoenix, AZ 85063-4188
Gilbert Heritage District Market
10 South Gilbert Road
Dee and John Logan, (623) 848-1234
YEAR-ROUND - Sat.
Call for other locations.

Prescott Farmers Market
by Town Square
P.O. Box 1748
Prescott, AZ 86302
Susan Crutcher, (520) 445-1771
SEASONAL - Sat.

arkansas

Dr. Craig Anderson
Extension Horticulturalist
Phone: (501) 575-2639

Arkansas County/North Farmers Market
700 South Main Street
Stuttgart, AR 72160
Pat West, (870) 282-3384
YEAR-ROUND - Tues./Thur./Sat.

Little Rock River Market
400 East Markham
Little Rock, AR 72201
Shannon Jeffery, (501) 375-2552
YEAR-ROUND

california

Randii MacNear
California Federation of Certified
  Farmers Markets
Phone: (530) 756-1695
Website: http://farmersmarket.ucdavis.edu

Sacramento Central Farmers Market
8th & W Street (under highway)
Sacramento, CA
Dan and Renae Best, (916) 688-0100
SEASONAL - Sun.

Davis Farmers Market
4th & C Streets, Central Park
Davis, CA 95617
Randii MacNear, (530) 756-1695
YEAR-ROUND - Wed./Sat.

San Francisco Ferry Plaza
  Farmers Market
Embarcadero & Green Streets
San Francisco, CA 94111
Sibella Kraus, (510) 528-6987
YEAR-ROUND - Sat./Sun./Tues.

Marin Farmers Market I
Marin County Civic Center
  Fairgrounds on Highway 101
San Rafael, CA 94915
Gail Hayden, (800) 897-3276
YEAR-ROUND - Thur./Sun.

Santa Barbara Farmers Markets
Cota & Santa Barbara Streets
Santa Barbara, CA 93101
Mark Sheridan, (805) 962-5354
YEAR-ROUND - Sat.
Call for other location.

Santa Monica Farmers Markets
Arizona Avenue & 2nd Street
Santa Monica, CA 90401
Laura Avery, (310) 458-8172
YEAR-ROUND - Wed./Sat.
Call for other locations.

colorado

Loretta Lopez
Colorado Dept. of Agriculture
Phone: (303) 239-4114

Denver Farmers Market
16th & Market Street
Denver, CO 80202
Shannon McCurry, (303) 887-3276
OPEN-AIR/SEASONAL - Sat.

Durango Farmers Market
13th & 3rd Avenue
Durango, CO 81302
Carol Clark, (970) 259-9339
OPEN-AIR/SEASONAL - Sat.

Ft. Collins Farmers Market
Steele's Market parking lot,
  west of College Avenue, across
  from Foothills Fashion Mall
Ft. Collins, CO 80524
Sara Buchleiter, (970) 495-4889
OPEN-AIR/SEASONAL - Wed./Sun.

Glenwood Springs Farmers Market
1605 Grand Avenue, downtown
Glenwood Springs, CO 81652
Ken and Gail Kuhns, Jr.
(970) 876-2850
OPEN-AIR/SEASONAL - Sat.

Pueblo Farmers Market
West 6th Street
Midtown Shopping Center
Pueblo, CO 81001
Farmers' Marketeers, (719) 583-6566
OPEN-AIR/SEASONAL - Fri.

connecticut

Rick Macsuga
Connecticut Dept. of Agriculture
Phone: (860) 713-2544
Website: www.state.ct.us/doag/

Darien Farmers Market
CVS parking lot
Darien, CT 06820
SEASONAL - Wed.

Stamford Farmers Market
Columbus Park on
  Main & West Park Place
Stamford, CT 06902
OPEN-AIR/SEASONAL - Mon./Thurs.

Stonington Farmers Market
Town Landing at fishing pier
Stonington, CT 06374
OPEN-AIR/SEASONAL - Sat.

West Hartford Farmers Market
LaSalle Road public parking
West Hartford, CT 06101
OPEN-AIR/SEASONAL - Tues./Thurs./Sat.

delaware

Melanie Rapp
Delaware Dept. of Agriculture
Phone: (302) 739-4811

Lewes Terminal Green Market
Ferry Terminal Area
Lewes, DE 19958
Becky Culler, (302) 739-4811
OPEN-AIR/SEASONAL - Wed./Sun.

Wilmington Farmers Market
8th & Orange Streets
Wilmington, DE 19801
Beverly Zimmerman, (302) 571-9088
YEAR-ROUND

district of columbia

Al Smith,
DC Federation of Farmers &
  Consumers Markets, Inc.
Phone: (202) 678-0610

FreshFarm Market
Dupont Circle, 20th Street, NW.
Washington, DC
Marlene Kweskin, (202) 659-5170
SEASONAL - Sun.

Eastern Market
7th & North Carolina Avenue, SE.
Washington, DC 20032
John Harrold, (202) 543-7293
YEAR-ROUND - Sat./Sun.

florida

Don Coker
Florida Dept. of Agriculture
Phone: (850) 921-1998
Website: www.fl-ag.com/farmmkt/city.htm

Clearwater Farmers Market
Station Square Park
Clearwater, FL 33758
Bob Fernandez, (813) 461-7674
YEAR-ROUND - Sat.

Haile Plantation Farmers Market
5300 SW 91st Terrace
Gainesville, FL
Rose Koenig, (352) 331-1804
SEASONAL - Thurs. or Sat.

Tallahassee Farmers Market
1415 Timberlane Road at Market Square
Tallahassee, FL 32301
Jimmy Mitchell, (912) 377-2313
YEAR-ROUND - Tues./Thur./Sat.

Union Street Farmers Market
20 SE 2nd Place in the Sun Center
Gainesville, FL
Charles Lybrand, (904) 462-3192
YEAR-ROUND - Wed.

georgia

Bob Meyer
Georgia Dept. of Agriculture
Phone: (404) 656-3680

Atlanta State Farmers Market
16 Forest Parkway
Forest Park, GA 30050
Mike Bonner, (404) 366-6910
YEAR-ROUND

Augusta State Farmers Market
1150 5th Street
Augusta, GA 30901
William J. Carroll, Jr., (706) 721-3004
YEAR-ROUND

Macon State Farmers Market
2055 Eisenhower Parkway
Macon, GA 31206
Doyce Mullis, (912) 752-1097
YEAR-ROUND

Savannah State Farmers Market
701 U.S. Highway 80, West
Savannah, GA 31408
Market Manager, (912) 966-7800
YEAR-ROUND

hawaii

Calvin Lee
Hawaii Dept. of Agriculture
Phone: (808) 973-9594
Fax: (808) 973-9590

Hilo Farmers Market
At the corner of Kamehameha
  and Mamo Streets
Hilo, Hawaii
Mike Rankin, (808) 969-9114
YEAR-ROUND - Wed./Sat.

idaho

Kim Murphy
Idaho Dept. of Agriculture
Phone: (208) 332-8538
Fax: (208) 334-2879

Moscow Farmers Market
4th & Main
Moscow, ID 83843
Mary Blyth, (208) 883-7036
OPEN-AIR/SEASONAL - Sat.

Twin Falls Farmers Market
K-Mart parking lot, 2318 Addison Road
Twin Falls, ID 83301
Steve Tanguy, (208) 734-8371
OPEN-AIR/SEASONAL - Tues./Sat.

illinois

Kent McFarland
Illinois Dept. of Agriculture
Phone: (217) 524-9131

Chicago Farmers Markets
27 markets
Connie Basemi, (312) 744-9187
OPEN-AIR/SEASONAL
Call for locations.

Land of Goshen Farmers Market
3457 Edwardsville Road
Edwardsville, IL 62025
Tammie Baker, (618) 656-1875
OPEN-AIR/SEASONAL

Carbondale Farmers Market
10160 Old Highway
Carbondale, IL 62920
Bonnie Newcomb, (618) 687-4281
OPEN-AIR/SEASONAL

Galena Farmers Market
Historic Market House
Commerce Street
Galena, IL 61036
Carmen Ferguson, (815) 777-1270
OPEN-AIR/SEASONAL

Monroe County Farmers Market
3rd Street, by Courthouse
Waterloo, IL 62298
Paul Merz, (618) 281-4147
OPEN-AIR/SEASONAL

indiana

Loni Davenport
Purdue University
Phone: (765) 494-1314
Fax: (765) 494-0391
Website: www.anr.ces.purdue.edu.anr/
   anr.farmersmkts.html

Corydon Farmers Markets
Parking lot of Jay-C Store
Old Capital Plaza Shopping Center
Corydon, IN 47112
Charles Hambley, (812) 968-3693
OPEN-AIR/SEASONAL - Fri./Sat.
Call for other location.

Lafayette Farmers Market
5th Street between Main and Columbia
Lafayette, IN 47901
Susan K. Smith
(765) 742-2313, Fax (765) 420-7435
OPEN-AIR/SEASONAL - Tues./Thurs./Sat.

Michigan City Farmers Market
8th & Washington Streets
Michigan City, IN 46360
Ed Kis
(219) 874-3647, Fax (219) 874-5727
SEASONAL - Sat.

South Bend Farmers Market
1105 Northside Boulevard
South Bend, IN 46615
Gene Hiatt
(219) 282-1259, Fax (219) 282-1250
SEASONAL - Tues./Thurs./Fri./Sat.

iowa

Barbara Lovitt
Iowa Dept. of Agriculture
Phone: (515) 281-8232

Cedar Rapids City Market
Riverside Roundhouse
1350 A Street, SW.
Cedar Rapids, IA 52404
Teresa White, (319) 398-5264
OPEN-AIR/SEASONAL - Mon./Wed./Fri.

Downtown Des Moines Farmers Market
4th & Court Avenues
Des Moines, IA 50309
Deb Burger, (515) 245-6625
OPEN-AIR/SEASONAL - Sat.

kansas

Karen Gast
Kansas State University
Phone: (785) 532-1439

Atchison Farmers Market
5th & Main Street
Atchison, KS 66002
Chamber of Commerce
(913) 367-2428
YEAR-ROUND - Mon./Sat.

Columbus Farmers Market
1300 East Maple
Columbus, KS 66725
Bob and Mary Soper, (316) 674-3099
YEAR-ROUND - Sat./Sun./Mon.

kentucky

Jim Mansfield
Kentucky Dept. of Agriculture
Phone: (502) 564-6676

louisiana

Jimmy Boudreaux
Louisiana Dept. of Agriculture
Phone: (225) 388-2222

Crescent City Farmers Market
Twomay Center, Loyola University
7214 St. Charles Avenue
New Orleans, LA 70118
Richard McCarthy
(504) 861-5898, Fax (504) 861-5833
Website: www.loyno.edu/ccfm
YEAR-ROUND - Sat.

Red Stick Farmers Market
300 North Boulevard
Baton Rouge, LA 70801
Chris Campany and Andrew Smiley
(225) 336-9532, Fax (225) 344-6171
YEAR-ROUND - Sat.

maine

Deanne Herman
Maine Dept. of Agriculture
Phone: (207) 287-7561

Camden Farmers Market
Colcord Street
Camden, ME 04843
John Barnstein, (207) 273-2809
OPEN-AIR/SEASONAL - Wed./Sat.

maryland

Tony Evans
Maryland Dept. of Agriculture
Phone: (410) 841-5770
Website: www.mda.state.md.us/
   farmmarket.htm

Anne Arundel County Farmers Market
Riva Road & Harry South
   Truman Parkway
Anne Arundel, MD 21012
Martin Zehner, (410) 798-5083
OPEN-AIR/SEASONAL - Sat.

Bel Air Farmers Market
Bond & Thomas Streets
Bel Air, MD 21014
John Sullivan, (410) 638-3254
OPEN-AIR/SEASONAL - Tues./Sat.

Chestertown Farmers Market
Park Row on the Fountain Park
Chestertown, MD 21620
Owen McCoy, (410) 639-7217
OPEN-AIR/SEASONAL - Sat.

Dobbins Center Farmers Market
Dobbin Road & Route 175
Columbia, MD 21046
Tom Owen, (301) 310-0707
OPEN-AIR/SEASONAL - Tues./Thurs.

massachusetts

David Webber
Massachusetts Dept. of Agriculture
Phone: (617) 727-3018, ext.179

Berkshire Area/Pittsfield Farmers Market
Route 8, Allendale Shopping Center
Pittsfield, MA 01237
Kenneth Wirtes, (413) 499-1012
OPEN-AIR/SEASONAL - Wed./Sat.

Copley Square Farmers Market
St. James Avenue
Boston, MA 02202
Federation of MA Farmers Markets
(413) 527-6572
SEASONAL - Tues./Fri.

Newton Farmers Market
Cold Spring Park, Beacon Street
Newton Highlands, MA 02165
Judy Dore, (617) 552-7120
OPEN-AIR/SEASONAL - Tues.

Scollay Square Farmers Market
Boston City Hall Plaza
Boston, MA 02202
Federation of MA Farmers Markets
(413) 527-6572
OPEN-AIR/SEASONAL - Mon./Wed.

michigan

Susan Smalley
Michigan State University
Phone: (517) 432-0049

Ann Arbor Farmers Market
315 Detroit Street
Ann Arbor, MI 48104
Maxine Rosasco, (734) 994-3276
YEAR-ROUND - Wed./Sat .

Detroit Eastern Market
2934 Russell Street
Detroit, MI 48207
Jesse Henderson, (313) 833-1560
YEAR-ROUND

minnesota
Vince Steffen
Minnesota Dept. of Agriculture
Phone: (651) 282-6806

Minneapolis Farmers Market
Off I-94, exit 230 (Lyndale Avenue)
Minneapolis, MN 55440
Larry Cermak, (612) 333-1718
SEASONAL - Daily

Rochester Downtown Farmers Market
1st Avenue
Rochester, MN 55904
Patty Eckdahl, (507) 753-2651
OPEN-AIR/SEASONAL - Sat.

St. Cloud Area Farmers Market
First American Bank on 12th
 & Division Streets
St. Cloud, MN 56301
(320) 398-6252
OPEN-AIR/SEASONAL
Call for other locations.

St. Paul Farmers Markets
290 East 5th Street
St. Paul, MN 55101
Patty Brand, (612) 227-6856
SEASONAL - Sat./Sun.
Call for other location.

mississippi
Billy Carter
Mississippi Dept. of Agriculture
Phone: (601) 354-6573
Website: www.mdac.state.ms.us/

Central Farmers Market
352 Woodrow Wilson
Jackson, MS 39216
Billy Carter, (601) 354-6573
SEASONAL

Meridian Area Farmers Market
1800 Main Street
Meridian, MS 39301
Jim Hollis, (601) 482-9764
SEASONAL

missouri
Tammy Bruckerhoff
Missouri Dept. of Agriculture
Phone: (573) 751-3394

City Market
5th & Walnut
Kansas City, MO 64108
Gary Goebel, (816) 842-1271
Website: http://kc-citymarket.com
OPEN-AIR/YEAR-ROUND

Soulard Farmers Market
730 Carroll Street
St. Louis, MO 63104
Sandra Zak
(314) 622-4180, Fax (314) 771-8762
OPEN-AIR/YEAR-ROUND

Columbia Farmers Market
Fairgrounds
Columbia, MO 65203
Eleanor Green, (573) 442-9215
OPEN-AIR/SEASONAL

Greater Springfield Farmers Market
Battlefield Mall at Sunset &
 Glenstone Avenues
Springfield, MO 65801
Roland Natzer, (417) 887-4156
OPEN-AIR/SEASONAL

montana
Louise Dix
AERO
Phone: (406) 443-7272

Missoula Farmers Market
917 Parkview Way
Missoula, MT 59803
William Taylor, (406) 721-2351
OPEN-AIR/SEASONAL

Gallatin Valley Farmers Market
608 South 7th Avenue
Bozeman, MT 59715
Joanne Jennings, (406) 586-9585
OPEN-AIR/SEASONAL

nebraska
Dick Arends
Nebraska Dept. of Agriculture
Phone: (402) 471-4876
Website: www.agr.state.ne.us

Lincoln Haymarket Farmers Market
Downtown, Haymarket District
Lincoln, NE 68508
Billene Nemec, (402) 435-7496
OPEN-AIR/SEASONAL - Sat.

Omaha Farmers Market
Old Market parking lot
11th & Jackson Street
Omaha, NE 68108
Vic Gutman, (402) 345-5401
OPEN-AIR/SEASONAL - Sat.

nevada
Shirley Adshade-Sponsler
Farmers Market Association
Phone: (775) 746-5024

Hometown Farmers Market
Downtown Sparks
Sparks, NV 89431
Andre Stigall, (702) 353-2291
SEASONAL - Thurs.

Henderson Farmers Market
Civic Center
Henderson, NV 89015
Michelle Romero, (702) 565-2474
YEAR-ROUND - Thurs.

new hampshire
Gail McWilliam
New Hampshire Dept. of Agriculture
Phone: (603) 271-3788

Manchester Farmers Market
Victory Park, Concord & Pine Streets
Manchester, NH 03101
Cathy Cook, (603) 645-6285
OPEN-AIR/SEASONAL - Thurs.

Portsmouth Farmers Market
Parrott Avenue parking lot
Portsmouth, NH 03801
Edie Barker, (603) 778-1039
OPEN-AIR/SEASONAL - Sat.

new jersey
Ronald Good
New Jersey Dept. of Agriculture
Phone: (609) 984-2278

Hoboken Farmers Market
River & Newark Streets
Hoboken, NJ 07030
Cynthia Siber, (201) 420-0313
SEASONAL - Tues.

Madison Farmers Market
Madison High School, Ridgedale Avenue
Madison, NJ 07940
Catherine Cropper, (973) 822-9351
OPEN-AIR/SEASONAL - Thurs.

Montclair Farmers Market
South Fullerton parking lot
Montclair, NJ 07043
Alison Barnett, (973) 783-8003
OPEN-AIR/SEASONAL - Sat.

Trenton Farmers Market
960 Spruce Street
Trenton, NJ 08648
Jack and Marci Ball, (609) 695-2998
YEAR-ROUND

new mexico

Pam Roy
Statewide Farmers Market Assoc.
Phone: (505) 983-4098

Albuquerque Growers Market
Caravan East parking lot
7605 Central Avenue, NE.
Albuquerque, NM 87110
Ed and Pat Shaffer, (505) 265-7250
OPEN-AIR/SEASONAL - Tues./Sat.

Sante Fe Farmers Market
In the rail yard, near train depot
Sante Fe, NM 87505
Pamela Roy, (505) 983-4098
OPEN-AIR/SEASONAL - Tues./Sat./Sun.

new york

Robert Lewis
New York Dept. of
  Agriculture & Markets
Phone: (718) 722-2830

Downtown Country Market
Main Street, between
  Court & Church Streets
Buffalo, NY 14203
Mary Dormer, (716) 856-3150
OPEN-AIR/SEASONAL - Thur.

Ithaca Farmers Market I
545 3d Street at Steamboat Landing
Ithaca, NY 14850
Becky Bosch, (607) 273-5626
SEASONAL - Sat./Sun.

Millbrook Farmers Market
Front Street at the
  corner of Franklin Avenue
Millbrook Village, NY 12545
Merribeth and Jeff Advocate
(914) 635-2281
OPEN-AIR/SEASONAL - Sat.

Warwick Valley Farmers Market
South Street parking lot
South Street & Railroad Avenue
Warwick, NY 10990
Linda Glohs, (914) 987-9990
OPEN-AIR/SEASONAL - Sun.

Union Square Greenmarket
Union Square Park, 17th & Broadway
Manhattan, NY 10003
Brendan Carr and Joel Patraker
(212) 477-3220
YEAR-ROUND - Mon./Wed./Fri./Sat.

north carolina

Louis Johnson
North Carolina Dept. of Agriculture
Phone: (919) 733-7136
Website: www.agr.state.nc.us.markets/
  facilit

Charlotte Regional Farmers Market
1801 Yorkmont Road
Charlotte, NC 28266
Frank Suddreth, (704) 357-1269
YEAR-ROUND - Tues./Sat.

The State Farmers Market
Off Lake Wheeler Road
Raleigh, NC 27611
Charles Edwards, (919) 733-7417
YEAR-ROUND - Mon.-Sat.

WNC (Asheville) Farmers Market
570 Brevard Road
Asheville, NC
Mike Ferguson, (828) 253-1691
YEAR-ROUND - Daily

Carrboro Farmers Market
Robeson Street
Carrboro, NC 27510
Kim Dawson, (910) 376-3237
OPEN-AIR/SEASONAL - Sat.

north dakota

Sara Wagner
North Dakota Dept. of Agriculture
Phone: (701) 328-2231
Website: www.state.nd.us/agr

Larry and Pat Shimek
15037 115th Ave SE
Bismarck, ND
Pat Shimek, (701) 673-3202
SEASONAL

Thorson Gardens
6 miles East of Wing on Hwy 36,
2 miles South
Wing, ND 58494
Steven and Roberta Thorson
(701) 943-2347
SEASONAL

ohio

Tim Sword
Ohio Dept. of Agriculture
Phone: (614) 752-9816
Website: www.state.oh.us/agr/

Athens Farmers Market
270 Highland Avenue
Athens, OH 45701
Dave Gutknecht, (740) 594-4990
YEAR-ROUND - Wed./Sat.

Findlay Market
Elder Street
Cincinnati, OH 45227
Tom Jackson, (513) 352-4638
YEAR-ROUND - Mon./Tues./Thur.

Toledo Farmers Market
P.O. Box 9294
Toledo, OH 43697
Luis Mikesell, (419) 255-6765
YEAR-ROUND - Mon.-Sat.

Pearl Alley Farmers Market I
Pearl Alley at Broad Street
Columbus, OH 43215
Frank Musson, (419) 674-4719
OPEN-AIR/SEASONAL - Tues./Fri.

oklahoma

Jason Harvey
Oklahoma Dept. of Agriculture
Phone: (800) 580-6543
Website: www.state.ok.us/~okag/
  aghome.html

Oklahoma City - John E. Kirkpatrick
OSU Horticulture Center
400 North Portland
Oklahoma City, OK 73107
Chris Kirby, (405) 945-3358
YEAR-ROUND - Wed./Sat.

Norman Farmers Market
615 East Robinson
Cleveland County Fairgrounds
Norman, OK 73071
Craig Evans, (405) 321-4774
OPEN-AIR/SEASONAL - Sat.

oregon

Cathi McLain
Oregon Dept. of Agriculture
Phone: (503) 872-6600
Website: www.oda.state.or.us

Beaverton Farmers Market
Washington St. btwn. 3rd & 5th Avenues
Beaverton, OR 97075
Ginger Rapport, (503) 643-5345
OPEN-AIR/SEASONAL - Sat.

Corvallis-Albany Farmers Market
City Hall Parking Lot
6th & Monroe
Corvallis, OR 97339
Rebecca Landis, (541) 752-1510
OPEN-AIR/SEASONAL - Sat.

Hollywood Farmers Market
Washington Mutual parking lot
4333 Northeast Sandy Boulevard
Portland, OR 97213
Suzanne Briggs, (503) 233-3313
OPEN-AIR/SEASONAL - Sat.

Lane County Farmers Market
East 8th & Oak Streets
Eugene, OR 97401
Noa O'Hare, (541) 431-4923
OPEN-AIR/SEASONAL - Tues./Sat.

pennsylvania

Michael Varner
Pennsylvania Dept. of Agriculture
Phone: (717) 787-2376
Website: www.pda.state.pa.us

Broad Street Market
1233 North 3rd Street
Harrisburg, PA 17105
(717) 236-7923
YEAR-ROUND - Thur./Fri./Sat.

Central Market
West King & Market Streets
Lancaster, PA 17603
(717) 291-4723
YEAR-ROUND - Tues./Fri./Sat.

Central Market House
34 West Philadelphia & Beaver Street
York, PA 17402
(717) 848-2243
YEAR-ROUND - Tues./Thur./Sat.

Lewisburg Farmers Market
Fairground Road
Lewisburg, PA 17837
(814) 237-1960
YEAR-ROUND - Wed.

Root's Country Market/Auction
705 Graystone Road
Manheim, PA 17545
(717) 898-7811
YEAR-ROUND - Tues.

rhode island

Peter Susi
Rhode Island Dept. of Agriculture
Phone: (401) 222-2781, ext. 4517

Aquidneck Growers Market
909 East Main Road, Route 138
Middletown, RI 02842
Lisa Lewis
(401) 848-0099, Fax (401) 847-0866
OPEN-AIR/SEASONAL - Wed./Sat.

South Kingstown Farmers Market
Wakefield - Marina Park
Kingston, RI 02881
Adrian Kovach, (401) 397-4702
OPEN-AIR/SEASONAL - Tues./Sat.
Call for other location.

south carolina

Tammy Griffin Koon
South Carolina Dept. of Agriculture
Phone: (803) 737-4664

Columbia State Farmers Market
1001 Bluff Road
Columbia, SC 29201
Lee Sowell, (803) 737-4664
YEAR-ROUND - daily

Greenville State Farmers Market
1354 Rutherford Road
Greenville, SC 29609
Jack Watson, (864) 244-4023
YEAR-ROUND - Mon.–Sat.

south dakota

Jon Farris
South Dakota Dept. of Agriculture
Phone: (605) 773-5436

Black Hills Farmers Market
Kansas City Street
Rapid City, SD 57701
Chuck and Betty Bruner
(605) 456-2171
OPEN-AIR/SEASONAL - Sat.
Call for other location.

Downtown Farmers Market, Main Street
East 10th Street & 1st Avenue
Sioux Falls, SD 57501
Boby Sandord, (605) 594-2135 or
Lorraine Niemeyer, (712) 753-2264
OPEN-AIR/SEASONAL - Wed./Sat.

tennessee

Stanley Trout
Tennessee Dept. of Agriculture
Phone: (615) 837-5160
Website: www.picktnproducts.org

11th Street Farmers Market
716 East 12th Street
Chattanooga, TN 37403
Karen Lamb, (423) 267-4492
YEAR-ROUND - daily

Knox County Regional Farmers Market
4700 New Harvest Lane
Knoxville, TN 37918
Karen Lamb, (423) 524-3276
YEAR-ROUND

Metro Farmers Market
900 8th Avenue North
Nashville, TN 37208
Jim Cupit, (615) 880-2001
YEAR-ROUND

Farmers Market at Agricenter
7777 Walnut Grove Road
Memphis, TN 38112
Charles Duvall, (901) 757-7790
OPEN-AIR/SEASONAL - daily

texas

Jim Jones
Texas Dept. of Agriculture
Phone: (512) 463-7563
Website: www.agr.state.tx.us

San Antonio Farmers Market
Olmos Basin Park
San Antonio, TX 78624
Kay Engel, (830) 997-1632
SEASONAL - Sat.

El Paso Farmers Market
6375 Montana
El Paso, TX 79902
Ignacio Padilla, (915) 859-2999
SEASONAL - Sat.

Ft. Worth Farmers Market
8101 Highway 80, West
Ft. Worth, TX 76141
(817) 341-0603
YEAR-ROUND - Sat./Sun.

Austin Farmers Market
6701 Burnet Road
Austin, TX 78757
(512) 454-1002
SEASONAL - Sat.

utah

Randy Parker
Utah Dept. of Agriculture
Phone: (801) 538-7108

Downtown Alliance Farmers Market
Pioneer Park, 300 West & 300 South
Salt Lake City, UT 84111
Brad Parkin, (801) 359-5118
OPEN-AIR/SEASONAL

Utah Farm Bureau Farmers Market
9865 South State Street
Sandy, UT 84070
Reed Balls
(801) 233-3000, Fax (801) 233-3030
Website: www.sbf.com/utfb
SEASONAL

vermont

Lindsey Ketchel
Vermont Dept. of Agriculture
Phone: (802) 828-3833
Website: www.state.vt.us/agric

Brattleboro Area Farmers Market
West Brattleboro at Route 9
Brattleboro, VT 05301
Ed Lopata, (802) 257-1272
OPEN-AIR/SEASONAL - Wed./Sat.

Burlington Farmers Market
City Hall Park
Burlington, VT 05402
Barbara Provost, (888) 889-8188
OPEN-AIR/SEASONAL - Sat.

Capital City Farmers Market
State & Elm Streets
Montpelier, VT 05601
Les Snow, (802) 426-3800
OPEN-AIR/SEASONAL - Sat.

Norwich Farmers Market
Route 5, South
Norwich, VT 05055
Robert Ward, (603) 763-4169
OPEN-AIR/SEASONAL - Sat.

virginia

Cathy Beicher
Phone: (804) 786-4046
Website: www.state.va.us/~vdacs/opms/
opmshome.htm

Charlottesville City Farmers Market
Carver Recreation Center
Charlottesville, VA 22906
Judy Marie Johnson, (804) 971-3271
OPEN-AIR/SEASONAL

Lynchburg Community Farmers Market
Main at 12th Street
Lynchburg, VA 24504
Tracy Trent, (804) 847-1499
OPEN-AIR/YEAR-ROUND

17th Street Farmers Market
17th & Main Streets
Richmond, VA 23232
Kathy Emerson, (804) 780-8597
OPEN-AIR/SEASONAL

Historic Roanoke City Farmers Market
Campbell Street Market Square
Roanoke, VA 24022
Dara Saunders, (540) 342-2028
YEAR-ROUND

washington

Washington State Farmers Market Assoc.
Phone: (206) 706-5198
Website: www.wafarmersmarkets.com

Bellingham Farmers Market
Railroad & Chestnut Avenues
Bellingham, WA 98225
Karen Durham, (360) 647-2060
OPEN-AIR/SEASONAL - Sat./Sun.

Moses Lake-Columbia Basin
  Farmers Market
Civic Center Park, downtown
Moses Lake, WA 98837
Bertha Wydler, (509) 787-1305
OPEN-AIR/SEASONAL - Sat.

Olympia Farmers Market
700 North Capitol Way
Olympia, WA 98507
Rick Castellano, (360) 352-9096
OPEN-AIR/SEASONAL - Mon./Sun.

Seattle-University District
  Farmers Market
Corner of Northeast 50th &
  University Way, NE.
Seattle, WA 98101
Chris Curtis, (206) 547-2278
OPEN-AIR/SEASONAL - Sat.

Wenatchee Valley Farmers Markets
Riverfront Park
Wenatchee, WA 98801
Valerie Schooler, (509) 884-7155
OPEN-AIR/SEASONAL - Wed./Sat.
Call for other locations.

west virginia

Robert Williams
West Virginia Dept. of Agriculture
Phone: (304) 558-2210

Capitol Market
800 Smith Street
Charleston, WV 25301
Henry Bender, (304) 558-0185
YEAR-ROUND - Mon./Sat./Sun.

Central City Market
555 14th Street, West
Huntington, WV 25704
Kenneth Bolen, (304) 634-9999
SEASONAL - Tues./Thurs./Sat.

wisconsin

Bob Williams
Wisconsin Dept. of Agriculture
Phone: (608) 224-5131

Madison Farmers Market
Capitol Square
Madison, WI 53714
Mary and Quentin Carpenter
(920) 563-5037
OPEN-AIR/SEASONAL - Sat.

West Allis Farmers Market
1559 South 65th Street
West Allis, WI 53214
Ronald Buege, (414) 543-2052
OPEN-AIR/SEASONAL - Tues./Thurs./Sat.

Hurley Farmers Market
Business Highway 51 & 10th Street
Hurley, WI 54534
John Sola, Sr., (715) 561-3158
OPEN-AIR/SEASONAL - Wed./Sat.

Sturgeon Bay Farmers Market
Market Square
Sturgeon Bay, WI 54235
Lee Peterson, (920) 746-2914
OPEN-AIR/SEASONAL - Sat.

wyoming

Ted Craig
Agriculture Business Division
Phone: (307) 777-6578

Buffalo Farmers Market
55 North Main
Buffalo, WY 82834
Roy Beck, (307) 684-9551
OPEN-AIR/SEASONAL

Powell Farmers Market
1257 State Road #9
Powell, WY 82435
Sharon Earhart, (307) 754-3826
OPEN-AIR/SEASONAL

index of recipes

Below are sources for various home furnishings shown in the photographs (any items not credited are privately owned).

jacket

BUFFET SETTING:
"Portofino" ivory plates from Italy—Zrike & Co., (973) 616-1668. "Mocha Grove" reproduction coffee table with linen top—Rhubarb Home, (212) 533-1817. "Linen" handmade bowl (Fig and Arugula Salad)—Luna Garcia, (800) 905-9975. "Chaco" stainless-steel flatware—Norstaal USA, (800) 404-5199. Cylinder glass pitcher; "Gibraltar" tumblers; throw pillows—Crate & Barrel, (800) 996-9960. White painted bench—Avery on Bond, (212) 614-1492. Striped napkins—Anthropologie, (800) 309-2500. "Tangerine" green and white 16-inch fruit platter on top of cereal bowl (Roasted Poussins)—Present Tense, (800) 282-7117.

spring

TABLE SETTING (PAGE 10):
Rendez-Vous" crystal champagne flutes—Baccarat, (800) 777-0100.

Spring Lunch for Two
ASPARAGUS, HAM, AND CHEESE MELTS (PAGE 12):
Ceramic plate—Fish's Eddy, (212) 420-9020. Beechwood flatware; linen napkin—Ad Hoc Softwares, (212) 925-2652.

Spring Dinner for Six
ASPARAGUS SOUP (PAGES 18 and 21):
Lusterware plates and bowls—for stores call Swid Powell, (800) 808-7943. Dupione silk napkins by Ann Gish—for stores call (805) 498-4447. "Royal" wineglasses with gold rims—for stores call the Moser Company, (800) 267-2155. "Reims" crystal wineglasses by Royales De Champagne—Marel Gifts, (800) 261-3501 or (516) 466-3118. Sterling wine goblet from York, England, circa 1829—F. Gorevic & Son, (212) 753-9319. Flowers—Zezé, (212) 753-7767. Cut-glass wine rinser, circa 1820 (on mantel)—Bardith, (212) 737-3775.

Elegant Spring Dinner for Six
MUSHROOM CONSOMMÉ WITH MORELS (PAGE 22):
"Truffle soup" bowls—Bridge Kitchenware Corp., (800) 274-3435.

spring recipes

FRESH PEA SOUP WITH TARRAGON (PAGE 26):
"Verdura" porcelain bowls and salad plates by Rosanna Imports—for stores call (206) 325-8883.
STUFFED RADISHES (PAGE 27):
Ceramic plate—Pottery Barn, (800) 922-5507.
SHRIMP AND ARTICHOKE (PAGE 31, TOP):
Sasaki "Colorstone" stoneware bowl and plate—for stores call Sasaki, (212) 686-5080.
SPRING VEGETABLE RAGOUT (PAGE 36):
French copper skillet—Bridge Kitchenware Corp., (800) 274-3435.

STRAWBERRY SHORTCAKE (PAGE 40):
Puiforcat "Rosebud" porcelain dessert plate—Baccarat, (800) 777-0100. "Windsor Shell" hand-forged sterling dessert fork and spoon—Old Newbury Crafters—Cardel Ltd., (212) 753-8880.

summer

Summer Lunch for Two
SPAGHETTI AND TOMATO SALAD (PAGE 46):
"Pale Wind" white glass dinner plate—for stores call Izabel Lam, (718) 797-3983. "Triangle" glass plate—for stores call Annieglass, (800) 347-6133. Napkin—Ad Hoc Softwares, (212) 925-2652.

Summer Dinner for Four
GRILLED COUNTRY RIBS (PAGE 50):
Earthenware dinner plate, vintage flatware, and cotton napkin—Pottery Barn, (800) 922-5507. "Courtly Check" enameled tin plate—MacKenzie-Childs Store, (212) 570-6050.
GINGERBREAD WITH NECTARINES AND CREAM (PAGE 53):
"Luna" white porcelain dessert plate—Calvin Klein, (800) 294-7978.

Alfresco Summer Dinner for Four
LOBSTER, POTATO, AND CORN SALAD (PAGE 54):
"Firmament Gold" crystal plate by Saint Louis (special order only)—Bergdorf Goodman, (212) 753-7300.

Summer Dinner from the Grill for Four
VEGETABLE KEBABS; HERBED STEAMED RICE (PAGE 58):
Ceramic platter by Skyros; hand-blown wineglasses—Hoagland's, 175 Greenwich Avenue, Greenwich, CT 06830. Flowers—Zezé, (212) 753-7767.

Summer Dinner for Six
ZUCCHINI AND YELLOW SQUASH WITH PESTO (PAGE 62):
"Quadrato" frosted glass plate—Pottery Barn, (800) 922-5507.
BROWN BUTTER ALMOND TORTE (PAGE 65):
"Star" ceramic plate—Fish's Eddy, (212) 420-9020.

summer recipes

CHILLED SOUPS (PAGE 66):
Pitchers and bowls—Crate & Barrel, (800) 996-9960. "Hoffman" stainless-steel soup spoons by David Mellor—Simon Pearce, (212) 421-8801. Napkins—Barneys New York, (212) 826-8900.
ZUCCHINI, MUSHROOM, AND PASTA PIE (PAGE 71):
Wooden bread board—Williams-Sonoma, (800) 541-2233.
HERBED TOMATO TARTS (PAGE 72):
Calphalon non-stick baking sheet—Bloomingdale's, (212) 355-5900.
GRILLED PORK CHOP (PAGE 73):
"Trellis" ceramic salad plate—Crate & Barrel, (800) 996-9960.

STEAMED VEGETABLES WITH BASIL PECAN PESTO (PAGE 76):
"Brasserie" porcelain dinner plate—Williams-Sonoma, (800) 541-2233.
SUGAR SYRUP (PAGE 84):
Highball glasses designed by Ward Bennett for Sasaki—Barneys New York, (212) 826-8900.

fall

Fall Brunch for Two
GOAT CHEESE, SWEET POTATO, AND CROUTON OMELET (PAGE 90):
Zinc-topped table with twig base—Intérieurs, (212) 343-0800.
VASE OF FLOWERS ON CHAIR (PAGE 92):
Matte earthenware vase—Luna Garcia, (800) 905-9975.

Fall Dinner for Four
HONEY POACHED PEARS—(PAGE 99):
Nineteenth-century Etruscan majolica dessert plates and cake stand; nineteenth-century Wedgwood majolica compote—J. Garvin Mecking, (212) 677-4316. Scof wood-handled spoon; picnic baskets—William-Wayne, (212) 288-9243.

Fall Supper for Four
SAUTÉED POLENTA WITH SWEET ITALIAN SAUSAGE (PAGE 100):
White porcelain plates and bowl, "Hudson Wood" flatware, square blackwood serving tray—Calvin Klein, (800) 294-7978.
PEPPERED PEARS, BLUE CHEESE, AND FRIED SAGE (PAGE 101):
"Kusuman" porcelain plates designed by Tricia Guild for Rosenthal— (800) 804-8070.

Fall Dinner for Six
ROASTED RED PEPPER AND GARLIC DIP WITH FENNEL (PAGE 104):
"Tortoise" wineglasses and bowl—for stores call Mesa International, (603) 456-2002. Vintage English silver-plate toast rack; Italian silver-plate tray—S. Wyler, Inc., (212) 879-9848. Vintage wood and silver bowl (with fruit)—J. Garvin Mecking, (212) 677-4316.
TABLE SETTING (PAGE 108):
"Naturalware" stoneware chargers; "Beekman" crystal wineglasses— for stores call Calvin Klein, (800) 294-7978. Nineteenth-century unglazed drabware plates by Wedgwood—Bardith, (212) 737-3775. Acrylic and stainless steel flatware by Sabre—Marel Gifts, (800) 261-3501. Horn-handled knives by Kirk & Matz— William-Wayne, (212) 288-9243. Vintage sterling-rimmed horn cups—Holland & Holland, (212) 752-7755. "Highlander Plaid" cotton fabric (place mats), available through decorators— Clarence House, (212) 752-2890.

fall recipes

GARLIC POTATO PURÉE WITH SHIITAKE RAGOUT (PAGE 110):
"Bacchanale" porcelain dinner and salad plates—Bernardaud, (212) 371-4300. "Trianon" sterling flatware—Tuttle La Préference, (617) 561-2200. "Moisson" crystal wineglasses— Hermès, (800) 441-4488. Silver-plate goblets; nineteenth-century ebony and ivory candlesticks; majolica urns, circa 1850— Yale R. Burge Antiques, (212) 838-4005. "Craquele Ottoman" cotton and viscose fabric (on table); "Sologne" cotton fabric (on sofa), both available through decorator—Clarence House, (212) 752-2890. Flowers—Castle & Pierpont, (212) 570-1284. Faux bois walls by Richard Pellicci, (914) 271-6710.
COLCANNON-STUFFED BRUSSELS SPROUTS (PAGE 114):
Marble dish—Gordon Foster, (212) 744-4922.
TURKEY, SQUASH AND LIMA BEAN POTPIE (PAGE 115):
Twelve-inch copper gratin dish (with stainless steel lining)— Bridge Kitchenware Corp., (800) 274-3435.
ROASTED ONION TARTS (PAGE 123, TOP):
Wedgwood "Countryware" service plates and "Edmeware" dinner plates—The Waterford Wedgwood Store, (212) 759-0500. Limoges "Blanc de Blanc" and "Promenade" service plates by Philippe Deshoulieres—for stores call (800) 993-2580. Marseilles tablecloth, circa 1870—Françoise Nunnallé, (212) 246-4281.
APPLE CIDER, ONION, AND RAISIN CHUTNEY (PAGE 124):
English glass honey jar, circa 1820—James II Galleries, Ltd., (212) 355-7040. "Arabesque" fibranne and silk fabric, available through decorator—Clarence House, (212) 752-2890.

winter

Winter Lunch for Two
FISH CHOWDER WITH HERBED OYSTER CRACKERS (PAGE 136):
Hand-thrown spongeware chowder bowl and plate; Nineteenth-century tole sugar bowl (with crackers, lid not shown), pewter spoon, bone and steel fork, silver filigree salt spoon, cotton towel, and napkin; eighteenth-century treen salt—Gail Lettick's Pantry & Hearth, (212) 532-0535.
CHEESE WITH QUINCE, GINGER, AND PECAN CONSERVE (PAGE 139):
"Craftworks" stoneware salad plate—for stores call Lindt-Stymeist, (510) 654-0413. Fabric by Silk Surplus—ABC Carpet & Home, (212) 473-3000.

Easy Winter Dinner for Four
HAM STEAK WITH CIDER RAISIN SAUCE (PAGE 140):
"Fine stem" wineglass—Calvin Klein, (800) 294-7978.
ORANGE TAPIOCA AND CRANBERRY PARFAITS (PAGE 143):
"Ovale" glasses by Carlo Moretti—Avventura, (212) 769-2510.

Casual Winter Dinner for Four
WARM BEET AND CARROT SALAD (PAGE 144):
"Rondure" stainless steel flatware—Dansk, (800) 293-2675.
LEMON-RUBBED CHICKEN LEGS WITH GARLIC AND ROSEMARY (PAGE 146):
"Colorstone Birch" dinner plate by Sasaki—for stores call (212) 686-5080. "Data" stainless steel flatware—Ikea, for stores call (410) 931-8940 (East Coast) or (818) 912-1119 (West Coast). Velvet pillow—Pottery Barn, (800) 922-5507.

Winter Brunch for Six
BROILED GRAPEFRUIT WITH VANILLA GINGER SUGAR (PAGE 148):
Baking dish—Bloomingdale's, (212) 355-5900. Champagne flutes—Crate & Barrel, (800) 996-9960.
CORNED BEEF HASH WITH FRIED EGGS (PAGE 150):
Eighteenth-century polychrome Delft charger; nineteenth-century breadboard—Gail Lettick's Pantry & Hearth, (212) 532-0535.

Winter Dinner for Six
TABLE SETTING (PAGES 152 AND 153):
Matte earthenware plates—Luna Garcia, (800) 905-9975. "Round" stemware and beakers (water)—Simon Pearce, (212) 421-8801. "Telluride" stainless-steel flatware; "Southern Plains Serape" striped cotton place mats—Ralph Lauren Home Collection, (212) 642-8700. Glass vase—Takashimaya, (212) 350-0100. "Dunbar" cotton napkins by Fallani and Cohn—for stores call (914) 365-3535. House designed and built by Servais Design & Construction, Inc., (510) 548-8453.
CHICKEN STEW WITH SAUSAGE (PAGE 155):
"Mediterranean Festival" Italian earthenware bowls and plates—Pottery Barn, (800) 922-5507.
FRESH APPLE CAKE WITH CHILE DE ÁRBOL CARAMEL GLAZE (PAGE 157):
"Flo Blue" English plates, circa 1870—More & More Antiques, (212) 580-8404.

winter recipes

SHERRIED PARSNIP SOUP WITH HAZELNUT PESTO (PAGE 158):
Colorstone bowl by Sasaki—for stores call (212) 686-5080.
MINESTRONE (PAGE 161):
Wineglass—Williams-Sonoma, (800) 541-2233. Cotton napkin—ABC Carpet & Home, (212) 473-3000. Oak slab table with ebony inlays—Daniel Mack Rustic Furnishings, (914) 986-7293.
GUMBO WITH MIXED GREENS AND RED BEANS (PAGE 162):
Hand-painted ceramic soup bowl and dinner plate by Eigen Arts—for stores call (201) 798-7310.
ROAST COD WITH POTATOES, ONIONS, AND OLIVES (PAGE 166):
Mexican hand-painted earthenware plate—Pan American Phoenix, (212) 570-0300. Earthenware baking dish—Bridge Kitchenware Corp., (800) 274-3435.
HAZELNUTS (PAGE 171):
Colorstone bowl by Sasaki—for stores call (212) 686-5080.
GOAT CHEESE MASHED-POTATO GRATIN (PAGE 174):
Apilco ovenproof porcelain dish—Bridge Kitchenware Corp., (800) 274-3435.
APPLE CHEDDAR BREAD PUDDING (PAGE 177):
Baking dish—Bridge Kitchenware Corp., (800) 274-3435.

credits

recipes

Grateful acknowledgment is made to the following contributors for permission to reprint recipes previously published in *Gourmet Magazine*.

Bruce Aidells and Denis Kelly
CHICKEN STEW WITH SAUSAGE, HOMINY, AND CRISPY ONIONS (PAGE 154).
Copyright © 1990.

Naomi Barry and Bettina McNulty
ZUCCHINI, MUSHROOM, AND PASTA PIE (PAGE 70).
Copyright © 1991.

Joyce Goldstein
ASPARAGUS SOUP WITH SAFFRON (PAGE 19).
Copyright © 1998.

Katherine Kagel and Stephanie Morris
FRESH APPLE CAKE WITH CHILE DE ÁRBOL CARAMEL GLAZE AND ÁRBOL CARAMEL GLAZE (PAGES 156 AND 157).
Copyright © 1998.

Jeanne Lemlin
BUTTERNUT SQUASH AND RED PEPPER CASSEROLE (PAGE 123).
Copyright © 1995.

Susan Herrmann Loomis
LOBSTER, POTATO, AND CORN SALAD WITH TARRAGON (PAGE 55).
Copyright © 1992.

Kemp Miles Minifie
STRAWBERRY SHORTCAKE, CREAM BISCUITS, AND BUTTERMILK BISCUITS (PAGES 40 AND 41).
Copyright © 1993.

Mary Taylor Simeti
BRAISED BASIL- AND GARLIC-STUFFED EGGPLANTS
from Pomp and Sustenance, Twenty-Five Centuries of Sicilian Food, by Mary Taylor Simeti (New York: Alfred A. Knopf, 1989).

Zanne Early Stewart
PEACH TARTES TATIN (PAGE 82).
Copyright © 1998.
SHRIMP AND ARTICHOKES IN PEPPERY BUTTER SAUCE (PAGE 30).
Copyright © 1995.
GOAT CHEESE MASHED-POTATO GRATIN (PAGE 174).
Copyright © 1993.

photography

The following photographers have generously given permission to reprint their photographs. Some of these photographs have previously appeared in *Gourmet Magazine*.

Cotten Alston
BASKETS OF PEACHES (PAGE 48). INDIANA BARN (PAGE 134). *Copyright © 1990.*

Richard Bowditch
SALAD GREENS (PAGES 11 AND 28). *Copyright © 1998.*

Mark Ferri
ASPARAGUS; CABBAGES AND CAULIFLOWER (PAGE 7). SHELL BEANS (PAGE 79). *Copyright © 1999.* ARTISANAL CHEESES (PAGE 113). *Copyright © 1997.*

Elisabeth Hughes
WALNUTS IN A BASKET (PAGE 133). *Copyright © 1997.*

Marry Kim
AT THE FARMERS MARKET (PAGES 180 AND 182). *Copyright © 1999.*

Geoff Lung
APPLES ON A BRANCH (PAGE 89). *Copyright © 1997.* SUGAR SHAKER (PAGE 97). *Copyright © 1998.*

Minh + Wass
JONAGOLD APPLES (PAGE 7). *Copyright © 1999.*

Steven Mark Needham
JERUSALEM ARTICHOKES (PAGE 96). LEEKS (PAGE 164). *Copyright © 1999.*

Julian Nieman
ONIONS, SHALLOTS, AND GARLIC (PAGE 105). *Copyright © 1997.*

Mathias Oppersdorff
SIGN NEAR BIRD-IN-HAND, PENNSYLVANIA (PAGE 88). *Copyright © 1989.*

Riley + Riley
JALAPEÑO PEPPERS (ENDSHEETS). *Copyright © 1998.*

Romulo Yanes
SUNFLOWERS IN FIELD (PAGE 6). *Copyright © 1998.*

If you are not already a subscriber to *Gourmet Magazine* and would be interested in subscribing, please call *Gourmet's* toll-free number, 1-800-365-2454. If you are interested in purchasing additional copies of this book or other *Gourmet* cookbooks, please call 1-800-245-2010.

artichokes spring APRICOTS asparagus AVOC

garlic chives MINT peas PEA SHOOTS purslane

spinach SPROUTS strawberries TARRAGON tatsoi

avocados summer FAVA BEANS green bean

RASPBERRIES celery SOUR CHERRIES corn CUCUMB

CANTALOUPE honeydew melons WATERMELON nectar

YELLOW SQUASH zucchini PATTYPAN tomatoes LEM

BRUSSEL SPROUTS

ONIONS PEARS

pumpkins

limabeans BEETS broccoli

DATES fennel GRAPES

SWEET POTATOES

chives

pomegranates

fall

ARUGULA

cauliflower CHERVIL

asian pears PERSIMMON

apples